# Machine Learning for Quants

*Algorithms for Predicting Market Movements*

William Johnson

Published by HiTeX Press

For permissions and other inquiries, write to:
P.O. Box 3132, Framingham, MA 01701, USA

# Contents

# Preface

Imagine standing in the heart of a bustling financial district, surrounded by towering skyscrapers that symbolize the relentless pursuit of wealth and knowledge. The air is thick with anticipation and the subtle hum of the markets, where fortunes can be made or lost in the blink of an eye. Welcome to the exhilarating world of quantitative finance, where data reigns supreme and machine learning algorithms have become the new alchemists, transforming raw information into actionable insights.

In today's fast-paced financial markets, traditional trading strategies are being upended by innovative approaches that harness the power of machine learning. The noise of human intuition is progressively being supplanted by data-driven decisions, as quants—that is, quantitative analysts and traders—use sophisticated algorithms to predict market movements and optimize trading strategies. This book, *Machine Learning for Quants: Algorithms for Predicting Market Movements*, embarks on a journey to unravel the intricate tapestry of machine learning techniques specifically tailored for the world of finance.

Our journey begins by laying a solid foundation in quantitative finance, exploring the fundamentals that underpin market behaviors and financial instruments. With a thorough understanding of these principles, we then delve into the heart of machine learning, demystifying its core concepts and different types—from supervised to unsupervised learning. As we progress, we meticulously guide you through the nuances of data preprocessing and feature engineering, crucial steps that transform raw financial data into a form ready for machine learning models.

The excitement truly begins as we explore various machine learning algorithms and their application in finance. From the simplicity of linear regression to the complexity of neural networks, we will explore how each algorithm can uncover hidden patterns in market data. Special emphasis will be placed on time series analysis, a critical component in understanding and predicting financial trends.

We provide a robust framework for evaluating and validating models, ensuring that your predictions are not only accurate but also reliable. The book continues with a deep dive into algorithmic trading strategies, revealing how to automate trades and exploit market inefficiencies. Risk management, a pillar of successful trading, is thoroughly examined, offering strategies to mitigate potential losses and safeguard investments.

The art of optimization is then introduced, highlighting techniques to fine-tune models and strategies for maximum efficacy. To solidify your understanding, we present a series of compelling case studies drawn from real-world financial markets. These practical examples will illustrate how machine learning is not just a theoretical exercise, but a powerful tool applied by leading financial institutions and hedge funds.

As you navigate through the pages of this book, you will acquire the skills and knowledge needed to harness the transformative power of machine learning in quantitative finance. Imagine the possibilities: the potential to predict market movements with uncanny accuracy, to design trading strategies that consistently outperform the market, and to manage risks with unparalleled precision.

So, are you ready to unlock the secrets of the markets and join the ranks of cutting-edge quants who are redefining the landscape of finance? Turn the page, and let the adventure begin. Dive into the meticulous world of data, algorithms, and finance with *Machine Learning for Quants: Algorithms for Predicting Market Movements*, and discover how you can transform information into wealth. Welcome aboard!

# Chapter 1

# Introduction to Quantitative Finance

**This chapter covers the fundamental principles of quantitative finance, beginning with an overview of financial instruments and markets. It explores key concepts such as return, risk, and alpha, and introduces essential statistical tools used in finance. Topics such as portfolio theory, the Capital Asset Pricing Model (CAPM), the Efficient Market Hypothesis, and arbitrage principles are discussed in detail. The chapter also provides an introduction to derivatives and fixed income securities, setting a solid groundwork for more advanced topics in quantitative finance.**

## 1.1 Fundamentals of Quantitative Finance

Quantitative finance is the application of mathematical models and computational techniques to understand and predict market behaviors. It is a field that combines finance, mathematics, statistics, and computer science, aiming to provide more precise and systematic ways to navigate financial markets. The essence of quantitative finance lies in its data-driven approach, utilizing historical data and algorithmic rigor to inform trading and investment decisions.

A pivotal aspect of quantitative finance involves understanding financial instruments and their respective markets. Financial instruments, ranging from simple equity stocks to complex derivatives, serve as the vehicles for trading value. Equally important is the comprehension of financial markets, where these instruments are exchanged, influenced by factors such as economic indicators, news events, and market sentiment.

Building on these foundational elements, the core of quantitative finance can be broken down into several key concepts:

**Return**: Return is the gain or loss generated on an investment over a specific period. It is typically expressed as a percentage of the investment's initial cost. Mathematically, if $P_0$ is the initial investment price and $P_t$ is the price at time $t$, the return $R$ over the period $t$ can be defined as:

$$R_t = \frac{P_t - P_0}{P_0}$$

For continuous compounding, where returns are reinvested continuously, the formula modifies using natural logarithms:

$$R_t = \ln\left(\frac{P_t}{P_0}\right)$$

**Risk**: In the context of finance, risk represents the uncertainty associated with the return on an investment. Quantifying risk is crucial for making informed investment decisions. One common measure of risk is volatility, often represented by the standard deviation $\sigma$ of returns. Higher volatility indicates greater risk and potential for unpredictable changes in value. The standard deviation of returns can be expressed as:

$$\sigma = \sqrt{\frac{1}{n-1}\sum_{i=1}^{n}(R_i - \bar{R})^2}$$

where $n$ is the number of observations, $R_i$ is the individual return, and $\bar{R}$ is the average return.

**Alpha**: Alpha ($\alpha$) measures an investment's performance relative to a benchmark index. Positive alpha indicates outperformance, while negative alpha signifies underperformance. Alpha can be mathematically expressed as:

$$\alpha = R_i - (R_f + \beta(R_m - R_f))$$

where $R_i$ is the investment's return, $R_f$ is the risk-free rate, $\beta$ is the sensitivity to the benchmark, and $R_m$ is the benchmark's return.

These concepts provide a framework for understanding other essential topics in quantitative finance. For instance, portfolio theory, introduced by Harry Markowitz, relies on the trade-off between return and risk to optimize the allocation of assets. Portfolio theory posits that diversified investments can achieve an optimal balance, reducing overall risk without sacrificing returns.

**Statistical Tools and Models**: Quantitative finance heavily relies on statistical tools to analyze and model market data. Descriptive statistics, such as mean, median, variance, and skewness, provide foundational insights into data distributions. Inferential statistics, including hypothesis testing and regression analysis, help in drawing conclusions and making predictions based on sample data. For example, the linear regression model can be used to predict future trends based on historical data. If $y$ is the dependent variable and $x$ is the independent variable, the regression model can be expressed as:

$$y = \alpha + \beta x + \epsilon$$

where $\alpha$ is the intercept, $\beta$ is the slope, and $\epsilon$ is the error term.

**Time Series Analysis**: This area of statistics focuses on analyzing data points collected or recorded at specific time intervals. It is particularly important in finance because market data is inherently sequential. Techniques like moving averages, autoregressive models (AR), and autoregressive integrated moving average models (ARIMA) are used to identify patterns and predict future prices. An AR model of order $p$, for instance, is represented as:

$$X_t = c + \phi_1 X_{t-1} + \phi_2 X_{t-2} + \cdots + \phi_p X_{t-p} + \epsilon_t$$

where $X_t$ is the current value, $c$ is a constant, $\phi$ represents the coefficients, and $\epsilon_t$ is the white noise error.

**Algorithmic Trading**: Algorithmic trading, or algo trading, uses computer algorithms to automatically execute trades based on predefined criteria. It leverages mathematical models to identify profitable opportunities and execute trades at high speeds and volumes. Key techniques include statistical arbitrage, market making, and the momentum strategy. One common model for execution is the volume-weighted average price (VWAP), which aims to execute orders in line with market volume:

$$\text{VWAP} = \frac{\sum_i^n (P_i \cdot V_i)}{\sum_i^n V_i}$$

where $P_i$ and $V_i$ are the price and volume of each trade.

Understanding these fundamentals equips traders and investors with the necessary tools to analyze market data, develop trading strategies, and manage investment portfolios efficiently. By leveraging the power of quantitative models and computational techniques, one can enhance decision-making processes, identify profitable opportunities, and ultimately achieve better financial outcomes.

## 1.2 Financial Instruments and Markets

Understanding financial instruments and markets is crucial for anyone looking to delve into quantitative finance. This section will demystify the various types of financial instruments and the markets where they are traded. A solid grasp of these concepts will serve as a foundation for more complex strategies discussed later in this book.

Financial instruments can be broadly classified into equity, debt, derivatives, and hybrid instruments. Each class has its distinct characteristics, risk profiles, and uses within a portfolio. Let's explore each type in detail.

**Equity Instruments:** These represent ownership interests in a company. Common examples include common stocks and preferred stocks.

- *Common Stocks:* These are shares that entitle the holder to a portion of the company's profits and carry voting rights. The return on investment comes from dividends and capital gains.
- *Preferred Stocks:* These shares generally don't provide voting rights but offer fixed dividends and have priority over common stock in the event of liquidation.

**Debt Instruments:** These are loans made by an investor to an entity. They typically offer regular interest payments and the return of principal upon maturity. Examples include bonds, debentures, and certificates of deposit (CDs).

- *Bonds:* These are long-term debt securities issued by corporations, municipalities, and governments that pay periodic interest and repay the principal at maturity.
- *Debentures:* Unsecured bonds that rely on the creditworthiness of the issuer rather than collateral.
- *Certificates of Deposit (CDs):* Time deposits offered by banks that pay a fixed interest rate for a specified period.

**Derivatives:** These are financial contracts whose value is derived from the performance of underlying assets, rates, or indices. Types of derivatives include futures, options, and swaps.

- *Futures:* Contracts to buy or sell an asset at a future date at a predetermined price.
- *Options:* Contracts that give the holder the right, but not the obligation, to buy or sell an asset at a specified price within a certain period.
- *Swaps:* Agreements to exchange cash flows or other financial instruments between parties.

**Hybrid Instruments:** These combine features of debt and equity instruments. For instance, convertible bonds can be turned into a predetermined number of common shares.

**Markets:** Financial instruments are traded in various markets, which can be categorized into primary and secondary markets, and further into organized exchanges and over-the-counter (OTC) markets.

**Primary Markets:** These are venues where new securities are issued. Examples include initial public offerings (IPOs) for stocks and bond issuances.

**Secondary Markets:** Once securities have been issued, they trade among investors in secondary markets. These markets provide liquidity and price discovery.

**Organized Exchanges:** These are formal markets with fixed trading rules and centralized locations, such as the New York Stock Exchange (NYSE) or the Chicago Board Options Exchange (CBOE).

**Over-the-Counter (OTC) Markets:** These are decentralized markets where participants trade directly with each other, often through electronic networks. Examples include the foreign exchange (Forex) market and bond markets.

**Market Efficiency:** The effectiveness of markets in reflecting information within the prices of traded assets is known as market efficiency. This concept is essential to understanding the rationale behind many trading and investing strategies.

Knowledge of financial instruments and markets is foundational for anyone involved in quantitative finance. By understanding these basics, you can better assess the risk-return profile of various instruments and navigate the complexities of the financial landscape. This understanding will bolster your ability to implement more sophisticated quantitative strategies as discussed in the subsequent sections.

## 1.3 Basic Statistical Concepts in Finance

In the realm of quantitative finance, a solid grasp of statistical concepts is indispensable. These concepts underpin the analytical tools and models that traders and investors use to interpret market data, estimate future movements, and make informed decisions. By understanding these statistical principles, one gains the ability to better manage risk and harness opportunities within the financial markets.

**Mean and Variance:** At the core of statistical analysis in finance are the measures of central tendency and variability. The arithmetic mean, or average, is a primary measure of central tendency, reflecting the expected value of a set of returns. Formally, the mean return $\mu$ of a portfolio or financial instrument is calculated as:

$$\mu = \frac{1}{N} \sum_{i=1}^{N} r_i$$

where $r_i$ denotes the return for the $i$-th period and $N$ is the total number of periods.

The variance $\sigma^2$, a measure of the dispersion of returns around the mean, is defined as:

$$\sigma^2 = \frac{1}{N}\sum_{i=1}^{N}(r_i - \mu)^2$$

Variance provides insight into the degree of risk associated with an investment, as higher variance indicates greater uncertainty in returns.

**Standard Deviation:** Building on the concept of variance, the standard deviation $\sigma$ is simply the square root of the variance. This measure is particularly useful because it is expressed in the same units as the returns themselves, facilitating a more intuitive understanding of risk. The standard deviation is given by:

$$\sigma = \sqrt{\sigma^2}$$

**Covariance and Correlation:** When considering a portfolio of multiple assets, it is crucial to understand how these assets move in relation to each other. Covariance and correlation are key metrics for this purpose. The covariance between two asset returns, $r_A$ and $r_B$, is defined as:

$$\text{Cov}(r_A, r_B) = \frac{1}{N}\sum_{i=1}^{N}(r_{A,i} - \mu_A)(r_{B,i} - \mu_B)$$

where $\mu_A$ and $\mu_B$ are the mean returns of assets $A$ and $B$, respectively. Positive covariance indicates that the returns move together, while a negative value suggests inverse movement.

To standardize this relationship, the correlation coefficient $\rho_{A,B}$ is employed, giving a dimensionless measure of the strength and direction of the relationship between two assets:

$$\rho_{A,B} = \frac{\text{Cov}(r_A, r_B)}{\sigma_A \sigma_B}$$

Here, $\sigma_A$ and $\sigma_B$ are the standard deviations of the returns of assets $A$ and $B$. Correlation values range from -1 to 1, with 1 signifying a perfect positive correlation, -1 a perfect negative correlation, and 0 indicating no linear relationship.

**Probability Distributions:** Returns in financial markets often assume specific probability distributions. The normal distribution is frequently used due to its well-understood properties and the application of the Central Limit Theorem, which states that the sum of many independent random variables tends toward a normal distribution, even if the original variables themselves are not normally distributed.

The probability density function (PDF) of a normal distribution with mean $\mu$ and standard deviation $\sigma$ is:

$$f(x) = \frac{1}{\sqrt{2\pi\sigma^2}} e^{-\frac{(x-\mu)^2}{2\sigma^2}}$$

This bell-shaped curve is symmetric about the mean, with its spread determined by the standard deviation. When modeling financial returns, the assumption of normality simplifies many analyses, although it is also acknowledged that financial returns exhibit skewness (asymmetry) and kurtosis (fat tails) that deviate from the normal distribution.

**Hypothesis Testing:** In finance, hypothesis testing is used to make inferences about the properties of financial instruments or the effectiveness of trading strategies. A common test is the null hypothesis $H_0$ (e.g., that a strategy does not produce alpha) against an alternative hypothesis $H_1$. The p-value obtained from statistical tests determines whether to reject $H_0$, with lower p-values indicating stronger evidence against $H_0$.

Consider a test for whether the mean return $\mu$ of a strategy is different from zero. The test statistic might be:

$$t = \frac{\bar{r}}{s/\sqrt{N}}$$

where $\bar{r}$ is the sample mean return, $s$ is the sample standard deviation, and $N$ is the number of observations. This $t$-statistic follows a Student's $t$-distribution under the null hypothesis.

**Linear Regression:** Linear regression is pivotal for modeling relationships between dependent and independent variables, widely applied in finance to understand and predict asset prices, risk premia, and other key financial metrics. A simple linear regression model can be expressed as:

$$r_i = \alpha + \beta x_i + \epsilon_i$$

where $r_i$ is the dependent variable (e.g., asset return), $x_i$ the independent variable (e.g., market return), $\alpha$ the intercept, $\beta$ the slope of the line, and $\epsilon_i$ the error term.

The parameters $\alpha$ and $\beta$ are estimated using the Ordinary Least Squares (OLS) method, minimizing the sum of squared residuals:

$$\text{RSS} = \sum_{i=1}^{N} (r_i - \hat{r_i})^2$$

where $\hat{r_i} = \alpha + \beta x_i$ are the predicted values.

Understanding these basic statistical concepts lays the foundation for the more advanced topics that follow, enabling traders and investors to critically evaluate financial models and approaches with a sound grounding in quantitative analysis. Having established this knowledge, one is well-prepared to delve into specific strategies and their applications in the myriad scenarios encountered in the financial markets.

## 1.4 Portfolio Theory

Portfolio theory, also known as modern portfolio theory (MPT), forms the backbone of various investment strategies employed by quants and financial analysts. It was introduced by Harry Markowitz in his seminal paper published in 1952, where he emphasized the importance of diversification and how investors can construct portfolios to maximize return for a given level of risk.

The primary objective of portfolio theory is to optimize the balance between risk and return. To achieve this, it employs quantitative methods to create a frontier known as the efficient frontier, which represents the set of optimum portfolios offering the highest expected return for a defined level of risk or the lowest risk for a given level of expected return.

**Expected Return and Variance of Portfolio**

To understand portfolio theory, we must first delve into the concepts of expected return and variance. Consider a portfolio consisting of $n$ assets, where $w_i$ represents the weight of asset $i$ in the portfolio, $R_i$ is the return of asset $i$, and $\bar{R}_i$ is the expected return of asset $i$. The expected return of the portfolio $\bar{R}_p$ can be defined mathematically as:

$$\bar{R}_p = \sum_{i=1}^{n} w_i \bar{R}_i$$

The variance of the portfolio, which measures the risk, depends not only on the variance of individual assets but also on the covariance between them. Let $\sigma_i^2$ be the variance of asset $i$, and $\sigma_{ij}$ be the covariance between asset $i$ and asset $j$. The variance of the portfolio $\sigma_p^2$ is given by:

$$\sigma_p^2 = \sum_{i=1}^{n} \sum_{j=1}^{n} w_i w_j \sigma_{ij}$$

For a two-asset portfolio, this can be simplified as:

$$\sigma_p^2 = w_1^2 \sigma_1^2 + w_2^2 \sigma_2^2 + 2 w_1 w_2 \sigma_{12}$$

where $\sigma_{12}$ is the covariance between the returns of assets 1 and 2.

**Diversification and the Efficient Frontier**

One of the key insights of portfolio theory is its advocacy for diversification. By combining assets with varying degrees of correlation, investors can create portfolios with lower risk than any individual asset on its own, without necessarily sacrificing expected return. The efficient frontier visually represents the optimal set of portfolios that offer the best possible expected return for a given level of risk.

Consider an investment opportunity set comprising all possible portfolios that can be constructed from $n$ assets. The efficient frontier is the upper edge of this set. Portfolios on the efficient frontier are "efficient" because it is impossible to obtain higher expected returns without increasing risk. Any portfolio lying below the efficient frontier is inefficient, as there exists another portfolio with higher expected return for the same or lower risk.

To construct the efficient frontier, one must solve the following optimization problem:

$$\min_{w} \sigma_p^2 \quad \text{such that} \quad \sum_{i=1}^{n} w_i \bar{R}_i = \bar{R}_p \quad \text{and} \quad \sum_{i=1}^{n} w_i = 1$$

where $w$ denotes the vector of portfolio weights, $\sigma_p^2$ is the portfolio variance, and $\bar{R}_p$ is the portfolio's expected return. This optimization involves finding the weights $w$ that minimize the portfolio variance for a given expected return, $\bar{R}_p$.

**Capital Market Line and the Optimal Portfolio**

Incorporating a risk-free asset into the analysis enhances the basic MPT. The combination of risky assets and a risk-free asset generates the Capital Market Line (CML). The CML illustrates the risk-return trade-off for efficient portfolios and provides a benchmark for assessing the performance of any portfolio.

The expected return of a portfolio combined with a risk-free asset is:

$$\bar{R}_c = R_f + \left( \frac{\bar{R}_p - R_f}{\sigma_p} \right) \sigma_c$$

where $R_f$ is the risk-free rate, $\bar{R}_p$ is the expected return of the tangency portfolio, $\sigma_p$ is the standard deviation of the tangency portfolio, and $\sigma_c$ is the standard deviation of the combined portfolio.

The slope of the CML, known as the Sharpe Ratio, is given by:

$$\text{Sharpe Ratio} = \frac{\bar{R}_p - R_f}{\sigma_p}$$

Investors seek to maximize the Sharpe Ratio, indicating they prefer higher excess returns per unit of risk.

Constructing an optimal portfolio involves selecting a mix of risky assets that lies on the tangency point of the efficient frontier and the CML. This tangency portfolio maximizes the Sharpe Ratio and represents the best possible capital allocation without additional risk.

**Implications and Applications of Portfolio Theory**

Portfolio theory has far-reaching implications for both individual and institutional investors. It serves as a foundation for various portfolio management strategies and aids in asset allocation decisions, performance evaluation, and risk management. Institutional investors, such as mutual funds, pension funds, and insurance companies, rely on portfolio theory to optimize their investment portfolios and meet their financial objectives.

Moreover, advancements in computational finance and machine learning have enabled the development of sophisticated models that further enhance portfolio optimization. Algorithmic trading systems, for instance, leverage portfolio theory to dynamically adjust asset weights in response to changing market conditions.

Portfolio theory's legacy endures, providing a structured and quantitative approach to constructing portfolios that balance risk and return.

As we delve into more advanced topics in quantitative finance, the principles of portfolio theory will continue to underpin our exploration of market dynamics and investment strategies.

## 1.5 Capital Asset Pricing Model (CAPM)

The Capital Asset Pricing Model (CAPM) is a cornerstone of modern financial theory, providing a framework to determine the expected return of an asset while accounting for its risk relative to the market. This model serves as a crucial tool in asset pricing and portfolio management, allowing investors to make informed decisions based on the trade-off between risk and return.

At its core, the CAPM posits that the expected return of a security or a portfolio is a function of the risk-free rate of return, the security's sensitivity to market movements (denoted by beta, $\beta$), and the expected return of the market. The relationship is mathematically expressed as:

$$E(R_i) = R_f + \beta_i(E(R_m) - R_f)$$

where:

- $E(R_i)$ is the expected return of asset $i$,
- $R_f$ is the risk-free rate of return,
- $\beta_i$ is the beta of asset $i$,
- $E(R_m)$ is the expected return of the market.

The risk-free rate, $R_f$, is typically represented by the yield on government securities, such as Treasury bills, which are considered free of default risk. The market return, $E(R_m)$, is the average return of a broad market index like the S&P 500. The beta $\beta_i$ measures the sensitivity of an asset's returns to the returns of the market. Essentially, it captures the systematic risk that cannot be diversified away.

**Understanding Beta**

Beta ($\beta$) is a fundamental concept in the CAPM and serves as a measure of an asset's market risk. A beta of 1 indicates that the asset's price moves in line with the market. A beta greater than 1 suggests that the asset is more volatile than the market, meaning it tends to amplify market movements. Conversely, a beta less than 1 implies that the asset is less volatile than the market.

Mathematically, beta is defined as:

$$\beta_i = \frac{\text{Cov}(R_i, R_m)}{\text{Var}(R_m)}$$

where Cov$(R_i, R_m)$ is the covariance between the asset's returns and the market returns, and Var$(R_m)$ is the variance of the market returns.

**Implications of CAPM**

The CAPM provides several critical insights for both investors and portfolio managers:

- **Risk and Return Relationship:** It quantifies the relationship between the expected return of an asset and its market risk, reinforcing the principle that higher risk (beta) should be compensated with higher expected returns.
- **Portfolio Allocation:** By using beta, investors can construct portfolios with a desired level of risk. For instance, if an investor seeks a low-risk portfolio, they can select assets with lower betas.
- **Performance Measurement:** CAPM serves as a benchmark for evaluating the performance of managed portfolios. By comparing the actual return to the expected return (predicted by CAPM), investors can assess whether a portfolio manager has delivered above-market performance (alpha).
- **Capital Market Line (CML):** The CAPM implies the existence of the Capital Market Line, which represents portfolios that optimally combine risk-free assets and the market portfolio. The CML equation is:

  $$E(R_p) = R_f + \left( \frac{E(R_m) - R_f}{\sigma_m} \right) \sigma_p$$

  where $E(R_p)$ is the expected return on the portfolio, $\sigma_p$ is the standard deviation of the portfolio returns, and $\sigma_m$ is the standard deviation of the market returns.

**Empirical Testing and Limitations**

Though widely used, the CAPM has faced empirical scrutiny. Studies have shown that:

- **Market Anomalies:** Certain anomalies, such as the size effect (small-cap stocks outperform large-cap stocks) and value effect (high book-to-market stocks outperform low book-to-market stocks), are not fully explained by CAPM.
- **Beta Instability:** Beta values can change over time, making predictions less reliable.
- **Assumption Limitations:** The model assumes homogeneous expectations and a single-period investment horizon, which might not reflect real-world conditions.

Despite these limitations, the CAPM's intuitive appeal and foundational role in finance make it a valuable model. It continues to be a vital tool for understanding risk and return dynamics and serves as a basis for more complex asset pricing models.

This understanding of the CAPM enables a deeper grasp of how market forces interact with individual asset returns, setting the stage for exploring more advanced methodologies in quantitative finance.

## 1.6 Efficient Market Hypothesis

The Efficient Market Hypothesis (EMH) is a cornerstone theory in the field of quantitative finance and serves as a foundational concept for understanding market dynamics. The EMH posits that financial markets are efficient in reflecting all available information at any given time, meaning that asset prices instantly adjust to new information, making it virtually impossible to consistently achieve returns that exceed average market returns on a risk-adjusted basis through either technical analysis or fundamental analysis.

The EMH can be categorized into three forms: weak, semi-strong, and strong. Each of these forms provides a different perspective on the level of market efficiency and the availability of information reflected in asset prices.

**Weak Form Efficiency** asserts that all past trading information is fully reflected in stock prices. This means that historical prices and data cannot be used to predict future movements because any patterns or trends that existed in the past have already been accounted for in current prices. As a result, technical analysis is deemed ineffective in producing consistent excess returns under this form of efficiency.

Mathematically, weak form efficiency can be expressed as:

$$P_t = P_{t-1} + \epsilon_t$$

where $P_t$ is the current price, $P_{t-1}$ is the previous price, and $\epsilon_t$ represents a random error term that is normally distributed with a mean of zero.

**Semi-Strong Form Efficiency** expands on the weak form by asserting that stock prices not only reflect all past trading information but also all publicly available information. This includes financial statements, news reports, earnings announcements, and macroeconomic indicators. In this form, neither fundamental analysis nor technical analysis can consistently generate excess returns, as all publicly accessible information is instantly incorporated into asset prices.

**Strong Form Efficiency** takes the hypothesis to its extreme, positing that stock prices reflect all information, both public and private (or insider information). This implies that no one, not even insiders with privileged information, can achieve consistently higher returns than the market. This form is often criticized and is less supported by empirical evidence, as it assumes perfect and instantaneous dissemination of all types of information.

The EMH has profound implications for traders, investors, and portfolio managers. For example, if markets are truly efficient, then active management strategies that attempt to pick individual stocks or time the market are unlikely to outperform passive strategies that seek to replicate market indices.

However, several anomalies and empirical challenges have been documented against the EMH, leading to the rise of behavioral finance—a field that examines how psychological factors and human behavior can result in market inefficiencies. Notable anomalies include the January effect, momentum, and the existence of bubbles and crashes which suggest that markets may not always function efficiently.

Despite these challenges, the EMH remains a critical theoretical framework for understanding modern financial markets. It emphasizes the difficulty of achieving consistent alpha—risk-adjusted excessive returns—and the importance of considering market efficiency when developing trading and investing strategies.

For a practical application, consider the implications of the EMH when constructing a portfolio. In an efficient market, a well-diversified portfolio that minimizes costs and aligns with the investor's risk tolerance and return objectives is typically more favorable than attempting to exploit perceived market inefficiencies through frequent trading.

Ultimately, while the Efficient Market Hypothesis may not fully capture all aspects of market behavior, it provides a foundational insight into the nature of financial markets and reinforces the importance of disciplined, long-term investment strategies over short-term speculation.

## 1.7 Arbitrage Principles

Arbitrage is a cornerstone concept in quantitative finance, underpinning many trading strategies and financial models. At its core, arbitrage involves exploiting price differentials of the same or similar assets across different markets or forms. This section delves into the principle of arbitrage, its types, significance, and application in real-world trading.

Arbitrage hinges on the notion that similar assets should not have divergent prices in different markets. When such price discrepancies are found, traders can simultaneously buy the undervalued asset and sell the overvalued one, locking in a risk-free profit. This process continues until the prices converge, thereby eliminating the arbitrage opportunity.

To thoroughly understand arbitrage, it is useful to classify it into three main types: pure arbitrage, risk arbitrage, and statistical arbitrage.

**Pure Arbitrage** refers to scenarios where a genuine risk-free profit can be earned by concurrently buying and selling equivalent assets in different markets. For instance, if a stock is trading for \$100 on the New York Stock Exchange (NYSE) and \$105 on the London Stock Exchange (LSE), a trader can buy the stock in NYSE and simultaneously sell it on LSE, realizing a risk-free gain of \$5 per share. Mathematically, such arbitrage can be represented as:

$$P_{NYSE} < P_{LSE} \implies \text{Buy on NYSE, Sell on LSE}$$

Pure arbitrage is relatively rare, appearing only when there are inefficiencies in the market, such as delays in price updates or temporary imbalances in supply and demand.

**Risk Arbitrage** (or merger arbitrage) involves taking positions based on the expected outcome of corporate events such as mergers, acquisitions, or bankruptcies. Here, the profit isn't entirely risk-free, as it depends on the successful completion of the corporate action. A common strategy involves buying the stock of a company being acquired (at a discount to the proposed acquisition price) and shorting the stock of the acquirer. The payoff depends on the deal going through, and the arbitrageur must evaluate the likelihood and risks associated with the outcome.

**Statistical Arbitrage** is a more complex form and relies on quantitative models to identify price discrepancies between related securities. These strategies use mean reversion principles, time-series analysis, and other statistical methods to detect temporary mispricings. For instance, pairs trading, a form of statistical arbitrage, involves two historically correlated stocks. When the spread between their prices deviates from the historical average, an arbitrage opportunity is identified: the underperforming stock is bought, and the outperforming one is shorted, anticipating that the spread will eventually revert to the mean.

These strategies can be formalized as:

$$\text{Spread} = P_A - P_B$$

$$\text{If Spread} > \text{Historical Average} \implies \text{Short } P_A\text{, Long } P_B$$

$$\text{Otherwise, Long } P_A\text{, Short } P_B$$

While arbitrage opportunities may seem ubiquitous in theory, several practical challenges must be considered. Transaction costs, such as commissions and bid-ask spreads, can erode profits. Additionally, arbitrage generally requires significant capital and quick execution capabilities to capitalize on fleeting opportunities. Regulation can also impact arbitrage by imposing restrictions on certain types of trades or short-selling.

Modern arbitrage strategies heavily incorporate algorithmic trading and high-frequency trading (HFT) to scan for and exploit minute price discrepancies in real-time. Advances in technology and access to vast amounts of data enable traders to develop sophisticated models to automate the identification and execution of arbitrage strategies.

Furthermore, mathematics plays a pivotal role in arbitrage. The fundamental theorem of asset pricing states that in the absence of arbitrage opportunities, there exists a risk-neutral measure under which the price of any asset equals its discounted expected future cash flows. This relation pinpoints the essence of arbitrage in maintaining market consistency and pricing fairness.

$$\text{Arbitrage-free price} = E_{\mathbb{Q}}\left[\frac{X}{1+r}\right]$$

Arbitrage thus serves a dual purpose: it presents profit opportunities for traders and ensures that markets remain efficient. By relentlessly seeking and exploiting price discrepancies, arbitrageurs drive prices towards equilibrium, reinforcing the principle that markets are self-correcting systems.

Understanding and employing arbitrage strategies allows investors to leverage temporary mispricings for profit while contributing to market stability. Whether through pure, risk, or statistical means, arbitrage remains a powerful tool within the arsenal of quantitative finance.

—

This section has elaborated on the fundamental principles, challenges, and applications of arbitrage in modern quantitative finance, setting the stage for more intricate concepts and strategies to follow in the subsequent sections.

## 1.8 Introduction to Derivatives

Derivatives are powerful financial instruments that derive their value from the performance of an underlying asset, index, or rate. These underlying entities could be stocks, bonds, commodities, currencies, interest rates, or market indexes. Derivatives are widely used in financial markets for hedging risks, speculation, and arbitrage. They are essential tools in the realm of quantitative finance, offering sophisticated mechanisms for managing and transferring risk.

To grasp the true utility and mechanics of derivatives, it is crucial to first understand the basic types and the theoretical underpinnings that drive their value and function. This section will cover the most common forms of derivatives—futures, forwards, options, and swaps—detailing their structures, uses, and the theoretical principles that govern their pricing.

At the heart of derivative pricing is the concept of *no-arbitrage*, which asserts that in an efficient market, identical assets must have the same price to prevent riskless profit opportunities. This principle is foundational in the theoretical models that we will explore in relation to each type of derivative.

### Futures and Forwards

Futures and forwards are agreements to buy or sell an asset at a predetermined future date for a price agreed upon today. While they are similar in purpose, there are key differences:

- *Forwards* are private contracts between two parties, typically customized and traded over-the-counter (OTC). They carry counterparty risk, as the agreement depends directly on the parties involved.
- *Futures* are standardized contracts traded on exchanges, benefiting from reduced counterparty risk due to the clearinghouse that acts as an intermediary.

The price of a forward or future contract, $F_t$, at time $t$ is given by the cost-of-carry model:

$$F_t = S_t e^{(r-q)(T-t)}$$

where $S_t$ is the spot price of the underlying asset, $r$ is the risk-free rate, $q$ is the dividend yield, and $(T-t)$ is the time to maturity of the contract.

### Options

Options grant the holder the right, but not the obligation, to buy (call option) or sell (put option) an asset at a specified price (strike price) on or before the expiration date. This unique feature introduces a non-linear payoff structure, providing strategic flexibility that can be tailored to a wide range of market scenarios. The value of an option can be understood in terms of its intrinsic and extrinsic value:

- *Intrinsic value* is the difference between the underlying asset's price and the strike price.
- *Extrinsic value* (or time value) encompasses the expectations of future volatility and time remaining until expiration.

The Black-Scholes-Merton model is a cornerstone in option pricing, assuming log-normal distribution of asset prices and deriving the price of a European call option:

$$C = S_0 N(d_1) - X e^{-rT} N(d_2)$$

where:

$$d_1 = \frac{\ln(\frac{S_0}{X}) + (r + \frac{\sigma^2}{2})T}{\sigma\sqrt{T}}, \quad d_2 = d_1 - \sigma\sqrt{T}$$

and $N(\cdot)$ represents the cumulative distribution function of the standard normal distribution, $S_0$ is the current price of the underlying asset, $X$ is the strike price, $\sigma$ is the volatility, $r$ is the risk-free interest rate, and $T$ is the time to maturity.

### Swaps

Swaps are agreements to exchange cash flows between two parties. The most prevalent types include interest rate swaps and currency swaps. In an interest rate swap, typically, one party exchanges fixed interest rate payments for floating rate payments tied to an index such as LIBOR (London Interbank Offered Rate). Swaps are primarily used for hedging and speculating on changes in interest rates or currency values.

The value of a swap is determined by the net present value (NPV) of the cash flows exchanged and can be expressed as:

$$\text{NPV}_{\text{swap}} = \sum_{i=1}^{n} \left( B_i^{\text{floating}} - B_i^{\text{fixed}} \right)$$

where $B_i^{\text{floating}}$ and $B_i^{\text{fixed}}$ are the respective cash flows from the floating and fixed legs of the swap at period $i$.

Through our journey in understanding these derivatives, we employ various pricing models and theories to assess their value and risk. A rigorous approach to these models offers invaluable insights into market dynamics and the strategies that can leverage these instruments effectively.

Derivatives not only provide mechanisms for hedging and risk management but also open avenues for strategic speculation and exploiting market inefficiencies. As we have only touched upon the basics foundational to derivatives, future chapters will delve into advanced models and real-world applications, introducing deeper quantitative techniques necessary for sophisticated trading strategies.

## 1.9 Fixed Income Securities and Interest Rate Models

Fixed income securities represent a crucial segment of the financial markets, encompassing a variety of instruments designed to provide regular income through interest payments. These securities are typically issued by governments, corporations, and other entities seeking to raise capital. In this section, we will delve into the characteristics of fixed income securities, explore various types such as bonds and treasury instruments, and introduce key concepts in interest rate modeling essential for pricing and risk management.

At the core of fixed income securities is the bond, a debt instrument that requires the issuer to pay the bondholder a specified interest (coupon) over a predetermined period, with the principal (face value) repaid at maturity. Bonds can differ significantly based on their issuers, maturity, coupon structure, and other attributes. Common categories include government bonds, corporate bonds, municipal bonds, and mortgage-backed securities, each with unique risk profiles and yields.

**Government Bonds** are typically considered low-risk investments, issued by sovereign states. Examples include U.S. Treasury securities (T-bills, T-notes, T-bonds) and other sovereign debt. Their safety stems from the issuing government's taxing power or ability to print currency.

**Corporate Bonds** are issued by companies to finance operations, expansion, or other expenditures. These carry higher risk compared to government bonds due to the potential default risk of the issuing entity. The creditworthiness of corporate bonds is assessed by rating agencies and reflected in their yield spreads over risk-free securities.

Municipal bonds, issued by states, municipalities, or counties, fund public projects such as schools and roads. Mortgage-backed securities pool together a collection of mortgages and sell the interests to investors, providing exposure to the real estate market.

Understanding the valuation of these securities relies on the concept of present value, where the future cash flows (interest and principal payments) are discounted back to their present value using an appropriate discount rate. The formula for the present value of a bond (without considering periodic coupon payments) is:

$$PV = \frac{C}{(1+r)^t} + \frac{F}{(1+r)^n}$$

where $C$ is the coupon payment, $r$ the discount rate, $t$ the period, and $F$ the face value of the bond repayable at maturity $n$. For coupon bonds, we sum the discounted cash flows received periodically until maturity.

Interest rate models come into play for more sophisticated analysis and management of fixed income securities. These models help in predicting future interest rate movements, valuing derivatives, managing risks, and constructing portfolios. We will focus on three primary frameworks: the **Vasicek Model**, the **Cox-Ingersoll-Ross (CIR) Model**, and the **Ho-Lee Model**.

The **Vasicek Model** assumes that interest rates follow a mean-reverting stochastic process described by the equation:

$$dr_t = a(b - r_t)dt + \sigma dW_t$$

Here, $r_t$ represents the interest rate at time $t$, $a$ the speed of reversion to the mean $b$, $\sigma$ the volatility, and $W_t$ a Wiener process. This model captures the tendency of rates to return to an average value over time, making it useful for long-term interest rate predictions.

The **CIR Model** builds on the Vasicek framework by incorporating the square root of the interest rate in the volatility term, ensuring non-negativity:

$$dr_t = a(b - r_t)dt + \sigma\sqrt{r_t}dW_t$$

This model is particularly advantageous in scenarios where the likelihood of negative interest rates must be minimized while preserving mean-reversion and realistic interest rate distribution properties.

The **Ho-Lee Model** takes a different approach by assuming that changes in the short rate follow a binomial process. It is represented as:

$$dr_t = \theta(t)dt + \sigma dW_t$$

where $\theta(t)$ function is deterministic and fitted to match the current term structure of interest rates. The Ho-Lee model is often used for fitting and valuing bond options and other derivatives.

Advanced interest rate models and more sophisticated fixed income strategies heavily rely on these foundational frameworks, each fitting varying market conditions and investment objectives. Mastery of these tools enables traders and portfolio managers to navigate the complexities of fixed income markets, optimizing portfolios to achieve desired risk-return profiles.

By efficiently utilizing interest rate models, investors can anticipate future fluctuations, hedge risks, and uncover opportunities in interest rate-sensitive instruments. Each model offers specific strengths, dictating its suitability for different financial scenarios and market dynamics. With these concepts well understood, we can now transition to exploring the application of machine learning in predicting market movements and refining quantitative strategies.

# Chapter 2

# Introduction to Machine Learning

**This chapter provides a comprehensive overview of machine learning concepts, starting with the basics and the different types of machine learning: supervised, unsupervised, and reinforcement learning. It covers key terms such as training, testing, and validation, and reviews common machine learning algorithms. The chapter also discusses evaluation metrics, overfitting and underfitting, and the bias-variance tradeoff. It introduces popular machine learning libraries and tools, outlines the steps in a typical machine learning workflow, and addresses common challenges in the field.**

## 2.1 What is Machine Learning?

Machine learning (ML) is a branch of artificial intelligence (AI) that enables systems to learn and improve from experience without being explicitly programmed. At its core, machine learning focuses on the development of algorithms that can analyze and learn from data, making predictions or decisions informed by this analysis. Unlike traditional programming, where a human provides specific instructions for every possible scenario, machine learning involves creating models that generalize from a set of examples, allowing the system to autonomously adapt to new and unseen data.

The process of machine learning typically begins with the collection of data. This dataset can include historical market prices, trading volumes, financial indicators, and other relevant variables. The next step involves selecting a suitable model or algorithm capable of learning from this data. Commonly used algorithms span a wide range, from linear regression and decision trees to more complex neural networks.

Once the data is gathered and the model is chosen, the data is divided into different subsets: a training set, used to teach the model; a validation set, employed to tune the model parameters; and a testing set, which assesses the model's performance on unseen data. This process ensures that the model can generalize well and is not merely memorizing the training data—a phenomenon known as overfitting.

To understand the essence of machine learning, consider the task of predicting stock prices. Traditional methods may involve building complex financial models or relying on expert judgment. In contrast, a machine learning approach might use historical price data as input to a model, training it to recognize patterns that precede price changes. Over time, the model refines its predictions by adjusting to new data and minimizing prediction errors.

Mathematically, if we denote our dataset as $\boldsymbol{X}$ (features) and $\boldsymbol{y}$ (target labels), the goal of machine learning is to find a function $f$ such that $y \approx f(X)$. Formally, we seek to minimize a loss function $L$ over the dataset:

$$\arg\min_{\theta} L(f_\theta(\boldsymbol{X}), \boldsymbol{y})$$

where $\theta$ represents the model parameters that we adjust during training. The loss function quantifies the difference between the predicted values and the actual target values, guiding the optimization process to improve model accuracy.

The success of machine learning heavily relies on the quality of the data and the relevance of the features used. Feature engineering, which involves selecting and transforming raw data into meaningful inputs for the model, is a critical step. It requires domain knowledge to identify which factors are likely to influence the outcome. For instance, in trading, features might include price trends, market sentiment, economic indicators, and company-specific news.

There are various types of machine learning, categorized based on the nature of the learning signal: supervised learning, where the model learns from labeled data; unsupervised learning, which deals with unlabeled data to find hidden patterns or structures; and reinforcement learning, where an agent learns by interacting with an environment and receiving feedback through rewards or penalties. These categories will be explored in greater detail in the next section.

The convergence of machine learning with trading and investing has led to the development of sophisticated trading strategies and enhanced risk management techniques. Algorithmic trading, for example, leverages machine learning to execute trades at optimal timings, often guided by real-time data analysis and predictive modeling. These innovations underscore the transformative potential of machine learning in the financial markets.

As you delve deeper into machine learning, you will encounter a rich landscape of algorithms, techniques, and tools designed to harness the power of data. The upcoming sections will provide a solid foundation on these topics, equipping you with the knowledge to apply machine learning effectively in your trading strategies.

## 2.2 Types of Machine Learning: Supervised, Unsupervised, Reinforcement

Machine learning can be categorized into three primary types: supervised learning, unsupervised learning, and reinforcement learning. Each type addresses different kinds of problems and utilizes distinct methods to derive patterns or make predictions from data. Understanding these types and their respective frameworks enables investors and traders to effectively apply machine learning techniques to predict market movements.

Supervised learning is one of the most widely used techniques in machine learning. It involves training a model on a labeled dataset, where the input data is paired with the correct output. The goal is for the model to learn the relationship between inputs and outputs so that it can predict the output for new, unseen inputs. This type of learning is analogous to a teacher supervising the learning process. Supervised learning can be further divided into two categories: regression and classification. Regression tasks predict continuous values, such as future stock prices. A common example of a regression algorithm is linear regression, where the relationship between the dependent variable and one or more independent variables is modeled by fitting a linear equation to the observed data. Mathematically, it can be represented as:

$$y = \beta_0 + \beta_1 x_1 + \cdots + \beta_n x_n + \epsilon$$

where $y$ is the dependent variable, $x_1, \ldots, x_n$ are the independent variables, $\beta_0, \ldots, \beta_n$ are the coefficients, and $\epsilon$ is the error term. Classification tasks, on the other hand, categorize inputs into discrete classes. For example, classifying whether a stock will go up or down the next day is a binary classification problem. Support Vector Machines (SVM) and Random Forests are popular algorithms used for classification tasks.

Unsupervised learning deals with unlabeled data, meaning the algorithm attempts to find patterns or intrinsic structures in the input data without any explicit instructions on what to look for. This type of learning is especially useful for exploratory data analysis, anomaly detection, and clustering. Clustering is a common unsupervised learning task where the goal is to group data points that are similar to each other. An example of a clustering algorithm is $k$-means clustering, which partitions the data into $k$ clusters, minimizing the variance within each cluster. The algorithm iteratively assigns data points to the cluster with the nearest centroid and then recalculates the centroids based on the current assignments. The process can be formalized as:

$$\text{argmin} \sum_{i=1}^{k} \sum_{x \in C_i} \|x - \mu_i\|^2$$

where $C_i$ represents the $i$-th cluster and $\mu_i$ is the centroid of the $i$-th cluster. Another example is Principal Component Analysis (PCA), which reduces the dimensionality of the data by transforming it into a new coordinate system where the greatest variances become the principal components.

Reinforcement learning is a type of machine learning where an agent learns to make decisions by interacting with an environment. The agent takes actions in the environment and receives feedback in the form of rewards or penalties. The objective is to learn a policy that maximizes the cumulative reward over time. This learning process involves exploration (trying new actions to discover their effects) and exploitation (choosing actions that are known to yield high rewards). Markov Decision Processes (MDP) are commonly used to model reinforcement learning problems, where the environment is a set of states, $S$, actions, $A$, transition probabilities, $P$, and rewards, $R$. The goal is to determine an optimal policy $\pi$ that maximizes the expected sum of the rewards:

$$\pi^* = \text{argmax}_\pi \mathbb{E}\left[\sum_{t=0}^{\infty} \gamma^t R(s_t, \pi(s_t))\right]$$

where $\gamma$ is the discount factor, and $s_t$ is the state at time $t$. Reinforcement learning algorithms include Q-learning and Deep Q-Networks (DQN), which use a neural network to approximate the Q-value function that represents the expected rewards for state-action pairs.

Understanding and leveraging these types of machine learning techniques allow traders and investors to build models that can predict market movements, identify trends, and optimize trading strategies more effectively. Seamlessly integrating supervised, unsupervised, and reinforcement learning approaches into an investment strategy can lead to more informed and profitable decision-making.

## 2.3 Key Concepts: Training, Testing, and Validation

A fundamental aspect of machine learning is the process of using data to build predictive models. This process is structured around three key concepts: training, testing, and validation. Each of these steps plays a vital role in ensuring that the model performs well not only on the data it was trained on, but also on unseen data.

The **training** phase involves feeding the machine learning algorithm a dataset, known as the training set, which contains both input features and corresponding target values. This is where the model learns the underlying relationships between the inputs and outputs. For instance, in supervised learning, the algorithm adjusts its internal parameters to minimize the difference between its predictions and the actual target values, using techniques such as gradient descent.

Mathematically, the training process can be represented as

$$\text{minimize} \sum_{i=1}^{n} L(y_i, f(x_i; \theta)),$$

where $L$ is the loss function, $y_i$ is the actual output, $f(x_i; \theta)$ is the model's prediction with parameters $\theta$, and $n$ is the number of training samples. The goal is to find the optimal set of parameters, $\theta^*$, that best fits the training data.

After training, the model is evaluated using a **testing** dataset. The testing phase is crucial because it measures the model's predictive performance on unseen data. This helps determine if the model has generalizable patterns or if it has merely memorized the training data, a problem known as overfitting. The testing set should be a representative sample from the same distribution as the training set but should not be used at all during training to prevent information leakage.

A common metric to evaluate the model's performance on the testing set is the Mean Absolute Error (MAE), which is defined as

$$\text{MAE} = \frac{1}{n}\sum_{i=1}^{n} |y_i - \hat{y}_i|,$$

where $\hat{y}_i$ represents the predicted value. Other evaluation metrics include Root Mean Squared Error (RMSE), R-squared score for regression tasks, and accuracy, precision, recall, and F1-score for classification tasks.

Finally, the **validation** process is used to fine-tune the model. It involves splitting the training set further into a separate validation set, which is used to tune hyperparameters—parameters that configure the learning process itself, such as learning rate or regularization strength. Cross-validation is a robust technique often employed here, wherein the training data is divided into $k$ subsets (folds). The model is trained on $k-1$ folds and validated on the remaining fold. This process is repeated $k$ times, and the model's performance is averaged over all $k$ rounds. This helps in making the model more resilient and less dependent on a particular split of the data.

Mathematically, cross-validation can be expressed as

$$\text{CV} = \frac{1}{k}\sum_{i=1}^{k} \text{ValError}_i,$$

where $\text{ValError}_i$ is the validation error of the model on the i-th fold. This provides a more reliable estimate of the model's performance and aids in hyperparameter tuning.

By understanding and correctly applying the concepts of training, testing, and validation, one can develop models that generalize well to new data, which is the ultimate objective of any predictive model in machine learning. These steps ensure that the model's performance is optimized and robust, providing confidence in its predictions when applied to real-world scenarios.

## 2.4 Common Machine Learning Algorithms

The landscape of machine learning is rich with a variety of algorithms, each suited for different types of tasks and data characteristics. This section delves into some of the most widely used machine learning algorithms, providing a detailed examination of their mechanics, strengths, and ideal application scenarios. Our exploration will encompass both supervised and unsupervised learning algorithms, given their prominence in practical applications.

**Linear Regression**

Linear regression is one of the simplest and most interpretable algorithms used primarily for regression tasks. It models the relationship between a dependent variable $y$ and one or more independent variables $X$ by fitting a linear equation to observed data. The linear regression model can be expressed as:

$$y = \beta_0 + \beta_1 x_1 + \beta_2 x_2 + \cdots + \beta_n x_n + \epsilon$$

where $\beta_0$ is the intercept, $\beta_1, \beta_2, \ldots, \beta_n$ are coefficients representing the weights of the features $x_1, x_2, \ldots, x_n$, and $\epsilon$ is the error term.

The objective is to minimize the mean squared error (MSE) between the predicted values and the actual values. This is achieved through methods such as Ordinary Least Squares (OLS). Linear regression is widely used due to its simplicity and efficiency, particularly in cases where the relationship between variables is approximately linear.

**Logistic Regression**

Despite its name, logistic regression is used primarily for classification problems. It models the probability that a given input belongs to a particular category. The logistic regression model can be expressed using the logistic function:

$$P(y = 1|X) = \frac{1}{1 + e^{-(\beta_0 + \beta_1 x_1 + \beta_2 x_2 + \cdots + \beta_n x_n)}}$$

where the logistic function maps any real-valued number into a value between 0 and 1. The model's output is interpreted as the probability of the input belonging to the positive class. By applying a threshold (typically 0.5), we can classify the input into one of the two classes. Logistic regression is particularly powerful for binary classification and can be extended to multiclass classification using techniques such as the One-vs-All approach.

### Decision Trees

Decision trees are versatile and intuitive algorithms that can be used for both classification and regression tasks. A decision tree algorithm recursively splits the feature space into regions through a series of if-else questions based on feature values. The resultant model resembles a tree where each node represents a feature, each branch represents a decision rule, and each leaf node represents an outcome.

The process of building a decision tree involves selecting the feature and threshold that result in the best partitioning of the dataset, which is often determined by metrics like Gini impurity or information gain for classification trees, and mean squared error for regression trees. Decision trees are easy to visualize and interpret, but they are prone to overfitting, making it crucial to incorporate techniques such as pruning.

### Random Forests

Random forests address the overfitting problem inherent in decision trees by aggregating multiple trees into an ensemble model. Each tree in a random forest is trained on a bootstrap sample (random subset) of the data, and at each split, a random subset of features is considered. The final prediction is obtained by averaging the predictions for regression or taking a majority vote for classification.

Random forests provide improvements in accuracy and robustness over single decision trees and are less sensitive to overfitting because the ensemble averaging process reduces variance.

### Support Vector Machines (SVM)

Support Vector Machines are powerful supervised learning models used for classification and regression tasks. SVMs work by finding the optimal hyperplane that maximizes the margin between the closest points of the different classes, known as support vectors. The objective is to maximize this margin, thus ensuring better generalization.

For linearly separable data, the SVM determines a linear hyperplane. For non-linearly separable data, SVMs can use kernel functions such as the radial basis function (RBF) to transform the feature space into higher dimensions where a hyperplane can neatly separate the classes. SVMs are particularly effective in high-dimensional spaces and are robust against overfitting, especially in scenarios with higher dimensionality than the number of samples.

**K-Nearest Neighbors (KNN)**

K-Nearest Neighbors is a simple, yet effective, non-parametric algorithm used for both classification and regression. The core idea is to predict the target value based on the $k$ closest training samples in the feature space. For classification, the predicted class is the majority class among the $k$ neighbors, while for regression, the prediction is the average of the target values of the $k$ nearest neighbors.

KNN is intuitive and easy to implement but can be computationally expensive with large datasets due to the necessity of storing and searching through all training examples. The choice of $k$ and the distance metric (e.g., Euclidean distance) are crucial for optimizing the algorithm's performance.

**K-Means Clustering**

K-Means is a popular unsupervised learning algorithm used for clustering. It partitions the dataset into $k$ clusters by minimizing the within-cluster sum of squares. The algorithm involves the following steps:

- Initialize $k$ centroids randomly.
- Assign each data point to the nearest centroid.
- Update the centroids to the mean of the assigned points.
- Repeat steps 2 and 3 until convergence.

The result is a partitioning of the dataset where intra-cluster variance is minimized. The choice of $k$ is critical and can be determined using methods like the elbow method.

**Principal Component Analysis (PCA)**

Principal Component Analysis is an unsupervised learning algorithm used for dimensionality reduction. It transforms the original features into a new set of orthogonal features called principal components, ordered by the amount of variance they capture from the data. The steps involve:

- Standardizing the data.
- Computing the covariance matrix.
- Calculating the eigenvectors and eigenvalues of the covariance matrix.
- Sorting the eigenvectors by their corresponding eigenvalues in descending order.
- Selecting the top $k$ eigenvectors to form the principal components.

By projecting the data onto these principal components, PCA reduces the dimensionality while retaining most of the variance, making it useful for visualization, noise reduction, and as a preprocessing step for other algorithms.

Incorporating these algorithms into your machine learning projects can significantly enhance predictive performance and provide robust solutions to complex financial problems. Understanding when and how to apply each algorithm is key to unlocking their full potential.

## 2.5 Evaluation Metrics for Machine Learning Models

Evaluating the performance of machine learning models is a critical step in the development and deployment of algorithms. Ensuring that models are performing as expected requires the use of well-defined metrics that quantify effectiveness in a manner appropriate to the goals of the task at hand. This section delves into various evaluation metrics, elucidating their relevance and application for both classification and regression tasks.

**Classification Metrics**

In classification problems, where the objective is to assign inputs to one of several predefined categories, several metrics are commonly employed:

- **Accuracy**: The proportion of correctly classified instances out of the total instances. While widely used, accuracy may not be suitable for imbalanced datasets.

$$\text{Accuracy} = \frac{\text{Number of correct predictions}}{\text{Total number of predictions}}$$

- **Precision, Recall, and F1-Score**: These metrics provide more granular insights, especially in imbalanced datasets:
  - **Precision**: The ratio of correctly predicted positive observations to the total predicted positives. It is critical when the cost of false positives is high.

    $$\text{Precision} = \frac{\text{True Positives}}{\text{True Positives + False Positives}}$$

  - **Recall (Sensitivity/True Positive Rate)**: The ratio of correctly predicted positive observations to all the positives in actual class. It is important when the cost of false negatives is high.

    $$\text{Recall} = \frac{\text{True Positives}}{\text{True Positives + False Negatives}}$$

  - **F1-Score**: The harmonic mean of Precision and Recall, providing a balance between the two.

    $$\text{F1-Score} = 2 \times \frac{\text{Precision} \times \text{Recall}}{\text{Precision + Recall}}$$

- **ROC-AUC (Receiver Operating Characteristic - Area Under Curve)**: This metric evaluates the trade-off between the true positive rate and false positive rate. The AUC metric summarizes the overall ability of the model to discriminate between positive and negative classes, with larger AUC values indicating better performance.

  $$\text{AUC} = \int_0^1 \text{TPR}(t) \cdot \text{FPR}(t)\, dt$$

- **Confusion Matrix**: A detailed breakdown of actual vs. predicted classifications, outlining true positives, true negatives, false positives, and false negatives. It serves as a foundation for many aforementioned metrics.

| | **Predicted Positive** | **Predicted Negative** |
|---|---|---|
| **Actual Positive** | True Positive (TP) | False Negative (FN) |
| **Actual Negative** | False Positive (FP) | True Negative (TN) |

- **Log-Loss (Logarithmic Loss)**: This metric quantifies the accuracy of probabilistic predictions. It penalizes false classifications and rewards probability scores closer to the actual class label.

$$\text{Log-Loss} = -\frac{1}{N}\sum_{i=1}^{N}[y_i \log(p(y_i)) + (1 - y_i)\log(1 - p(y_i))]$$

**Regression Metrics**

For regression tasks, where the goal is to predict continuous values, different metrics are more appropriate:

- **Mean Absolute Error (MAE)**: The average absolute difference between predicted and actual values. It is simple to interpret and provides a linear scale of error magnitude.

$$\text{MAE} = \frac{1}{N}\sum_{i=1}^{N}|y_i - \hat{y}_i|$$

- **Mean Squared Error (MSE)**: The average of squared differences between predicted and actual values. MSE penalizes larger errors more significantly, making it useful when larger errors are particularly undesirable.

$$\text{MSE} = \frac{1}{N}\sum_{i=1}^{N}(y_i - \hat{y}_i)^2$$

- **Root Mean Squared Error (RMSE)**: The square root of MSE, bringing the error metric back to the original scale of the data. It emphasizes larger errors more than MAE.

$$\text{RMSE} = \sqrt{\frac{1}{N}\sum_{i=1}^{N}(y_i - \hat{y}_i)^2}$$

- **R-squared (Coefficient of Determination)**: It measures the proportion of variance in the dependent variable that is predictable from the independent variables. An R-squared of 1 indicates perfect prediction, while 0 indicates that the model fails to predict the variance.

$$R^2 = 1 - \frac{\sum_{i=1}^{N}(y_i - \hat{y}_i)^2}{\sum_{i=1}^{N}(y_i - \bar{y})^2}$$

Selecting the appropriate evaluation metric is contingent on the specific goals of the machine learning task and the characteristics of the data. By comprehensively understanding and applying these metrics, practitioners can effectively assess model performance, ensuring that models not only perform well on training data but also generalize properly to unseen data, thereby making sound financial predictions and decisions based on accurate and reliable models.

## 2.6 Overfitting and Underfitting

Understanding the concepts of overfitting and underfitting is crucial for anyone involved in machine learning, particularly in the realm of financial markets where predictive accuracy can significantly impact trading decisions. Both phenomena are related to how well a machine learning model generalizes from its training data to unseen data.

Overfitting occurs when a model learns not only the underlying patterns in the training data but also the noise and outliers. As a result, it performs exceptionally well on the training data but poorly on new, unseen data. This is because the model becomes too complex, capturing spurious patterns that do not generalize. Mathematically, overfitting is often observed when the model's accuracy on the training set continues to increase while its performance on the validation or test set starts to deteriorate.

Conversely, underfitting happens when a model is too simple to capture the underlying structure of the data. This often occurs if the model has too few features, or if the algorithm used is not capable of learning the complexity present in the data. Underfitting is easily detectable when both the training and validation errors are high, indicating that the model hasn't learned enough from the data.

Let us delve deeper into these concepts with some examples and equations. Consider a dataset represented as $\{(x_i, y_i)\}_{i=1}^{N}$, where $x_i$ represents the input features and $y_i$ the corresponding labels. Assume we are trying to fit a polynomial regression model of degree $d$ to this data.

The model is defined as:

$$\hat{y} = \sum_{j=0}^{d} \beta_j x^j$$

For a linear regression model (where $d = 1$), there is a risk of underfitting if the data relationship is inherently non-linear. On the other hand, choosing a high degree polynomial (e.g., $d = 15$) might lead to overfitting, capturing noise along with the actual signal.

The bias-variance tradeoff provides a theoretical framework to understand overfitting and underfitting. Bias refers to the error introduced by approximating a real-world problem, which may be complex, by a simplified model. Variance refers to the error introduced by the variability of the model prediction for different training sets. Mathematically, the total error can be decomposed as:

$$\text{Total Error} = \text{Bias}^2 + \text{Variance} + \text{Irreducible Error}$$

High bias (leading to underfitting) typically corresponds to oversimplified models, whereas high variance (leading to overfitting) corresponds to overly complex models.

To avoid overfitting and underfitting, several strategies can be employed:

- **Cross-Validation**: Cross-validation, particularly k-fold cross-validation, allows the model to be trained and validated on different subsets of the data, ensuring that performance metrics are obtained from multiple perspectives. This helps in tuning model complexity effectively.

- **Regularization**: Techniques such as Lasso (L1 regularization) and Ridge (L2 regularization) add a penalty to the loss function, discouraging overly complex models. The Lasso regularizer adds a sum of the absolute values of the coefficients:

  $$\text{Lasso: } \hat{\beta} = \arg\min_{\beta} \left\{ \sum_{i=1}^{N} (y_i - y_i)^2 + \lambda \sum_{j=1}^{d} |\beta_j| \right\}$$

  While the Ridge regularizer adds a sum of the squares of the coefficients:

$$\text{Ridge: } \hat{\beta} = \arg\min_{\beta} \left\{ \sum_{i=1}^{N} (y_i - \hat{y}_i)^2 + \lambda \sum_{j=1}^{d} \beta_j^2 \right\}$$

Here, $\lambda$ is the regularization parameter that controls the amount of shrinkage: the larger the value of $\lambda$, the more the coefficients are shrunk towards zero.

- **Pruning**: In decision trees and ensemble methods such as random forests, pruning techniques are used to cut back extra branches that do not contribute to the final prediction. This effectively reduces overfitting by limiting the model's capacity.

- **Early Stopping**: During training of neural networks, early stopping can be employed to monitor the model's performance on a validation set, halting training when performance stops improving. This prevents the model from learning noise in the training data.

- **Increasing Training Data**: More data can help the model to generalize better, reducing both bias and variance. This is particularly useful when synthetic data generation techniques can be applied.

It is important to regularly evaluate your model on an independent test set to ensure it performs well on unseen data. Visual aids, such as learning curves, can also be used to diagnose overfitting and underfitting. A learning curve plots the training and validation error over a varying number of training instances and can clearly depict the relationship between model complexity and performance.

Balancing a model's complexity to maximize predictive performance is a delicate and critical process. Addressing overfitting and underfitting effectively will enable you to develop robust machine learning models that deliver reliable and actionable insights, particularly in trading and investing where market conditions constantly evolve.

## 2.7 Bias-Variance Tradeoff

Understanding the bias-variance tradeoff is crucial for developing proficient machine learning models, particularly in the context of financial markets where predictive accuracy is paramount. This tradeoff arises from the challenge of balancing a model's ability to both predict outcomes accurately and generalize well to unseen data.

Bias refers to the error introduced by approximating a real-world problem, which may be intricate, by a simpler model. High bias typically indicates that the model is not complex enough to capture the underlying structure of the data, resulting in underfitting. An underfit model may ignore relevant relationships between input and output variables, producing predictions that are consistently off from the actual values observed in the market.

Variance, on the other hand, refers to the model's sensitivity to small fluctuations in the training dataset. High variance indicates that the model is overly complex, capturing noise along with the intended data pattern. Such models suffer from overfitting, where the intricate noise within the training dataset is learned as if it was a true data signal, leading to poor predictive performance on new, unseen data.

To illustrate this tradeoff mathematically, consider the expected prediction error for a target variable $Y$ and input variable $X$. The expected squared error can be decomposed as follows:

$$\mathbb{E}\left[(Y - \hat{f}(X))^2\right] = \left(\text{Bias}[\hat{f}(X)]\right)^2 + \text{Var}[\hat{f}(X)] + \sigma^2$$

where:

- $\hat{f}(X)$ is the prediction model.
- Bias$[\hat{f}(X)]$ measures the error due to the model's assumptions not fitting the data well.
- Var$[\hat{f}(X)]$ measures the variability of the model prediction for different training sets.
- $\sigma^2$ is the irreducible error, inherent in the variability of the target variable.

The goal is to minimize the total error, which involves finding a balance between bias and variance. As a practical step, financial quants often employ various techniques to manage this tradeoff:

- **Model Selection**: Choosing the right model complexity is pivotal. Linear models may have low variance but high bias, while more flexible models like decision trees may have low bias but high variance. Models like Random Forests or Gradient Boosting provide a middle ground by averaging multiple models.

- **Regularization**: Techniques such as Lasso (L1 regularization) and Ridge (L2 regularization) introduce additional terms to the loss function to penalize extreme parameter values, thus controlling the variance without significantly increasing bias.

- **Cross-Validation**: This involves partitioning the dataset into multiple subsets, training the model on one subset and validating it on another. Cross-validation helps in ensuring that the model generalizes well by providing a more accurate estimate of model performance on unseen data.

- **Ensemble Methods**: Combining the predictions of multiple models to create a meta-model. This can help in reducing variance without significantly affecting bias. Techniques include bagging, boosting, and stacking, each contributing to lowering prediction errors.

- **Feature Engineering**: Transforming input features or adding interaction terms can help in reducing bias by capturing more complex relationships in the data. However, it is important to monitor the model's performance to ensure that this does not lead to an increase in variance.

- **Data Augmentation and Collection**: In financial markets, where historical data is extensive, one can increase the robustness of models to variance by incorporating more data points. Enhanced datasets help in reducing the effects of noise on model training, thus balancing the bias-variance ratio.

In trading and investing, especially where algorithmic strategies are employed, the implications of the bias-variance tradeoff are profound. Models must not only be accurate in-sample but must also perform robustly out-of-sample, under different market conditions. Avoiding overfitting is essential, as models that perform well on historical data but poorly on future data can lead to significant financial losses.

Deploying machine learning in trading requires an iterative approach towards tuning models. A balance must be struck between capturing the underlying financial signals (low bias) and maintaining generalizability across various market scenarios (low variance). By systematically applying the discussed techniques, quants can develop models that are both precise and robust, ultimately aiding in more effective prediction of market movements.

## 2.8 Machine Learning Libraries and Tools

The proliferation of machine learning has been significantly bolstered by the development of powerful, user-friendly libraries and tools. These resources simplify the implementation of complex algorithms and facilitate the building, training, and evaluation of machine learning models. Whether you are a novice embarking on your machine learning journey or an experienced quant refining your models, harnessing the right tools can markedly enhance your workflow. In this section, we delve into some of the most prominent machine learning libraries and tools, elucidating their features and usage scenarios.

Python's dominance in the machine learning arena is largely attributable to its extensive and versatile libraries. Here are some of the most widely used Python libraries:

**Scikit-learn**: Scikit-learn is a robust library that provides simple and efficient tools for data mining and data analysis. It is built on NumPy, SciPy, and matplotlib. Scikit-learn supports a range of machine learning models, including linear regression, support vector machines, decision trees, and ensemble methods like random forests.

- Installation: $ pip install scikit-learn
- Example usage:

```
from sklearn.model_selection import train_test_split
from sklearn.linear_model import LogisticRegression
from sklearn.metrics import accuracy_score

# Load dataset
X, y = load_iris(return_X_y=True)

# Split the dataset
X_train, X_test, y_train, y_test = train_test_split(X, y, test_size=0.2,
    random_state=42)

# Train the model
model = LogisticRegression()
model.fit(X_train, y_train)

# Predict and evaluate
y_pred = model.predict(X_test)
print("Accuracy:", accuracy_score(y_test, y_pred))
```

**TensorFlow**: Created by the Google Brain team, TensorFlow is an open-source library designed for high-performance numerical computations. It is particularly popular for deep learning applications. TensorFlow allows users to construct and train neural networks through a flexible platform that can run on CPUs, GPUs, and TPUs.

- Installation: $ pip install tensorflow
- Example usage:

```
import tensorflow as tf
from tensorflow.keras.models import Sequential
from tensorflow.keras.layers import Dense

# Build a simple neural network
model = Sequential([
    Dense(128, activation='relu', input_shape=(784,)),
    Dense(10, activation='softmax')
])

# Compile the model
model.compile(optimizer='adam', loss='sparse_categorical_crossentropy',
      metrics=['accuracy'])

# Train the model
model.fit(x_train, y_train, epochs=10)
```

**Keras**: Keras is an API designed for human beings, not machines. Keras follows best practices for reducing cognitive load: it offers consistent and simple APIs, minimizes the number of user actions required for common use cases, and provides clear and actionable error messages. While initially independent, Keras is now integrated into TensorFlow, providing an easy-to-use interface for building and training neural networks.

- Installation: Included with TensorFlow, no separate installation needed.
- Example usage: See TensorFlow example above.

**PyTorch**: Developed by Facebook's AI Research lab, PyTorch has gained immense popularity due to its flexibility and dynamic computational graph. PyTorch is favored for research and development, particularly in the deep learning community, owing to its intuitive design and ease of use.

- Installation: $ pip install torch
- Example usage:

```
import torch
import torch.nn as nn
import torch.optim as optim
from torch.utils.data import DataLoader

# Define a simple neural network
class SimpleNN(nn.Module):
    def __init__(self):
        super(SimpleNN, self).__init__()
        self.fc1 = nn.Linear(784, 128)
        self.relu = nn.ReLU()
        self.fc2 = nn.Linear(128, 10)

    def forward(self, x):
        x = self.fc1(x)
        x = self.relu(x)
        x = self.fc2(x)
        return x

# Instantiate the model, define loss and optimizer
model = SimpleNN()
criterion = nn.CrossEntropyLoss()
optimizer = optim.Adam(model.parameters(), lr=0.001)

# Training loop
for epoch in range(10):
    for batch in DataLoader(train_dataset, batch_size=64, shuffle=True):
        inputs, targets = batch
        outputs = model(inputs)
        loss = criterion(outputs, targets)
        optimizer.zero_grad()
        loss.backward()
        optimizer.step()
```

R, a language known for its strength in statistical analysis, also offers powerful libraries for machine learning:

**caret**: The caret package in R provides a comprehensive suite of functions to streamline the model training process for complex regression and classification problems. It includes tools for data splitting, pre-processing, feature selection, model training, and tuning.

- Installation: install.packages("caret")
- Example usage:

```
library(caret)
data(iris)

# Split the dataset
set.seed(123)
trainIndex <- createDataPartition(iris$Species, p = .8, list = FALSE, times =
    1)
trainData <- iris[trainIndex, ]
testData <- iris[-trainIndex, ]
```

```
# Train a model
model <- train(Species ~ ., data = trainData, method = "rf")

# Make predictions and evaluate
predictions <- predict(model, testData)
confusionMatrix(predictions, testData$Species)
```

**xgboost**: Known for its efficiency and scalability, xgboost is widely used for optimizing decision tree based algorithms. It is a favorite in machine learning competitions such as those hosted on Kaggle.

- Installation: install.packages("xgboost")
- Example usage:

```
library(xgboost)
data(iris)

# Convert data to matrix form
X <- as.matrix(iris[, -5])
y <- as.numeric(iris$Species) - 1

# Train an xgboost model
dtrain <- xgb.DMatrix(data = X, label = y)
model <- xgboost(data = dtrain, max.depth = 3, eta = 1, nrounds = 10,
      objective = "multi:softprob", num_class = 3)

# Predict
pred <- predict(model, X)
pred <- matrix(pred, nrow = 3, ncol = length(pred) / 3)
pred <- max.col(t(pred)) - 1
accuracy <- mean(pred == y)
print(paste("Accuracy:", accuracy))
```

Beyond individual libraries, several integrated development environments (IDEs) and platforms further enhance the machine learning workflow:

**Jupyter Notebooks**: An open-source web application that allows you to create and share documents containing live code, equations, visualizations, and narrative text. Jupyter supports numerous programming languages, including Python, R, and Julia.

- Installation: $ pip install jupyter

**Google Colab**: A free, cloud-based service that facilitates the execution of Python code via the web browser. Colab provides access to GPUs and TPUs, making it an excellent resource for training complex deep learning models.

- Access: https://colab.research.google.com/

**GitHub**: A platform for version control and collaborative work, GitHub allows you to manage and share your machine learning projects. It integrates well with various CI/CD tools, enhancing the automated deployment of models.

- Access: https://github.com/

The right combination of libraries and tools can streamline your machine learning projects, allowing you to focus on refining your models and extracting actionable insights. With the capabilities of these resources at your fingertips, you are well-equipped to tackle the most challenging problems in the field of quantitative finance and beyond.

## 2.9 Steps in a Machine Learning Workflow

The machine learning workflow is a structured approach to developing predictive models. It involves a series of consecutive and interdependent steps designed to transform raw data into actionable insights. Understanding this workflow is crucial for both novice and experienced traders who wish to leverage machine learning for predicting market movements. Let us delve into each step with detailed explanations and practical implications.

The first step in the workflow is **Data Collection**. This involves gathering relevant data from various sources such as historical price data, trading volumes, economic indicators, and sentiment data from news or social media. Quality and quantity of data are pivotal at this stage. Inadequate or low-quality data can lead to weak models that fail to capture the underlying market dynamics. Utilize APIs, databases, and web scraping to compile a comprehensive dataset.

Once the data is collected, **Data Preprocessing** comes next. This step includes cleaning the data, handling missing values, detecting outliers, and normalizing or standardizing the data. For financial data, it's essential to manage anomalies such as stock splits or dividends that might introduce noise. Transformations like logarithmic returns can also be applied to stabilize the variance. Proper data preprocessing ensures that the dataset is clean and compatible with various machine learning algorithms.

Following preprocessing, **Feature Engineering** is performed. Feature engineering involves creating new features or modifying existing ones to improve the performance of the model. This could include technical indicators like moving averages, relative strength index (RSI), or Bollinger Bands. Feature selection techniques, such as correlation analysis or using algorithms like LASSO, help in identifying the most relevant features to use in the model, ultimately enhancing its predictive power.

Next is the crucial step of **Splitting the Dataset**. The data must be divided into training, validation, and test sets. This is typically done in a ratio such as 70-15-15 or 80-10-10. The training set is used to train the model, the validation set helps in tuning parameters and avoiding overfitting, and the test set evaluates the model's performance on unseen data. It's important to ensure that the split is done in a manner that preserves the temporal order of financial data to avoid look-ahead bias.

The **Model Selection** step involves choosing the appropriate machine learning algorithm for the problem at hand. Common algorithms include linear regression, decision trees, random forests, support vector machines (SVM), and neural networks. The choice of model depends on various factors such as the nature of the data, the complexity of the problem, and the specific objectives of the trading strategy. Trying multiple models and comparing their performances is a good practice.

After selecting the model, the next step is **Model Training**. During this phase, the chosen algorithm learns from the training data. It adjusts its parameters to minimize the prediction error through optimization techniques such as gradient descent. Monitoring the learning process and preventing issues like overfitting through techniques like cross-validation and regularization are integral to developing a robust model.

**Model Evaluation** follows model training. Using the validation and test sets, the model's performance is assessed using various metrics such as mean squared error (MSE), mean absolute error (MAE), accuracy, precision, recall, and the F1 score. For financial applications, metrics like Sharpe Ratio or maximum drawdown might also be relevant. These metrics help in understanding the strengths and weaknesses of the model, guiding further improvements.

The next step, **Model Tuning**, involves optimizing the model's hyperparameters to enhance its performance. Techniques like grid search, random search, or Bayesian optimization can be employed. The process is iterative, often requiring multiple trials and adjustments to strike an optimal balance.

Once the model is tuned, **Model Deployment** is the step where the model is put into production. This can involve integrating the model with trading platforms, setting up automated trading algorithms, or providing decision support for discretionary trading. Ensuring the model works seamlessly in a live environment is critical.

Finally, **Monitoring and Maintenance** ensures that the model continues to perform well over time. Financial markets are dynamic, and models might degrade as market conditions change. Continuous monitoring, periodic retraining with new data, and performance review ensure the model's longevity and reliability.

Each step in the machine learning workflow is interrelated and pivotal to developing effective market prediction models. A diligent and iterative approach can significantly enhance the probability of success when utilizing machine learning in trading and investing.

## 2.10 Challenges in Machine Learning

Machine learning has revolutionized the field of quantitative finance and trading, offering powerful tools to predict market movements and optimize trading strategies. However, deploying machine learning models in real-world financial markets presents numerous challenges that practitioners must navigate. This section delves into key obstacles, providing insights into how these challenges can be addressed effectively.

One of the primary challenges in machine learning for finance is **data quality and availability**. Financial markets generate massive amounts of data daily, but not all of this data is reliable or accessible. Historical data may contain gaps, inaccuracies, or biases, which can significantly impact the performance of machine learning models. Moreover, obtaining high-quality, granular data often requires substantial financial resources. To mitigate this, quants must implement robust data cleaning and preprocessing techniques. Utilizing data imputation methods for missing values and performing rigorous outlier detection can help improve data quality. Additionally, strategies such as combining multiple data sources can enhance data availability and robustness.

Another significant challenge is **non-stationarity** of financial data. Unlike in many other domains, financial time series are inherently non-stationary, meaning that their statistical properties, such as mean and variance, change over time. This non-stationarity introduces complexity in model training and validation, as patterns detected during the training phase may not hold in the future. Techniques like time-series decomposition and state-space modeling can be applied to address non-stationarity. Moreover, adaptive algorithms that can update themselves with new data in real-time are valuable in managing changing market conditions.

**Model interpretability** is another critical issue in the application of machine learning to finance. Many advanced machine learning models, such as deep learning networks, operate as "black boxes," providing limited insight into how they make predictions. This lack of transparency can be problematic, especially in highly regulated environments where model decisions must be justifiable. To enhance interpretability, practitioners can employ models that are inherently more transparent, such as linear regression, or use post-hoc interpretability techniques like SHAP (SHapley Additive exPlanations) values, which explain individual predictions by attributing the importance of each feature.

Financial markets are also characterized by **high noise-to-signal ratios**, where relevant signals are often obscured by noise. This makes it challenging to extract valuable insights and can lead to models overfitting to noise rather than identifying true underlying patterns. Employing regularization techniques and cross-validation methods can help prevent overfitting. Furthermore, integrating domain expertise with machine learning can provide a more nuanced understanding of the signal, improving model robustness.

**Real-time implementation** of machine learning models presents another layer of complexity. Financial markets demand rapid decision-making, often within milliseconds. Deploying models in such environments requires not only efficient algorithms but also reliable and low-latency infrastructure. This involves optimizing code for speed, using high-performance computing resources, and employing latency-sensitive data feeds.

Lastly, **regulatory and ethical considerations** in machine learning are paramount in finance. Models must comply with stringent regulations to prevent market manipulation and ensure fairness. Ethical considerations, such as avoiding biased decision-making and ensuring equitable access to financial services, are increasingly under scrutiny. Quants must work closely with compliance teams to ensure that their models adhere to all relevant legal and ethical standards.

Navigating these challenges requires a combination of technical expertise, domain knowledge, and strategic foresight. By proactively addressing data quality issues, adapting to non-stationarity, enhancing model interpretability, managing noise, optimizing for real-time implementation, and adhering to regulatory standards, quants can harness the full potential of machine learning to drive innovative and effective trading strategies.

# Chapter 3

# Data Preprocessing for Financial Data

**This chapter delves into the essential steps for preparing financial data for machine learning models. It begins by explaining the nature of financial data and methods for data collection. The chapter addresses handling missing data, data cleaning techniques, normalization, standardization, and feature scaling. It also covers working with time series data, handling outliers, and various data transformation techniques. Finally, the chapter discusses data augmentation strategies to enhance the quality and utility of financial datasets.**

## 3.1 Understanding Financial Data

Financial data forms the backbone of any trading and investing strategy. It includes a wide range of information, from stock prices and trading volumes to economic indicators and market sentiments. To effectively utilize machine learning for predicting market movements, it is critical to understand the nuances of this data, how it is structured, and its unique characteristics.

Financial data can be categorized into several types: price data, fundamental data, technical indicators, and alternative data. Each type of data offers unique insights and can be used complementarily to inform trading decisions.

Price data includes the open, high, low, and close prices of a financial instrument, along with the trading volume. This is the most fundamental form of financial data, and it is the starting point for most analysis. Understanding the patterns and behaviors in price movements is crucial. For instance, price data can exhibit trends, cycles, and support and resistance levels. These patterns can be identified using various statistical and visual techniques, such as moving averages and candlestick charts.

Fundamental data refers to the financial health and performance of a company and typically includes metrics like revenue, earnings, profit margins, and balance sheet items. This data helps in assessing the intrinsic value of a stock, guiding long-term investment decisions. Key financial ratios such as Price-to-Earnings (P/E), Price-to-Book (P/B), and Return on Equity (ROE) are derived from fundamental data and are instrumental in evaluating whether a stock is undervalued or overvalued.

Technical indicators are mathematical calculations based on price, volume, or open interest of a security. Common technical indicators include the Moving Average Convergence Divergence (MACD), Relative Strength Index (RSI), and Bollinger Bands. These indicators help in identifying the momentum, volatility, and strength of a price movement, thus assisting in making short-term trading decisions.

Alternative data encompasses non-traditional data sources that provide additional insights into market behavior. Examples include sentiment analysis from social media, foot traffic data for retail stores, satellite imagery for agriculture analysis, and more. The rise of big data and advancements in data analytics have made alternative data an essential tool for gaining an edge in the market.

Financial data is inherently non-stationary, meaning its statistical properties change over time. This characteristic makes financial data analysis particularly challenging. Unlike other forms of data, financial data is influenced by a variety of unpredictable factors including economic news, geopolitical events, and market sentiment shifts. The real-time nature of financial markets adds another layer of complexity, with data streaming in continuously and requiring timely analysis and response.

It is also important to consider the frequencies at which financial data is available. Data can be intra-day (minute-by-minute), daily, weekly, monthly, or even annual. The choice of frequency affects the type of analysis that can be performed. For instance, high-frequency trading strategies rely on intra-day data, while long-term investment strategies may focus on daily or monthly data.

In handling financial data, one must account for various market anomalies and biases. For instance, the "Monday effect" refers to the tendency of stock returns to be lower on Mondays. Another example is the "holiday effect," where trading volumes and market returns can be influenced by the time of the year. Recognizing and adjusting for these anomalies is critical when preprocessing data for machine learning models.

Moreover, financial data is often subject to survival bias, especially in historical data, where only information on companies that have survived until today is available. This can skew analysis and predictive models unless properly adjusted.

Lastly, regulatory constraints and data privacy concerns play a significant role in financial data management. Adhering to regulations such as the General Data Protection Regulation (GDPR) is essential for ensuring ethical and legal compliance when handling sensitive financial information.

Understanding these aspects of financial data lays the groundwork for effective data preprocessing, which is the next step in preparing data for machine learning models. By appreciating the complexity and the distinctive characteristics of financial data, traders and investors can better navigate the challenges and leverage the opportunities it presents.

## 3.2 Data Collection Methods

Effective data collection is the bedrock of any machine learning model, particularly in the realm of financial markets where data drives decision-making. Collecting high-quality financial data ensures that models are built on a solid foundation, leading to more reliable predictions and strategies. In this section, we explore various methods for gathering financial data, providing insights on where to source accurate and relevant information, and detailing the steps involved in the process.

First and foremost, understanding the types of financial data available is crucial. Financial data comes in various forms, including price data, volume data, fundamental data, and macroeconomic indicators. Price data encompasses the historical prices of securities, such as stocks, bonds, and derivatives. Volume data represents the number of shares or contracts traded over a given period. Fundamental data includes financial statements, earnings reports, and other company-specific information. Macroeconomic data involves broader economic indicators like GDP, interest rates, and inflation rates.

Several primary sources exist for collecting financial data, including exchanges, regulatory bodies, financial news platforms, and specialized data providers. Each source has its strengths and is suited for different types of data.

Exchanges such as the New York Stock Exchange (NYSE), Nasdaq, and global counterparts are direct sources of price and volume data. They provide raw, high-frequency data that is vital for high-frequency trading algorithms and other quantitative models. Most exchanges offer data subscription services, supplying real-time and historical data.

Regulatory agencies like the Securities and Exchange Commission (SEC) in the United States provide in-depth fundamental data through mandatory filings such as 10-K and 10-Q reports. These filings offer a treasure trove of information on a company's financial health, management discussions, and market risks. Accessing these reports is typically free through platforms like the SEC's EDGAR database.

Financial news platforms, including Bloomberg, Reuters, and CNBC, are excellent sources of both real-time market updates and historical data. They often provide comprehensive coverage, including market analyses, company news, and macroeconomic indicators. These platforms may require subscriptions, which can be costly, but the breadth and depth of data available can be invaluable.

Specialized data providers like Quandl, FactSet, and Morningstar offer custom datasets tailored to specific needs. They aggregate data from multiple sources, including exchanges, regulatory filings, and proprietary research, providing a one-stop shop for complex data requirements. These services often come with sophisticated data retrieval tools and APIs, facilitating easy integration with machine learning models.

Now, let's consider the mechanics of data collection. Collecting data involves both automated and manual processes, depending on the source and the type of data required. Automated data collection uses APIs (Application Programming Interfaces) to retrieve large volumes of data quickly and accurately. For instance, many exchanges and data providers offer APIs that allow users to programmatically access their data services. This is especially useful for frequent, systematic data retrieval in algorithmic trading and backtesting models.

Manual data collection, while more labor-intensive, is sometimes necessary for niche or less-structured data sources. This might involve scraping websites for specific financial news articles or manually downloading and parsing PDF files from regulatory filings. Technologies like web scraping libraries (e.g., BeautifulSoup in Python) and Optical Character Recognition (OCR) tools can assist in the extraction of structured data from unstructured sources.

Data storage and management also play a pivotal role in the collection process. Effective storage solutions ensure that data is readily accessible and securely maintained. Relational databases like MySQL and PostgreSQL are commonly used for storing structured financial data, offering robust query capabilities and data integrity. For handling large volumes of high-frequency data, NoSQL databases like MongoDB or time-series databases like InfluxDB are preferred due to their scalability and efficiency in managing time-indexed records.

Finally, it's essential to ensure the quality and consistency of collected data. Regular data audits and validation checks help identify and correct discrepancies, ensuring that the data used in models is accurate and reliable. Techniques such as cross-referencing data from multiple sources and implementing automated error-checking algorithms are vital.

Combining these diverse data collection methods equips financial analysts and quants with a rich dataset, forming the backbone of any sophisticated financial model. By understanding the nuances of each method and carefully managing the collected data, one can significantly enhance the effectiveness and accuracy of machine learning models in predicting market movements and optimizing investment strategies.

## 3.3 Handling Missing Data

Financial datasets often contain missing values due to various reasons, such as reporting errors, market closures, or data transmission issues. Properly handling missing data is crucial as it can significantly affect the performance of machine learning models. This section will explore different methods for detecting, analyzing, and addressing missing data in financial datasets, ensuring the integrity and reliability of your machine learning models.

When first encountering a dataset, it is essential to perform an initial assessment to understand the extent and pattern of missing data. This can be achieved by constructing a missing data matrix or plotting heatmaps to visualize the locations and proportions of missing values. Once the scope of missing data is identified, selecting an appropriate strategy for addressing these gaps is the next step.

Several strategies are available to handle missing data, and the choice of method depends on the nature of the data and the specific context of the analysis. Here we will examine the most commonly used techniques:

- **1. Deletion Methods:**
  - *Listwise Deletion:* This method involves removing entire rows where any value is missing. It is straightforward to implement but can result in significant data loss if the dataset contains a high proportion of missing values.
  - *Pairwise Deletion:* Instead of removing entire rows, this method uses all available data points for each calculation. It allows for more flexible use of the dataset but can lead to inconsistencies and biased estimates in the analysis.
- **2. Imputation Methods:**
  - *Mean/Median/Mode Imputation:* Replacing missing values with the mean, median, or mode of the available data in the same column is a common approach. While simple, it may not be suitable for datasets with a high density of missing values or for data with complex patterns.
  - *Forward/Backward Fill:* This time series–specific technique fills missing values using the previous or next available value. It preserves temporal continuity but assumes that consecutive values are similar, which may not always be the case.
  - *Linear Interpolation:* This method estimates missing values based on linear trends in the data. It is particularly useful for time series data, where it can produce more accurate and smooth imputations.
  - *K-Nearest Neighbors (KNN) Imputation:* This machine learning–based method identifies the K nearest observations using a distance metric and imputes missing values based on a weighted average of these neighbors.

KNN is robust but computationally intensive, especially for large datasets.

- *Multiple Imputation by Chained Equations (MICE):* This advanced technique creates multiple imputed datasets by iteratively estimating the missing values using a series of regression models. MICE accounts for uncertainty in the imputation process and provides more reliable statistical inferences.

- **3. Model-Based Methods:**
  - *Expectation-Maximization (EM):* This iterative method estimates the parameters of a statistical model that describes the data and then uses these estimates to impute missing values. EM is powerful but requires assumptions about the underlying data distribution and model structure.
  - *Machine Learning Models:* Machine learning algorithms, such as decision trees, random forests, and neural networks, can be trained to predict missing values based on the patterns in the dataset. These models can capture complex relationships and dependencies, making them effective for complex datasets with intricate missing data patterns.

It is important to note that handling missing data is not a one-time process but an iterative and continuous effort throughout the data preprocessing stage. The choice of method should be guided by the nature of the financial data, the amount of missing data, and the specific requirements of the machine learning model.

Ultimately, the goal is to ensure that the dataset is both complete and representative, allowing the machine learning model to learn effectively and generalize well to unseen data. By carefully addressing missing data, you enhance the reliability and predictive power of your model, paving the way for more accurate and robust financial predictions.

## 3.4 Data Cleaning Techniques

Data cleaning is a critical step in the preprocessing pipeline, ensuring that the dataset is free of errors and inconsistencies that could corrupt the results of your machine learning models. Due to the inherent noise and complexity of financial data, meticulous attention to cleaning techniques is essential. This section will delve into various strategies for ensuring data integrity, enhancing the reliability of your subsequent analysis and modeling efforts.

Before applying any cleaning techniques, it is crucial to conduct an initial examination of the data to identify potential issues. Inspect the dataset for anomalies, inconsistencies, and inaccuracies, paying close attention to the nature of financial data, such as outliers or data points that defy expected market behavior.

One effective method for cleaning data is the detection and correction of outliers. Outliers can significantly skew model outcomes, especially in financial datasets where market anomalies can occur. We use statistical methods or clustering algorithms to identify and manage these outliers appropriately. For instance, one can employ the Z-score method, where outliers are defined as data points that fall beyond a certain number of standard deviations from the mean. The formula for the Z-score is given by:

$$Z = \frac{(X - \mu)}{\sigma}$$

where $X$ represents the data point, $\mu$ is the mean, and $\sigma$ denotes the standard deviation. Data points with a $|Z|$ value greater than a predefined threshold (commonly 3) are considered outliers and can either be removed or adjusted.

Another common issue in financial datasets is dealing with duplicated entries. These can arise due to data aggregation from multiple sources, errors in data feeds, or transactional inconsistencies. Identifying duplicates can be straightforward with methods such as checking for exact row matches or more advanced techniques like fuzzy matching, which accounts for slight variations in otherwise identical records. In LaTeX, this can be approached programmatically with the pseudocode below:

```
# Pseudocode for the detection of duplicate rows.
for i in range(len(dataset)):
    for j in range(i + 1, len(dataset)):
        if dataset[i] == dataset[j]:
            mark_as_duplicate(dataset[j])
```

Missing values present another significant challenge. We covered handling missing data comprehensively in a previous section, but it's essential to reiterate its importance within data cleaning. Strategies like imputation (mean, median, mode), interpolation, or deletion of incomplete records ensure the dataset remains robust. More sophisticated techniques might involve the use of predictive models to estimate missing values based on other features within the dataset.

Data consistency checks are also crucial. Financial data might contain inconsistencies like mismatched formats (e.g., date formats differing across records), heterogeneous data sources leading to differing conventions in numerical formats (commas versus periods for decimal points), and misalignment in temporal records. Ensuring uniformity in data formats across the dataset is vital for reliable analysis. This can involve converting all dates to a standard format (e.g., ISO 8601), normalizing numerical fields to a consistent decimal format, and aligning time series data to a common frequency if they come from different sources.

Additionally, financial datasets often include categorical data like stock symbols, market sectors, or transaction types. Cleaning these categories entails ensuring there are no spelling errors, consistent usage of symbols, and non-overlapping categories. Tools such as regular expressions and predefined dictionaries of valid categories can identify and correct these inconsistencies.

Finally, data integrity should be monitored continually through iterative checks as new data is incorporated. Automation of cleaning routines using scripts and pipeline tools can help maintain data quality over time. For instance, using Python's Pandas library can streamline many of these tasks:

```
import pandas as pd

# Example of removing duplicates and handling missing data using Pandas
df = pd.read_csv('financial_data.csv')
df.drop_duplicates(inplace=True)
df.fillna(df.mean(), inplace=True)
```

Adhering to a rigorous data cleaning protocol is fundamental. It ensures that anomalies, errors, and inconsistencies are methodically addressed, thereby reducing the risk of downstream issues in analytical or machine learning models. This meticulous approach not only enhances the quality of your predictions but also builds the foundation for more advanced techniques and analyses presented in subsequent chapters.

## 3.5 Normalization and Standardization

Normalization and standardization are fundamental preprocessing steps crucial for preparing financial data for machine learning models. These techniques ensure that the data is in a suitable format for algorithms to process effectively, enhancing model performance and convergence during training.

Normalization refers to the process of scaling individual samples to have unit norm, often to bring all values into the range [0, 1] or [-1, 1]. This technique is particularly useful when the scale of different features varies significantly. A common normalization technique is min-max scaling, defined mathematically as:

$$X' = \frac{X - X_{\text{min}}}{X_{\text{max}} - X_{\text{min}}}$$

where $X$ is an original value, $X_{\text{min}}$ and $X_{\text{max}}$ are the minimum and maximum values of the dataset, respectively. This transformation ensures that all data points are within the specified range, contributing to faster convergence and improved numerical stability of machine learning models.

Standardization, on the other hand, entails transforming the data to have a mean of zero and a standard deviation of one. This approach is essential when the model assumptions or algorithms (e.g., linear regression, PCA) require data to follow a standard Gaussian distribution. The formula for standardization is:

$$X' = \frac{X - \mu}{\sigma}$$

where $X$ is the original value, $\mu$ is the mean of the dataset, and $\sigma$ is the standard deviation. By transforming data in this manner, we enable models to process features on a comparable scale, which can significantly impact the performance of gradient-based optimization algorithms.

In financial data preprocessing, normalization and standardization aid in handling features such as stock prices, trading volumes, volatility, and returns, which often exhibit varied scales and distributions. Consider a scenario where stock prices range from tens to hundreds, while trading volumes span millions. Directly feeding such disparate data into a machine learning model could lead to suboptimal learning, as the model may disproportionately focus on features with larger magnitudes.

The choice between normalization and standardization depends largely on the specific machine learning algorithm in use and the nature of the financial data. Algorithms such as k-nearest neighbors (KNN) and artificial neural networks (ANNs), which rely on distance metrics, typically benefit from normalization. Conversely, algorithms like support vector machines (SVMs) and linear regression models perform better with standardized data.

For time series data, an additional consideration is the temporal dimension. When normalizing or standardizing financial time series, it is vital to apply these transformations in a way that respects the temporal order, avoiding data leakage between training and validation sets. Rolling window techniques are often employed, where calculations for mean and standard deviation (for standardization) or min and max values (for normalization) are done over a moving window, defined as:

$$\mu_t = \frac{1}{N} \sum_{i=t-N+1}^{t} X_i$$

$$\sigma_t = \sqrt{\frac{1}{N} \sum_{i=t-N+1}^{t} (X_i - \mu_t)^2}$$

for a window size $N$. This approach maintains the temporal ordering and prevents future information from influencing past data, preserving the integrity of the financial time series for predictive modeling.

Implementing normalization and standardization in a machine learning pipeline also involves practical considerations. Libraries such as Scikit-learn in Python offer robust implementations of these preprocessing steps, allowing for seamless integration into model training workflows. For instance, the following code illustrates the use of the 'MinMaxScaler' and 'StandardScaler' classes, which enable efficient application of these techniques:

```
# Example using MinMaxScaler
from sklearn.preprocessing import MinMaxScaler

scaler = MinMaxScaler(feature_range=(0, 1))
scaled_data = scaler.fit_transform(original_data)

# Example using StandardScaler
from sklearn.preprocessing import StandardScaler
```

```
scaler = StandardScaler()
standardized_data = scaler.fit_transform(original_data)
```

These implementations abstract the underlying computations, permitting financial quants to focus on higher-level model development and strategy optimization.

Careful preprocessing through normalization and standardization can significantly enhance the predictive power and reliability of machine learning models in financial markets. By equalizing feature scales and distributions, we create a more stable foundation for model training, leading to more nuanced and accurate predictions of market movements.

## 3.6 Feature Scaling

Feature scaling is an essential preprocessing step in machine learning, particularly when working with financial data. The goal of feature scaling is to ensure that all features contribute equally to a model's performance, which is crucial given the diverse range of magnitudes and units associated with financial data. This section delves into the methods of feature scaling, their importance, and practical applications in financial datasets.

In financial data, different features can vary drastically. For example, stock prices might range from a few dollars to several thousand dollars, while trading volume could span from hundreds to millions. These disparities can skew the performance of machine learning algorithms, especially those sensitive to feature magnitudes like gradient descent-based models and distance-based models (e.g., k-nearest neighbors and support vector machines).

**Why Feature Scaling is Important**

Machine learning algorithms often perform better when numeric attributes are on a similar scale. Consider models relying heavily on matrix operations – gradients calculated during training can be disproportionately influenced by features with larger magnitudes. This can lead to suboptimal performance and longer convergence times. Without scaling, the feature with the largest range may dominate the cost function, leading the algorithm to weight other features less effectively.

Moreover, algorithms like Principal Component Analysis (PCA) and clustering techniques such as K-means also assume that all features contribute equally to the analysis. Feature scaling ensures that distance metrics and variance calculations are not biased by differing feature scales, thereby improving the robustness and reliability of these models.

**Common Feature Scaling Techniques**

There are several methods to scale features, each suited to specific types of data and modeling requirements. The most commonly used techniques include:

- **1. Min-Max Scaling (Normalization):**

  Min-Max scaling transforms features to lie within a specified range, typically [0, 1]. This is achieved using the formula:

  $$X' = \frac{X - X_{min}}{X_{max} - X_{min}} \tag{3.1}$$

  Where $X$ is the original feature, $X_{min}$ and $X_{max}$ are the minimum and maximum values of the feature, and $X'$ is the scaled value. Normalization is particularly useful when dealing with features that need to be bounded within a certain range, preserving the relationships and variance within the data.

- **2. Standardization (Z-score Normalization):**

  Standardization rescales features so they have a mean of zero and a standard deviation of one. It adjusts the distribution of the data to align with a standard normal distribution:

  $$X' = \frac{X - \mu}{\sigma} \tag{3.2}$$

  Where $X$ is the original feature, $\mu$ is the mean, $\sigma$ is the standard deviation, and $X'$ is the standardized value. Standardization is preferred when financial data features have different units and the model assumptions include normally distributed data.

- **3. Robust Scaling:**

  Robust scaling uses the median and the interquartile range (IQR) to scale features, making it less sensitive to outliers:

  $$X' = \frac{X - \text{Median}(X)}{\text{IQR}(X)} \tag{3.3}$$

The interquartile range is defined as the difference between the 75th and 25th percentiles. Robust scaling is useful in datasets with significant outliers, ensuring they do not unduly affect the scaling process.

### Practical Implementation in Financial Data

When applying feature scaling in financial datasets, the following practical steps can enhance the preprocessing stage:

- **Consistency Across Training and Test Data:** It is crucial to fit the scaling transformation on the training data and subsequently apply it to the test data. This ensures that the test set is not exposed to information from the training process, preserving the integrity of model evaluation.
- **Handling Time Series Data:** For time series financial data, scaling should be performed in a manner that avoids data leakage. One effective strategy is to scale data within a rolling window, computing scaling parameters over this window and applying them as you move through the series.
- **Dealing with Outliers:** The presence of outliers can distort standard scaling methods. Consider using robust scaling or applying transformations (e.g., logarithmic transformation) before scaling to mitigate the impact of extreme values.

### Example: Scaling Stock Price Data

Consider a dataset containing daily stock prices and trading volume for several companies. Here is a simple example of how Min-Max scaling can be applied using Python's scikit-learn library:

```
from sklearn.preprocessing import MinMaxScaler
import pandas as pd

# Example stock price data
data = {
    'Stock A': [150, 155, 160, 165, 170],
    'Volume A': [2000, 3000, 4000, 5000, 6000]
}
df = pd.DataFrame(data)

# Initialize Min-Max Scaler
scaler = MinMaxScaler()

# Fit and transform the data
scaled_data = scaler.fit_transform(df)
```

```
# Convert scaled data back to DataFrame
scaled_df = pd.DataFrame(scaled_data, columns=df.columns)

print(scaled_df)
```

This example demonstrates how raw stock prices and volume are scaled to a range of [0, 1], facilitating uniform feature contributions to subsequent machine learning models.

As we continually handle financial datasets, recognizing the importance of feature scaling and meticulously applying suitable methods can profoundly impact the performance and accuracy of our models. This essential step anchors our data preprocessing endeavors, ensuring that our machine learning algorithms are well-prepared to capture and learn from the intricate patterns in financial markets.

## 3.7 Working with Time Series Data

Understanding how to effectively work with time series data is crucial for any quantitative analyst or financial engineer. Financial markets generate vast amounts of time-ordered data, encompassing prices, volumes, and other market indicators over time. Unlike typical datasets, time series data has unique properties that require specialized techniques for preprocessing and analysis.

Time series data is characterized by sequences of data points, typically measured at uniform time intervals. In financial contexts, this might include daily stock prices, minute-by-minute trade volumes, or high-frequency tick data. The inherent temporal structure in time series data introduces dependencies between observations, making traditional data preprocessing techniques inadequate.

**1. Time Series Characteristics**

The key characteristics of time series data include:

- *Temporal Dependence*: Observations depend on previous values due to trend, seasonality, and autocorrelation.
- *Stationarity*: A time series is considered stationary if its statistical properties do not change over time.
- *Trend and Seasonality*: Trends refer to long-term upward or downward movements, while seasonality involves repeating patterns at regular intervals.

These characteristics necessitate different handling techniques compared to time-independent data.

**2. Handling Temporal Dependencies**

One of the primary concerns when working with time series data is to respect the temporal dependencies. This means ensuring that the data used for training models does not "leak" future information. To preserve the integrity of the temporal order:

- *Lag Features*: Create lagged versions of features, where the prediction of an observation at time $t$ might depend on its value at time $t-1, t-2$, etc.
- *Rolling Window Statistics*: Use rolling window statistics (mean, standard deviation) to capture local patterns and reduce noise.
- *Expanding Windows*: Consider aggregating data by expanding windows which include all observations up to a certain time point, offering a cumulative summary.

Lag features and rolling window techniques help incorporate the temporal structure into the models.

**3. Stationarity and Differencing**

Many time series models, especially statistical ones like ARIMA, assume stationarity. Therefore, transforming non-stationary series into stationary ones is often required. Stationarity can be tested using methods like the Augmented Dickey-Fuller (ADF) test. If a series is non-stationary, differencing is a common technique:

$$y'_t = y_t - y_{t-1}$$

where $y'_t$ is the differenced series. Additional transformations, such as logarithmic scales, can also stabilize variance in the series.

**4. Seasonal Decomposition**

Seasonal decomposition is used to decompose a time series into trend, seasonal, and residual components:

$$y_t = T_t + S_t + R_t$$

where $T_t$ represents the trend component, $S_t$ the seasonal component, and $R_t$ the residual component. Decomposition can be additive or multiplicative, depending on the nature of the series.

Applying proper decomposition techniques allows more effective modeling by isolating various underlying processes within the data.

**5. Data Resampling and Frequency Conversion**

Financial data might be recorded at various frequencies, such as daily, hourly, or by the minute. Aggregating or resampling this data to uniform frequency can be necessary:

- *Upsampling*: Increasing the frequency of the data, often involving interpolation.
- *Downsampling*: Reducing the frequency of the data, such as taking daily closing prices from minute-by-minute trading data.

Effective resampling can help normalize the dataset and align different data sources.

**6. Handling Missing Values**

Missing data is particularly challenging in time series due to temporal dependencies. Standard imputation techniques might not suffice, so consider:

- *Forward/Backward Filling*: Impute missing values based on the last or next available observations.
- *Interpolation*: Linear or polynomial interpolation to estimate the missing values based on adjacent data points.

Choosing the appropriate method to handle missing values ensures data consistency without introducing biases.

**7. Time Series Smoothing**

Smoothing techniques help reduce noise and reveal underlying patterns:

- *Moving Averages*: Simple moving average (SMA) and exponential moving average (EMA) to smooth short-term fluctuations.
- *Exponentially Weighted Moving Average (EWMA)*: Gives more weight to recent observations, useful for capturing recent trends.

Applying smoothing techniques can enhance model performance by filtering out noise from the data.

The meticulous preprocessing of time series data lays a strong foundation for developing robust predictive models. By carefully addressing temporal dependencies, ensuring stationarity, adequately handling seasonal components, and skillfully managing missing values and smoothing, we enhance the effectiveness and reliability of machine learning models tailored for financial forecasting.

## 3.8 Handling Outliers

Outliers present a unique challenge in financial data preprocessing. These are data points that significantly differ from the majority of the data, often arising from errors, unusual market events, or genuine yet rare occurrences. Successfully handling outliers is crucial for the robustness of machine learning models, as unaddressed outliers can skew results, leading to misleading predictions and impaired model performance.

Outliers in financial data could be due to several factors such as sudden market news, data entry errors, or illiquid trading periods. Identifying and treating these outliers appropriately is a critical step in data preprocessing. Not all outliers are detrimental; some may provide valuable insights into market anomalies. The first step in handling outliers is to comprehend their origin and impact on the dataset.

Various statistical and visualization techniques can aid in identifying outliers:

**Density-Based Spatial Clustering of Applications with Noise (DBSCAN):** This algorithm is effective for identifying outliers based on data density. Points in low-density regions are flagged as outliers.

**Visualization:** Scatter plots, box plots, and histograms can visually highlight outliers. For instance, box plots use the interquartile range (IQR) to detect anomalies.

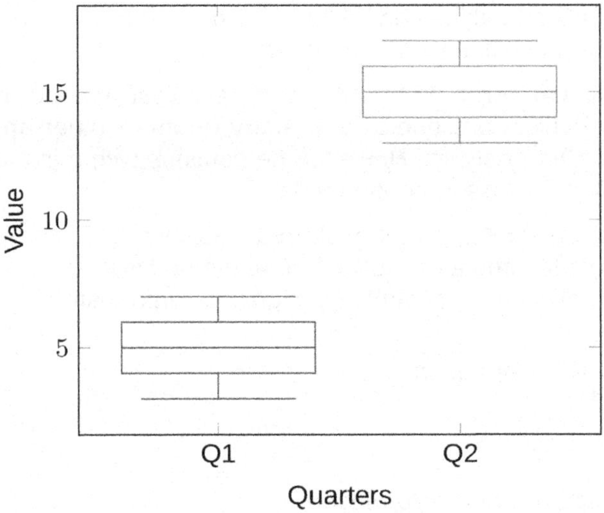


Figure 3.1: Example of Box Plot for Different Quarters

**Statistical Methods:**

**Z-Score:** Calculates how many standard deviations a data point is from the mean. A common threshold for identifying outliers is a Z-score greater than 3 or less than -3.

$$Z = \frac{X - \mu}{\sigma}$$

where $X$ is the data point, $\mu$ is the mean, and $\sigma$ is the standard deviation.

**IQR Method:** Data points outside $1.5 \times$ IQR above the third quartile or below the first quartile are considered outliers.

$$\text{IQR} = Q3 - Q1$$
$$\text{Lower Bound} = Q1 - 1.5 \times \text{IQR}$$
$$\text{Upper Bound} = Q3 + 1.5 \times \text{IQR}$$

**MAD (Median Absolute Deviation):** Offers a robust measure that is less sensitive to extreme values.

$$\text{MAD} = \text{median}(|X - \text{median}(X)|)$$

Once identified, outliers can be handled in several ways depending on their cause and influence on the dataset:

**Removing Outliers:** This is often the simplest method, particularly when the outliers are due to data entry errors or other anomalies irrelevant to the analysis. However, be cautious with this method as it can result in the loss of important data.

**Transformation:** Applying transformations such as log or square root can mitigate the impact of outliers. This method is useful when outliers are a natural occurrence and hold significant information.

- *Log Transformation:*

$$X' = \log(X + 1)$$

- *Square Root Transformation:*

$$X' = \sqrt{X + 1}$$

**Imputation:** Replacing outliers with mean, median, or a specific value can be effective. Imputation is particularly useful when the outliers are not many and removing them would not significantly affect the overall data distribution.

**Capping:** Limiting the extreme values within a threshold range. This can involve setting upper and lower bounds based on quantiles, thereby reducing the effect of outliers without entirely removing them.

$$X_{capped} = \begin{cases} \text{Upper Bound} & \text{if } X > \text{Upper Bound} \\ \text{Lower Bound} & \text{if } X < \text{Lower Bound} \\ X & \text{otherwise} \end{cases}$$

The decision to keep, transform, or remove outliers should be guided by the specific context of your financial analysis. Consider the following:

**Domain Knowledge:** Understanding the nature and domain of your financial data aids in making informed decisions about outliers. Consulting with market analysts and subject matter experts can provide insight into whether certain outliers carry meaningful patterns or can be discarded.

**Model Sensitivity:** Different machine learning models react differently to outliers. For instance, linear regression is highly sensitive, whereas tree-based models like Random Forests are less so. Testing multiple approaches and evaluating model performance can guide the best strategy.

Handling outliers effectively can significantly enhance the quality and reliability of your financial models. By combining statistical methods with domain knowledge, you can ensure your preprocessing steps align with the ultimate goal of robust and accurate market predictions.

## 3.9 Data Transformation Techniques

The ability to transform data is a cornerstone skill in the arsenal of any quantitative analyst or data scientist working with financial datasets. Data transformation involves modifying data attributes to facilitate data analysis or improve the performance of machine learning models. This section explores various transformation techniques, providing an understanding of their purpose and how to implement them effectively.

- **1. Log Transformation:** One of the most commonly used transformations in financial data analysis is the logarithmic (log) transformation. It is particularly useful for stabilizing variance, normalizing distributions, and handling multiplicative relationships in data such as returns.

  Mathematically, the log transformation is represented as:

  $$X_{\text{log}} = \text{log}(X + c)$$

  where $X$ is the original data, and $c$ is a constant added to shift the data to avoid taking the logarithm of zero.

  Implementing log transformation helps in linearizing exponential trends in data. For instance, if we have daily stock prices and want to analyze percentage returns, the log transformation aids by converting multiplicative effects into additive ones, making linear models more effective.

- **2. Differencing:** When working with time series data, handling trends and seasonality is vital. Differencing is a technique that involves subtracting the previous observation from the current observation to remove trends and stabilize the mean of a time series.

Differencing can be mathematically described as:

$$Y_t = X_t - X_{t-1}$$

where $Y_t$ is the differenced series, $X_t$ is the original series, and $X_{t-1}$ is the previous observation.

This transformation is widely used to make time series data stationary, a prerequisite for many statistical models, including ARIMA (AutoRegressive Integrated Moving Average) models.

- **3. Box-Cox Transformation:** The Box-Cox transformation is a family of power transformations that can stabilize variance and make data more normally distributed. It is defined as:

$$Y_{\text{BoxCox}} = \begin{cases} \frac{(X^\lambda - 1)}{\lambda}, & \lambda \neq 0 \\ \log(X), & \lambda = 0 \end{cases}$$

  where $X$ is the original data and $\lambda$ is the transformation parameter. The optimal value of $\lambda$ is usually determined via maximum likelihood estimation.

  This transformation is flexible and can handle a variety of data distributions, making it valuable for preprocessing financial data that exhibit non-constant variance or skewness.

- **4. Normalization and Standardization:** While normalization and standardization were discussed earlier in the chapter, revisiting these techniques in the context of transformation emphasizes their role in preparing data for machine learning models. Normalization techniques such as Min-Max scaling or Z-score transformation help in transforming the data into a suitable range or scale, essential for algorithms sensitive to the magnitude of data points, like k-Nearest Neighbors (k-NN) or Support Vector Machines (SVM).

  Normalization can be defined as:

$$X_{\text{norm}} = \frac{X - X_{\text{min}}}{X_{\text{max}} - X_{\text{min}}}$$

  Standardization can be described as:

$$X_{\text{std}} = \frac{X - \mu}{\sigma}$$

where $X$ is the original data, $X_{\text{min}}$ and $X_{\text{max}}$ represent the minimum and maximum values, while $\mu$ and $\sigma$ denote the mean and standard deviation of the data, respectively.

These transformations ensure that each feature contributes equally to the analysis or modeling process.

- **5. Polynomial Transformation:** Polynomial transformations are used to capture non-linear relationships by adding polynomial terms of the features. For example, given a feature $X$, a polynomial transformation of degree 2 would create new features $X^2$, allowing linear models to fit non-linear data.

  Mathematically, this can be represented as:

  $$X_{\text{poly}} = [X, X^2, X^3, \ldots, X^d]$$

  where $d$ denotes the degree of the polynomial.

  This technique is especially useful in regression modeling where relationships between predictor variables and the response variable are not linear.

Each of these transformations addresses specific issues within financial datasets and prepares the data for subsequent modeling, analysis, and visualization. Selecting the appropriate transformation depends on the nature of the data and the specific requirements of the machine learning algorithms being employed. Understanding and applying these techniques elevates the quality of the data and, by extension, the robustness of the models built upon it.

## 3.10 Data Augmentation for Financial Data

Data augmentation is a critical technique in machine learning, especially when dealing with limited datasets. It involves generating new data from existing datasets to improve the robustness and generalization of machine learning models. In the context of financial data, augmentation can be particularly challenging due to the intricate nature of market movements and the time-dependent structure of the data. However, several strategies can be applied effectively to create enriched datasets that better capture the complexities of financial markets.

First, let us introduce the concept of data augmentation in financial datasets. Typically, data augmentation in image processing might involve transformations such as rotation, scaling, or cropping, which are straightforward in their implementation. In financial data, however, one must be cognizant of the temporal component and the structural properties of the time series.

One common approach to augmenting financial data is bootstrapping, a statistical method that involves resampling with replacement. This technique can create new time series that maintain the essential statistical properties of the original dataset. By generating multiple different resample datasets, one can train models to be more robust against variations in the data.

$$X_i^* = X_{S(i)} \quad \text{for} \quad i = 1, \ldots, n$$

where $S(i)$ is an independent draw from the set $\{1, \ldots, n\}$ with replacement.

Another effective method is the use of sliding windows. In this technique, overlapping windows of fixed length are extracted from the time series data. Each window can serve as an independent training instance, while the overlap ensures that the temporal context is preserved. Parameter selection, such as the window size and the stride (i.e., the number of steps by which the window is moved), is crucial to balance redundancy and variability.

$$\text{Window}_j = \{X_{t+j}, X_{t+j+1}, \ldots, X_{t+j+k-1}\}, \quad j = 0, s, 2s, \ldots$$

where $s$ is the stride and $k$ is the window size.

Synthetic data generation through models such as Generative Adversarial Networks (GANs) has also shown promise. GANs can learn the underlying distribution of the financial data and generate realistic synthetic samples. Training a GAN involves a generator model $G$ that produces synthetic data and a discriminator model $D$ that attempts to distinguish between real and synthetic data. The training process is a minimax game:

$$\min_G \max_D \mathbb{E}_{x \sim p_{\text{data}}(x)}[\log D(x)] + \mathbb{E}_{z \sim p_z(z)}[\log(1 - D(G(z)))]$$

A related approach is the use of variational autoencoders (VAEs), which can capture the latent space of the data and generate new samples by decoding random points from this space. VAEs are particularly suitable when the goal is to ensure that the generated data preserves the underlying patterns and distributions observed in historical data.

$$\mathcal{L}(\theta, \phi; x, z) = \mathbb{E}_{q_\phi(z|x)} [\log p_\theta(x|z)] - D_{\text{KL}} (q_\phi(z|x) || p_\theta(z))$$

For time series data, techniques like time warping and permutation can also add valuable variability. Time warping involves stretching or compressing the time dimension of the data, whereas permutation adjusts the order of observations while maintaining the overall structure. When applying these methods, it is essential to ensure that the integrity and the autocorrelation structure of the original data are not overly disrupted.

Lastly, augmentation through transformation methods, such as Fourier transforms and wavelet transforms, can expose additional features and patterns within the data. These methods transform the original time-series data into a different domain (frequency for Fourier, time-frequency for wavelets), where augmentation can be applied before transforming back to the time domain. This can reveal hidden patterns and provide new insights for the model to learn from.

Through these data augmentation techniques, we can significantly enhance the robustness and performance of our machine learning models. By methodically applying these methods, we not only expand the dataset but also introduce controlled variability that promotes generalization and adaptability in predictive models.

# Chapter 4

# Feature Engineering

**This chapter explores the critical role of feature engineering in machine learning for finance. It starts by defining feature engineering and its importance, followed by techniques for feature selection. The chapter covers creating financial indicators, dimensionality reduction, and handling categorical data. It also discusses generating features from time series data, interaction features, polynomial features, and feature extraction using Principal Component Analysis (PCA). Automated feature engineering tools are introduced, along with best practices to ensure effective feature transformation and selection.**

## 4.1 What is Feature Engineering?

Feature engineering is a fundamental part of the machine learning pipeline that involves the creation, transformation, and selection of variables (features) that effectively represent the underlying patterns in the data used for building predictive models. This process is crucial in ensuring that machine learning algorithms can efficiently learn from the data and produce accurate predictions.

In essence, feature engineering bridges the gap between raw data and the machine learning models that analyze this data. This practice is not merely a technical task but an art that requires both domain knowledge and an understanding of the underlying mechanics of various machine learning algorithms. By transforming raw data into meaningful features, we can provide models with the insights necessary to capture complex relationships and improve their performance.

Feature engineering can be broadly classified into three main activities:

- **Feature creation**
- **Feature transformation**
- **Feature selection**

Feature creation involves generating new features based on existing data. For instance, in financial applications, one might derive moving averages, momentum indicators, or volatility measures from historical price data. These derived features can encapsulate important information that is otherwise hidden in the raw data.

Feature transformation includes techniques like normalization, standardization, or encoding categorical variables. These transformations ensure that features are in a suitable form for machine learning algorithms, which often perform better when data is scaled consistently and categorical variables are represented numerically.

Feature selection, on the other hand, involves identifying the most relevant features to use in a model. This step is vital as it helps in reducing the dimensionality of the dataset, mitigating overfitting, and enhancing computational efficiency. Techniques for feature selection might include statistical tests, wrapper methods like recursive feature elimination, or embedded methods such as LASSO regression.

The importance of feature engineering cannot be overstated in the context of financial data, which often exhibits intricate patterns and dependencies that need careful representation. Financial markets generate vast amounts of data with complex structures, incorporating multiple asset prices, economic indicators, corporate events, and more. Feature engineering allows us to distill this complexity into simpler, more manageable pieces of information that machine learning models can process effectively.

Moreover, in quantitative finance, domain-specific knowledge plays a pivotal role. Knowing which financial indicators or economic factors are likely to be influential can guide the feature engineering process. For instance, in stock price prediction, features like price-to-earnings ratio, dividend yield, and trading volume might be more pertinent than just the raw prices themselves.

Effective feature engineering leads to improved model accuracy and robustness, often making the difference between a profitable trading strategy and an ineffective one. It is a continuous and iterative process; as new data becomes available and market conditions evolve, the features might need to be reevaluated and adjusted accordingly.

To summarize, feature engineering forms the backbone of any successful application of machine learning in finance. It involves the creative and informed transformation of raw data into features that represent the underlying phenomena of interest. In the next sections, we will delve deeper into specific techniques and best practices for creating, transforming, and selecting features to enhance your machine learning models in quantitative finance.

## 4.2 Importance of Feature Engineering in Finance

In the realm of financial market analysis, the concept of feature engineering stands as a cornerstone for the development of robust and predictive machine learning models. Its importance cannot be overstated, as the very quality and performance of these models rely heavily on the features that are engineered from raw data. Understanding and applying feature engineering effectively can transform ordinary datasets into a wealth of predictive insights, ultimately driving more informed and accurate trading decisions.

At its core, feature engineering involves the process of selecting, modifying, and creating new features from existing data to improve the performance of machine learning algorithms. In finance, where the data is inherently noisy and complex, this becomes particularly crucial. The intricate nature of financial data demands a sophisticated approach to feature engineering, going beyond the mere selection of relevant predictors to include the creation of new, informative features that capture the underlying market dynamics.

One of the primary reasons feature engineering is so vital in finance is because financial markets are influenced by a multitude of factors – some are apparent while others are hidden beneath layers of market data. A well-engineered feature can unveil these hidden patterns, allowing machine learning models to capture the nuanced relationships and dependencies that drive market movements. By transforming raw data into meaningful features, quants can enhance the predictive capabilities of their models, leading to more accurate forecasts and strategies.

Moreover, feature engineering helps in dealing with the challenges posed by high-dimensional data. Financial data often contains an overwhelming number of variables, many of which may be irrelevant or redundant. Identifying and engineering the right features helps in reducing dimensionality, which not only improves the performance efficiency of models but also mitigates the risk of overfitting. By focusing on the most informative aspects of the data, quants can build models that generalize better to unseen data, thus providing more reliable predictions.

Another significant aspect of feature engineering in finance is its role in facilitating interpretability. Financial models, particularly those employed in trading and investment, benefit greatly from being interpretable. Stakeholders, including portfolio managers and risk analysts, need to understand how the model derives its predictions and the factors that influence its decisions. Well-crafted features that are intuitive and aligned with established financial theories can make the models more transparent and the results more actionable. This trust in the model's outputs can lead to better adoption and reliance on the predictive insights it provides.

The significance of feature engineering extends further into the realm of integrating domain knowledge with data science. Financial markets are governed by principles and factors that are well-understood by practitioners. Feature engineering provides a platform for incorporating this expert knowledge into machine learning models. For instance, creating financial indicators like moving averages, volatility measures, and momentum indicators can embed market insights directly into the features used by the model. This synergy between domain expertise and computational algorithms enhances the overall robustness and relevance of the model's predictions.

Additionally, the dynamic nature of financial markets necessitates continuous adaptation of models. As market conditions change, so do the relationships between different variables. Feature engineering plays a critical role in this adaptive process by enabling ongoing refinement and recalibration of features in response to new market data. This ensures that the models remain relevant and continue to provide accurate predictions in the face of evolving market dynamics.

One must also consider the impact of feature engineering on model validation and backtesting. Effective feature engineering contributes to more robust validation procedures by ensuring that the features used are stable and predictive over different time periods and market conditions. This robustness is crucial for backtesting trading strategies, as it provides greater confidence that the performance observed historically is likely to persist in future trading environments.

In the domain of algorithmic trading, where decisions are made in milliseconds, the efficiency of feature engineering can also influence the speed and responsiveness of trading algorithms. Creating features that can be computed quickly and efficiently allows trading systems to react promptly to market signals, which can be a decisive factor in the competitive landscape of high-frequency trading.

Thus, the importance of feature engineering in finance is manifested in its ability to uncover hidden market patterns, reduce dimensionality, facilitate interpretability, integrate domain knowledge, enable model adaptability, enhance validation processes, and improve computational efficiency. By investing time and expertise in the art and science of feature engineering, quants can harness the full power of machine learning to achieve more accurate and actionable trading and investment strategies. As financial markets continue to grow in complexity, the role of feature engineering will undoubtedly become even more pivotal in driving the next generation of predictive models.

## 4.3 Feature Selection Techniques

Feature selection is a pivotal step in the machine learning pipeline, particularly in the context of finance where the datasets are often multidimensional and complex. Selecting the most relevant features can lead to significant enhancements in model performance, interpretability, and computational efficiency. This section delves into various techniques used for feature selection, aligning with the overarching goal of refining the feature set to improve the predictive power of machine learning models.

Feature selection techniques can be broadly categorized into three groups: filter methods, wrapper methods, and embedded methods. Each category encompasses several strategies, offering a diverse toolkit for quants to tailor their feature selection process to the specific needs of their models and datasets.

**Filter Methods:** These methods rely on statistical measures to score and rank features independently of any machine learning algorithm. By evaluating the intrinsic properties of features, filter methods can swiftly eliminate irrelevant or redundant features.

One of the simplest filter methods is the *variance threshold*. Features with low variance are unlikely to be informative for predictive modeling since they do not change much across different samples. The variance threshold technique sets a minimum variance threshold, discarding features below this threshold.

$$\text{Var}(X_i) < \sigma^2_{\text{min}} \quad \Rightarrow \quad \text{Discard } X_i$$

Another popular filter method is *correlation analysis*. Features highly correlated with the target variable are considered informative, while those with high inter-feature correlation are redundant.

$$\text{Corr}(X_i, y) > \rho_{\text{max}} \quad \Rightarrow \quad \text{Select } X_i$$
$$\text{Corr}(X_i, X_j) > \rho_{\text{max}} \quad \Rightarrow \quad \text{Discard } X_i \text{ or } X_j$$

**Wrapper Methods:** In contrast to filter methods, wrapper methods evaluate feature subsets by training and evaluating a model on each subset. This iterative process aims to identify the feature subset that maximizes model performance.

The *sequential feature selection* approach includes both forward and backward strategies. Forward selection starts with an empty set, adding features one by one based on the model's performance improvement. Conversely, backward elimination starts with the full set, progressively removing the least important features.

```
# Pseudocode for Forward Selection
Initialize empty feature set F
for each feature combination k do
    Train model with F + k
    Evaluate model performance
    if performance improves
        Add k to F
```

Wrapper methods can be computationally expensive, especially with large feature sets, but they often yield superior performance due to their tailored feature subset evaluation.

**Embedded Methods:** Embedded methods integrate feature selection within the model training process, often leveraging the model's own mechanisms to rank and select features. These techniques offer a balance between the independence of filter methods and the exhaustive search of wrapper methods.

One common embedded method is *Regularization*. Regularization techniques like Lasso (L1 regularization) add a penalty to the model's loss function, shrinking less important feature coefficients to zero.

$$\min\left(\frac{1}{n}\sum_{i=1}^{n}(y_i-\hat{y_i})^2+\lambda\sum_{j=1}^{p}|\beta_j|\right)$$

Tree-based models, such as *Random Forests* and *Gradient Boosting Machines*, naturally incorporate feature selection by determining feature importance during the model training phase. Features that split the data more effectively are ranked higher, providing an intrinsic measure of relevance.

$$\text{Feature Importance}=\sum_{\text{trees}}\frac{\Delta\text{Impurity}}{\text{Total Nodes}}$$

Successfully applying these feature selection techniques can lead to a more robust, interpretable, and computationally efficient model. By carefully selecting features, quants can ensure that their machine learning models are both powerful and parsimonious, aligning with the broader objectives of financial modeling and prediction.

## 4.4 Creating Financial Indicators

Creating financial indicators is a pivotal part of feature engineering in machine learning models for finance. These indicators, derived from raw data such as stock prices, volumes, and volatility, can provide critical insights into market movements and trends. By transforming raw data into meaningful features, we can enhance the predictive power of our models. This section will delve into some of the most widely-used financial indicators, including their definitions, calculations, and applications.

Financial indicators can be broadly categorized into three types: trend indicators, momentum indicators, and volatility indicators. Each group provides unique insights into the market, and their combination can create a robust feature set for machine learning models.

**Trend Indicators:** Trend indicators help in identifying the direction of the market. One of the simplest and most powerful trend indicators is the *Moving Average* (MA). The moving average smooths out price data by creating a constantly updating average price, thereby helping to identify the direction of the trend over a certain period. The two most common types are the Simple Moving Average (SMA) and the Exponential Moving Average (EMA). The SMA is calculated as:

$$\text{SMA}(t) = \frac{1}{N} \sum_{i=0}^{N-1} P(t-i) \tag{4.1}$$

where $P(t)$ is the price at time $t$, and $N$ is the number of periods. The EMA, on the other hand, gives more weight to recent prices and is calculated using:

$$\text{EMA}(t) = P(t) \cdot \left(\frac{2}{N+1}\right) + \text{EMA}(t-1) \cdot \left(1 - \frac{2}{N+1}\right) \tag{4.2}$$

Another widely used trend indicator is the *Moving Average Convergence Divergence* (MACD). It is the difference between a short-term EMA and a long-term EMA, calculated as follows:

$$\text{MACD}(t) = \text{EMA}_{\text{short}}(t) - \text{EMA}_{\text{long}}(t) \tag{4.3}$$

**Momentum Indicators:** Momentum indicators measure the rate of change of prices and can help identify the strength of a trend. The *Relative Strength Index* (RSI) is a popular momentum indicator that oscillates between 0 and 100. It is calculated as:

$$\text{RSI}(t) = 100 - \frac{100}{1 + \text{RS}(t)} \tag{4.4}$$

where $\text{RS}(t)$ is the average gain of up periods during the specified time frame divided by the average loss of down periods. An RSI above 70 indicates that the asset may be overbought, while an RSI below 30 indicates it may be oversold.

Another momentum indicator is the *Stochastic Oscillator*, which compares a particular closing price with its price range over a specified period of time. It consists of two lines: %K and %D. These are calculated as follows:

$$\%K = \frac{P(t) - \text{L14}}{\text{H14} - \text{L14}} \times 100 \tag{4.5}$$

$$\%D = \text{SMA}_3(\%K) \tag{4.6}$$

where $P(t)$ is the current closing price, *L14* is the lowest price over the last 14 periods, and *H14* is the highest price over the last 14 periods. The %D line is a 3-period simple moving average of the %K line.

**Volatility Indicators:** Volatility indicators measure the degree of variation of a trading price series over time. The *Bollinger Bands* are one of the most commonly used volatility indicators. These bands are plotted at standard deviation levels above and below a simple moving average of the price. The standard Bollinger Bands are calculated as follows:

$$\text{Upper Band} = \text{SMA}(t) + k \cdot \sigma \tag{4.7}$$

$$\text{Lower Band} = \text{SMA}(t) - k \cdot \sigma \tag{4.8}$$

where $\sigma$ is the standard deviation of the closing prices over the same period used for the SMA, and $k$ is the number of standard deviations typically set to 2.

Another volatility indicator is the *Average True Range* (ATR), which measures market volatility by decomposing the entire range of an asset price for that period. The ATR is typically derived from the 14-period moving average of true ranges. The true range is the greatest of the following:

$$\text{Current High} - \text{Current Low} \tag{4.9}$$
$$|\text{Current High} - \text{Previous Close}| \tag{4.10}$$
$$|\text{Current Low} - \text{Previous Close}| \tag{4.11}$$

Once these financial indicators are calculated, they can be integrated into a machine learning model as features. These features can help the model infer patterns and relationships that are not readily apparent in raw data. Additionally, using a combination of trend, momentum, and volatility indicators can provide a comprehensive view of the market, allowing for better predictive accuracy.

The creation of these indicators must align with the trading strategy and objectives. For example, short-term traders might focus more on momentum indicators, whereas long-term investors might prioritize trend indicators. Automated tools and libraries, such as ta-lib in Python, can facilitate the efficient computation of these indicators, allowing traders to focus on leveraging them effectively within their predictive models.

## 4.5 Dimensionality Reduction

In the realm of financial machine learning, dimensionality reduction stands as a pivotal technique to enhance model performance and interpretability. As financial datasets often encompass a multitude of features, the curse of dimensionality can lead to overfitting, increased computational costs, and diminished predictive power. By reducing the number of features, we can focus on the most informative aspects of the data, fostering better model generalization and more efficient processing.

Dimensionality reduction can be broadly categorized into feature selection and feature extraction. While feature selection involves choosing a subset of existing features, feature extraction transforms the original features into a reduced set of new features. Here, we will delve into two primary methods of feature extraction: Principal Component Analysis (PCA) and Linear Discriminant Analysis (LDA).

**Principal Component Analysis (PCA)**

PCA is a statistical technique that transforms the original correlated features into a set of uncorrelated components, known as principal components. These components are linear combinations of the original features and are orthogonal to each other, ensuring no redundancy. The primary goal of PCA is to capture the maximum variance in the data with the fewest number of principal components.

Mathematically, the PCA process involves the following steps:

1. **Standardize the Data:** Ensure that each feature has a mean of 0 and a standard deviation of 1:

$$Z = \frac{X - \mu}{\sigma}$$

where $X$ is the original data matrix, $\mu$ is the mean, and $\sigma$ is the standard deviation.

2. **Compute Covariance Matrix:** Derive the covariance matrix of the standardized data:

$$C = \frac{1}{n-1} Z^T Z$$

3. **Eigen Decomposition:** Perform eigen decomposition on the covariance matrix to obtain the eigenvalues and eigenvectors:

$$C = P\Lambda P^T$$

where $P$ is the matrix of eigenvectors and $\Lambda$ is the diagonal matrix of eigenvalues.

4. **Select Principal Components:** Choose the top k eigenvectors (principal components) that correspond to the largest eigenvalues, capturing the most variance in the data.

5. **Transform Data:** Project the original data onto the selected principal components:

$$Z_{\text{PCA}} = ZP_k$$

Here's a simple example of implementing PCA using Python's scikit-learn library:

```
from sklearn.decomposition import PCA
from sklearn.preprocessing import StandardScaler

# Standardize the data
scaler = StandardScaler()
X_std = scaler.fit_transform(X)

# Apply PCA
pca = PCA(n_components=2)
X_pca = pca.fit_transform(X_std)

print(f"Explained variance ratio: {pca.explained_variance_ratio_}")
```

PCA's ability to reduce dimensionality while retaining most of the data's variance makes it particularly useful in financial analysis, where datasets can be vast and complex.

**Linear Discriminant Analysis (LDA)**

LDA is another dimensionality reduction technique, primarily used in classification problems. Unlike PCA, which focuses on maximizing variance, LDA aims to maximize the separation between different classes. It projects the data onto a lower-dimensional space where the classes are as distinct as possible.

The LDA process includes:

1. **Compute the Mean Vectors:** Calculate the mean vector for each class:

$$\mu_k = \frac{1}{n_k} \sum_{i \in C_k} x_i$$

where $n_k$ is the number of instances in class k, and $C_k$ is the set of instances in class k.

2. **Compute Scatter Matrices:** - *Within-class scatter matrix:*

$$S_W = \sum_k \sum_{i \in C_k} (x_i - \mu_k)(x_i - \mu_k)^T$$

- *Between-class scatter matrix:*

$$S_B = \sum_k n_k(\mu_k - \mu)(\mu_k - \mu)^T$$

where $\mu$ is the overall mean vector.

3. **Eigen Decomposition:** Compute the eigenvectors and eigenvalues for the matrix:

$$S_W^{-1} S_B$$

4. **Select Linear Discriminants:** Choose the top k eigenvectors that correspond to the largest eigenvalues.

5. **Transform Data:** Project the data onto the selected linear discriminants.

Example of implementing LDA using Python:

```
from sklearn.discriminant_analysis import LinearDiscriminantAnalysis as LDA

# Apply LDA
lda = LDA(n_components=2)
X_lda = lda.fit_transform(X_std, y)

print(f"Explained variance ratio: {lda.explained_variance_ratio_}")
```

In financial applications, LDA is particularly valuable in tasks such as credit scoring, where separating different categories (e.g., good vs. bad credit) is crucial.

By integrating dimensionality reduction techniques like PCA and LDA into your workflow, you can enhance both the efficiency and effectiveness of your machine learning models, ultimately leading to more robust and insightful financial analysis.

## 4.6 Handling Categorical Data

When delving into machine learning applications for financial markets, handling categorical data becomes pivotal. Unlike continuous numerical data, categorical data comprises discrete values, which can represent various attributes such as sector classifications, credit ratings, or even binary indicators like whether an asset is included in a specific index. Properly processing these categories can significantly impact the performance of machine learning models.

Given the nuanced characteristics of categorical data, the initial step involves understanding the types of categorical variables: nominal and ordinal. Nominal variables have no inherent order, such as stock ticker symbols or industry sectors. Ordinal variables possess a meaningful sequence, like credit ratings (e.g., AAA, AA, A) or risk levels (e.g., low, medium, high). This distinction influences the choice of encoding techniques.

One of the most common methods for handling nominal data is one-hot encoding. This technique creates binary columns for each category, with a value of 1 indicating the presence of the category and 0 otherwise. For example, if we have a categorical variable representing sectors with "Technology", "Healthcare", and "Finance" as values, one-hot encoding transforms this into three binary columns. The primary advantage of one-hot encoding is its simplicity and direct applicability in many machine learning algorithms.

Original $\rightarrow$ One-Hot Encoded

| Technology | Healthcare | Finance |
|---|---|---|
| 1 | 0 | 0 |
| 0 | 1 | 0 |
| 0 | 0 | 1 |

While one-hot encoding is widely used, it can lead to a curse of dimensionality problem if the categorical variable has numerous distinct levels. This is particularly pertinent in cases like stock identifiers, which might include thousands of ticker symbols, resulting in a sparse and high-dimensional dataset. To mitigate this, alternative techniques like target encoding can be employed. Target encoding assigns a value to each category based on the target variable's mean (e.g., stock return). Although more succinct, it requires careful handling to prevent data leakage or overfitting, commonly addressed by proper cross-validation.

For ordinal data, where an inherent sequence exists, label encoding or ordinal encoding is appropriate. This method assigns integers to the labels in a way that preserves their ordinal nature. Consider credit ratings with values "AAA" as 1, "AA" as 2, and "A" as 3. By assigning integers, ordinal encoding maintains the ranking order, allowing machine learning models to infer relationships effectively:

$$\text{Credit Rating} \rightarrow \text{Encoded}$$

| Credit Rating | Encoded |
|---|---|
| AAA | 1 |
| AA | 2 |
| A | 3 |

However, ordinal encoding should be applied judiciously in regression settings, as it imposes a linear relationship which may not accurately reflect real-world scenarios. Alternative approaches, such as binning categorical variables into meaningful intervals or quantile bucketing, help in capturing the underlying distribution without inflating dimensionality.

Lastly, embedding techniques, particularly advantageous for high-cardinality categorical variables, offer a powerful alternative. Leveraging domain knowledge and neural networks, embeddings transform categorical variables into dense vectors of continuous values, capturing intricate relationships between categories. For instance, stock ticker symbols can be embedded into a lower-dimensional space where each dimension encapsulates hidden patterns or sectoral correlations. Embeddings have gained traction in sophisticated machine learning models and algorithms, including deep learning, where they seamlessly integrate with neural network architectures to enrich feature sets.

| Category | Embedding Dimension 1 | Embedding Dimension 2 |
|---|---|---|
| AAA | -0.1 | 0.2 |
| AA | 0.4 | -0.3 |
| A | 0.1 | 0.5 |

While embeddings require extensive training data and computational power, they enhance the model's ability to learn complex interactions, especially when dealing with vast and diverse financial datasets.

Effectively handling categorical data can elevate the predictive accuracy of machine learning models in variable financial markets. Balancing simplicity and sophistication in encoding methods is crucial, ensuring that each technique aligns with the dataset's peculiarities and the model's requirements. By thoughtfully navigating categorical data preprocessing, quantitative analysts can unlock more nuanced insights and bolster their algorithmic trading strategies.

## 4.7 Generating Features from Time Series Data

In the realm of financial modeling, time series data is ubiquitous, representing sequences of data points indexed in time order. Generating features from this data type involves capturing meaningful patterns and relationships that can enhance predictive models. The ability to effectively harness time series data can significantly bolster the predictive power of machine learning algorithms in trading and investing.

Understanding the unique characteristics of time series data is paramount. Unlike cross-sectional data, where observations are independent, time series data points are sequential and often exhibit temporal dependencies. This inherent structure necessitates specialized techniques for generating features that can capture trends, seasonalities, and other temporal patterns.

One fundamental approach to feature generation from time series data is the creation of lag features. Lag features involve shifting the time series to create new variables that represent past values of the original series. For instance, given a time series $\{y_t\}$, where $t = 1, 2, \ldots, T$, a lag feature with a lag of 1 can be represented as $y_{t-1}$. Mathematically, this can be expressed as:

$$L_k(y_t) = \{y_{t-k}\}, \quad \text{for } k = 1, 2, \ldots$$

where $L_k$ denotes the lag operator for lag $k$. By including lagged versions of a time series, models can utilize past information to make future predictions.

Another critical technique is the computation of moving averages. Moving averages smooth out short-term fluctuations and highlight longer-term trends or cycles, allowing for better trend recognition. The formula for a simple moving average (SMA) over a window size $N$ is:

$$\text{SMA}_N(y_t) = \frac{1}{N} \sum_{i=0}^{N-1} y_{t-i}$$

Variations such as the exponentially weighted moving average (EWMA) place more emphasis on recent observations, which can be beneficial in rapidly changing markets. The EWMA is calculated as:

$$\text{EWMA}_\alpha(y_t) = \alpha y_t + (1-\alpha)\text{EWMA}_\alpha(y_{t-1})$$

where $\alpha$ is the smoothing factor, ranging between 0 and 1.

Seasonal decomposition is another powerful tool for generating features from time series data. This involves breaking down the time series into its constituent components: the trend, seasonal, and residual components. By isolating the seasonal and trend components, models can better differentiate between regular periodic patterns and irregular fluctuations. A common method is to use the STL (Seasonal and Trend decomposition using Loess) algorithm, which decomposes time series as follows:

$$y_t = T_t + S_t + R_t$$

where $T_t$, $S_t$, and $R_t$ represent the trend, seasonal, and residual components, respectively.

In addition to trends and seasonality, volatility measures such as the standard deviation or variance over rolling windows can provide valuable features indicating market instability or risk. The rolling standard deviation over a window size $N$ is given by:

$$\text{RollingStd}_N(y_t) = \sqrt{\frac{1}{N}\sum_{i=0}^{N-1}(y_{t-i} - \text{SMA}_N(y_t))^2}$$

For financial time series, it is also essential to consider more sophisticated statistical properties such as autocorrelation and partial autocorrelation, which measure the correlation of a time series with its own past values. Autocorrelation function (ACF) and partial autocorrelation function (PACF) can uncover significant lags in data, aiding in model selection and feature generation.

Beyond these traditional methods, advancements in machine learning have introduced automated approaches for feature extraction from time series data. Techniques such as Fourier Transforms and Wavelet Transforms can convert time series into the frequency domain, revealing periodicities and hidden patterns not evident in the time domain.

The Discrete Fourier Transform (DFT) is defined as:

$$X_k = \sum_{t=0}^{N-1} y_t e^{-i2\pi kt/N}, \quad k = 0, 1, \ldots, N-1$$

where $N$ is the number of observations, and $i$ is the imaginary unit. By examining the magnitude and phase of the transformed series, significant periodic components can be identified.

Wavelet Transforms, on the other hand, allow multi-resolution analysis, capturing both time and frequency information. This method is beneficial for non-stationary time series, as it can elucidate localized features within the data.

Integrating these various techniques for generating features from time series data can significantly enhance the performance of predictive models in finance. Traders and investors can better grasp the temporal dynamics of financial markets, leading to more informed and strategic decision-making. As we delve deeper into the intricacies of feature engineering, the fusion of traditional statistical methods with modern machine learning approaches will continue to yield powerful tools for quants.

## 4.8 Interaction Features and Polynomial Features

In the realm of machine learning for finance, boosting the performance of predictive models often involves transforming the input features into a form that better captures the complexities of the data. Two powerful techniques in this regard are interaction features and polynomial features. These methods create new features from the original ones, embedding intricate relationships and nonlinear patterns that might otherwise be missed by the model.

Interaction features are generated by combining two or more existing features to capture their joint effect. For instance, if two features, $x_1$ and $x_2$, might individually have some predictive power, their interaction, $x_1 \times x_2$, could reveal additional insight into the data. This approach is particularly valuable in finance, where the interplay between different market indicators can provide a clearer signal for predicting stock movements.

Mathematically, if we have a data set with features $\boldsymbol{x} = [x_1, x_2, \ldots, x_n]$, an interaction feature for two features $x_i$ and $x_j$ can be represented as:

$$z_{ij} = x_i \times x_j$$

This interaction term $z_{ij}$ becomes a new feature in our dataset. For example, when analyzing stock data, interacting the volume of trades with the price might uncover patterns that neither could reveal on its own.

Generating Interaction Terms in Python

```
import pandas as pd
import numpy as np

# Sample DataFrame with financial features
df = pd.DataFrame({
    'feature1': np.random.randn(100),
    'feature2': np.random.randn(100)
})

# Creating an interaction feature
df['interaction'] = df['feature1'] * df['feature2']
```

Polynomial features take this idea a step further by considering not just interactions but also the higher-order terms of a single feature. For instance, a polynomial feature of degree 2 for a feature $x_i$ would include $x_i^2$. These new terms allow the model to understand and fit more complex nonlinear relationships in the data.

If $x_i$ is a feature, the polynomial features of degree $d$ for $x_i$ would include terms such as:

$$x_i, x_i^2, x_i^3, \ldots, x_i^d$$

Combining polynomial features with interaction terms yields a feature set that reflects both the nonlinearities within individual features and the interactions between them.

For instance, if we have original features $x_1$ and $x_2$, polynomial features of degree 2 would include:

$$x_1, x_2, x_1^2, x_2^2, x_1 \times x_2$$

In Python, polynomial features can be generated using the 'PolynomialFeatures' class from the 'sklearn.preprocessing' module:

Generating Polynomial Features in Python

```
from sklearn.preprocessing import PolynomialFeatures

# Sample DataFrame with financial features
```

```
df = pd.DataFrame({
    'feature1': np.random.randn(100),
    'feature2': np.random.randn(100)
})

# Creating polynomial features of degree 2
poly = PolynomialFeatures(degree=2, include_bias=False)
poly_features = poly.fit_transform(df[['feature1', 'feature2']])

# Convert to DataFrame for better visualization
poly_df = pd.DataFrame(poly_features, columns=poly.get_feature_names_out(['
    feature1', 'feature2']))
```

These transformations facilitate capturing the intricate patterns and dependencies within financial data, enabling models to make more accurate predictions. When selecting the degree of polynomial features, it is crucial to balance model complexity and overfitting. High-degree polynomials can model complex relationships but also run the risk of fitting noise in the training data.

To determine the necessary transformations, it is beneficial to explore the data and domain knowledge pertinent to finance. Certain financial theories and empirical studies underline the importance of specific interactions or nonlinearities, which can guide the feature engineering process.

By crafting these sophisticated features, we can enhance the predictive power of our models, capturing the dynamics of financial markets more effectively. The inclusion of interaction and polynomial features transforms our dataset into a richer landscape, teeming with potential for uncovering hidden trends and making more informed investment decisions.

## 4.9 Feature Extraction using Principal Component Analysis (PCA)

Principal Component Analysis (PCA) is a powerful statistical technique commonly used in machine learning and finance for feature extraction and dimensionality reduction. This section delves into the intricacies of PCA, explaining its utility in transforming high-dimensional data into a lower-dimensional space without significant loss of information. By understanding and applying PCA, traders and quants can enhance their predictive models' efficiency and performance.

PCA works by identifying the directions (principal components) in which the variance of the data is maximized. These directions are orthogonal to each other, ensuring that they capture the most significant features of the dataset while minimizing redundancy. Let's walk through the process of performing PCA, from the mathematical foundations to its practical application in financial datasets.

**Mathematical Foundations of PCA:**

Consider a dataset $\boldsymbol{X} \in \mathbb{R}^{n \times p}$, where $n$ is the number of observations and $p$ is the number of features. The first step in PCA is to center the data by subtracting the mean of each feature from the data points, resulting in a mean-centered dataset $\boldsymbol{X}_{centered}$.

$$\boldsymbol{X}_{centered} = \boldsymbol{X} - \bar{\boldsymbol{X}}$$

Next, we compute the covariance matrix $\boldsymbol{S}$ of the centered data:

$$\boldsymbol{S} = \frac{1}{n-1} \boldsymbol{X}_{centered}^T \boldsymbol{X}_{centered}$$

The covariance matrix $\boldsymbol{S}$ is a $p \times p$ matrix that describes the variance and covariance of the features.

To identify the principal components, we need to solve the eigenvalue decomposition of the covariance matrix $\boldsymbol{S}$:

$$\boldsymbol{S}\boldsymbol{V} = \boldsymbol{V}\boldsymbol{\Lambda}$$

Here, $\boldsymbol{V}$ is a matrix whose columns are the eigenvectors (principal components) of $\boldsymbol{S}$, and $\boldsymbol{\Lambda}$ is a diagonal matrix containing the corresponding eigenvalues. The eigenvalues represent the amount of variance explained by each principal component. By ordering the eigenvalues in descending order and selecting the top $k$ eigenvalues and their corresponding eigenvectors, we can reduce the dimensionality of the dataset.

The transformed dataset $\boldsymbol{X}_{PCA}$ in the lower-dimensional space is obtained by projecting the original data onto the selected principal components:

$$\boldsymbol{X}_{PCA} = \boldsymbol{X}_{centered} \boldsymbol{V}_k$$

Where $\boldsymbol{V}_k$ consists of the top $k$ eigenvectors.

**Practical Application of PCA in Finance:**

In financial markets, PCA can be used to condense complex datasets like stock prices, returns, or financial ratios into a more manageable number of features. This is particularly useful for mitigating the curse of dimensionality and reducing noise in the data.

For example, consider a portfolio of stocks whose daily returns are our features. Rather than working with potentially hundreds of correlated returns, PCA allows us to extract a few key components that capture the majority of the variance in the returns, simplifying the analysis while retaining essential information.

**Step-by-step Implementation:**

- **Standardize the Data:** Given the varying scales of financial data, it's crucial to standardize the features before applying PCA. This can be achieved using the StandardScaler from the sklearn library in Python:

```
from sklearn.preprocessing import StandardScaler
scaler = StandardScaler()
X_scaled = scaler.fit_transform(X)
```

- **Apply PCA:** Using the PCA module from sklearn, fit the PCA model on the standardized data and transform it:

```
from sklearn.decomposition import PCA
pca = PCA(n_components=k) # Select number of components
X_pca = pca.fit_transform(X_scaled)
```

- **Analyze the Results:** The principal components can be analyzed to understand their contribution to the total variance. The explained variance ratio can help determine the number of components to retain:

```
explained_variance = pca.explained_variance_ratio_
```

  By plotting the cumulative explained variance, one can choose an appropriate $k$ that captures a high percentage of the variance (commonly 95

```
import matplotlib.pyplot as plt
plt.plot(np.cumsum(explained_variance))
plt.xlabel('Number of Components')
plt.ylabel('Cumulative Explained Variance')
plt.show()
```

By incorporating PCA into the feature engineering process, we can streamline the input data for machine learning models, improving their performance and robustness. This technique is especially valuable in scenarios where the dataset is large or contains multicollinear features, as it helps to focus on the most informative components while reducing dimensionality and potential overfitting.

Mastering PCA not only enhances model efficiency but also provides deeper insights into the underlying structure of financial data, enabling traders and quants to make more informed decisions. As we continue to build on the foundational aspects of feature engineering, PCA stands out as an essential tool in the quantitative finance toolkit.

## 4.10 Automated Feature Engineering Tools

Automated feature engineering tools are revolutionizing the way financial analysts and data scientists create predictive models. These tools utilize machine learning algorithms to generate, evaluate, and select the most relevant features, significantly reducing the manual effort involved in the feature engineering process. By leveraging automated methods, one can enhance the efficiency and accuracy of predictive models while maintaining a high degree of flexibility and scalability.

Modern automated feature engineering tools encompass various strategies and packages that cater to diverse financial data scenarios. Let's delve into some of the most popular tools and their applications in finance.

One widely adopted tool is FeatureTools, which implements a method called Deep Feature Synthesis (DFS). DFS automatically constructs features by stacking multiple primitive operations, such as aggregations and transformations, on raw data. A typical use case in finance could involve generating time-based features like moving averages, cumulative sums, and rolling statistics, which are crucial for stock price prediction.

Example of Deep Feature Synthesis using FeatureTools.

```
import featuretools as ft
import pandas as pd

# Sample dataframe with stock prices
data = {
    'date': pd.date_range(start='1/1/2020', periods=100),
    'stock_price': np.random.rand(100)
}
```

```
df = pd.DataFrame(data)

# Create an entity set and add the dataframe
es = ft.EntitySet(id='stock_data')
es = es.entity_from_dataframe(entity_id='prices', dataframe=df, index='date')

# Automatically generate features using DFS
feature_matrix, feature_defs = ft.dfs(entityset=es, target_entity='prices')

# View the generated feature matrix
print(feature_matrix.head())
```

Another valuable tool is AutoFeat, which focuses on feature generation, selection, and transformation. AutoFeat uses a combination of mathematical transformations and interactions between features to create a comprehensive set of potential features. This process is particularly beneficial when dealing with non-linear relationships in financial data.

Creating interaction features with AutoFeat.

```
from autofeat import AutoFeatRegressor
import numpy as np

# Sample dataset
np.random.seed(0)
X = np.random.rand(100, 5)
y = X[:, 0] * X[:, 1] + X[:, 1]**2 - X[:, 2]

# Initialize the AutoFeat regressor
model = AutoFeatRegressor()
X_transformed = model.fit_transform(X, y)

# View transformed features
print(X_transformed.head())
```

TPOT (Tree-based Pipeline Optimization Tool) is another powerful tool that automates the machine learning pipeline, including feature engineering, model selection, and hyperparameter optimization. By using genetic programming, TPOT optimizes feature sets and identifies the best models, making it particularly useful for complex financial datasets that require extensive feature interactions.

DataRobot is a commercial automated machine learning platform that integrates feature engineering as part of its end-to-end model building process. DataRobot uses proprietary algorithms to automatically generate, select, and evaluate features. This platform is ideal for financial institutions seeking a comprehensive, scalable solution for predictive modeling.

It is essential to understand that although these automated tools significantly streamline the feature engineering process, human expertise is irreplaceable. The analyst's domain knowledge is crucial for interpreting results, understanding feature importance, and ensuring that the generated features make economic sense. Combining automated tools with expert insights allows financial analysts to build robust and interpretable models effectively.

Exploring various automated feature engineering tools and incorporating them into the financial modeling workflow can immensely benefit practitioners by saving time, improving model performance, and maintaining data integrity. These tools serve as powerful allies, augmenting the traditional feature engineering process and paving the way for more advanced and accurate financial predictions.

## 4.11 Feature Engineering Best Practices

Feature engineering plays a pivotal role in the success of machine learning models in finance. It involves creating, selecting, and transforming raw data into meaningful inputs that enhance the predictive power of algorithms. This section outlines several best practices that can significantly improve the quality of your features, thereby boosting model performance and reliability.

One essential practice in feature engineering is understanding the domain context of your data. Financial markets are driven by complex dynamics, including economic indicators, market sentiment, and geopolitical events. Therefore, it's crucial to have a deep understanding of the market in which you're operating. This knowledge will help you design features that capture relevant patterns and signals. For instance, incorporating industry-specific indicators such as the price-to-earnings ratio, trading volume, and volatility indices can provide valuable insights into stock movements.

Another best practice is to maintain a balance between simplicity and complexity. While complex features might capture intricate relationships in the data, they also introduce the risk of overfitting, especially when the dataset is limited. Simpler features are often more interpretable and generalize better to unseen data. Start with basic features and gradually introduce complexity as needed, ensuring that each added feature contributes to the model's performance.

Consistency in data preprocessing is also critical. The preprocessing steps applied to training data must be identical to those applied to new, unseen data. This includes handling missing values, scaling numerical features, and encoding categorical variables. Inconsistent preprocessing can lead to significant discrepancies between training and real-world performance, rendering the model ineffective. Using automated pipelines, such as those provided by libraries like scikit-learn, can ensure that preprocessing steps are consistently applied.

Careful handling of multicollinearity is another important aspect. Multicollinear features provide redundant information, which can inflate variance and destabilize model coefficients. When features are highly correlated, it may be beneficial to remove one of the correlated features or apply dimensionality reduction techniques, such as Principal Component Analysis (PCA), to mitigate multicollinearity. Regular checks for correlation and appropriate mitigation strategies can maintain the robustness of your model.

Feature scaling is paramount in algorithms that rely on distance metrics, such as k-nearest neighbors and support vector machines, or those that use gradient descent optimization, like neural networks. Standardizing features to have zero mean and unit variance, or normalizing them to a specific range, ensures that all features contribute equally to the distance calculations or optimization process. This step can dramatically improve model convergence and performance.

The temporal nature of financial data necessitates particular attention to time-based features. Avoid data leakage by ensuring that future information is not used in constructing features for past data points. This means that when creating features from time series data, ensure that only past values are used to predict future outcomes. For example, rolling averages or lagged features should be computed using historical data up to the current point in time.

Furthermore, consider the interpretability of the features you engineer. Transparent and explainable models can provide actionable insights and build trust among stakeholders. Features based on known financial theories and economic principles are often more interpretable than those derived from complex transformations. Explainability is particularly important in compliance-heavy fields like finance, where understanding model predictions can lead to better decision-making processes.

To summarize, effective feature engineering is a blend of domain expertise, thoughtful design, and rigorous validation. By integrating these best practices into your workflow, you can create powerful and reliable features that enhance the predictive capabilities of your machine learning models. Continuously iterating and refining your feature sets in response to model performance metrics will ensure that your models remain robust and effective in dynamic financial markets.

# Chapter 5

# Supervised Learning

**This chapter provides an in-depth look at supervised learning techniques used in quantitative finance. It begins by explaining the fundamentals of supervised learning and introduces various algorithms, including linear regression, logistic regression, decision trees, random forests, and support vector machines (SVM). The chapter also covers neural networks and gradient boosting machines. Additionally, it addresses hyperparameter tuning and reviews crucial model evaluation metrics, ensuring robust and reliable model performance for financial applications.**

## 5.1 What is Supervised Learning?

Supervised learning is a fundamental concept in machine learning and plays a crucial role in quantitative finance. It involves using a labeled dataset to train a model, enabling it to make predictions or decisions based on new, unseen data. This section delves into the essential principles of supervised learning, providing a comprehensive overview that will form the foundation for more advanced topics discussed later in the chapter.

At its core, supervised learning operates on a simple premise: given a set of input-output pairs, the objective is to learn a mapping from inputs to outputs. This mapping should be robust enough to generalize well to new data. In the context of quantitative finance, these inputs, or features, could include a variety of market indicators such as historical prices, trading volumes, and economic indicators, while the outputs could represent target variables like future stock prices or the likelihood of a credit default.

Consider the formal definition of supervised learning. Let $\boldsymbol{X} \in \mathbb{R}^{n \times p}$ be a matrix of $n$ observations and $p$ features, and let $\boldsymbol{y} \in \mathbb{R}^n$ be a vector of corresponding target values. The goal is to find a function $f : \mathbb{R}^p \to \mathbb{R}$ such that $f(\boldsymbol{x}_i) \approx y_i$ for each observed pair $(\boldsymbol{x}_i, y_i)$. Mathematically, this can be formulated as:

$$f^* = \arg\min_f \mathbb{E}_{(\boldsymbol{X},\boldsymbol{y})}[L(f(\boldsymbol{X}), \boldsymbol{y})],$$

where $L$ is a loss function that quantifies the discrepancy between the predicted and actual values. Common loss functions include the mean squared error (MSE) for regression tasks and the cross-entropy loss for classification tasks.

The process of supervised learning involves several key steps:

- **Data Collection and Preprocessing:** The first step is to gather a relevant labeled dataset. In finance, this might involve compiling historical price data, macroeconomic indicators, and other financial metrics. Preprocessing steps such as normalization, handling missing values, and feature engineering are crucial to prepare the data for effective modeling.

- **Model Selection:** Choosing an appropriate model is critical. This chapter will cover various models, including linear regression, decision trees, and neural networks. Each model has its own strengths and weaknesses, and the choice depends on the specific characteristics of the problem at hand.

- **Training:** Once a model is selected, it is trained using the labeled dataset. This involves optimizing the model parameters to minimize the loss function on the training data. Techniques such as gradient descent are commonly used to perform this optimization.

- **Evaluation:** After training, the model's performance is evaluated using separate validation data that was not seen during training. This helps in assessing the model's ability to generalize to new, unseen data. Key evaluation metrics, such as accuracy, precision, recall, and mean absolute error, will be discussed in later sections.

- **Hyperparameter Tuning:** Models often have hyperparameters that need to be fine-tuned to achieve optimal performance. Techniques like cross-validation and grid search are employed to systematically explore different combinations of hyperparameters.
- **Deployment:** Once a model has been trained and tuned, it can be deployed in a production environment where it makes predictions on new data. In the financial context, this might involve predicting stock prices, assessing credit risks, or executing algorithmic trades.

To illustrate the concept of supervised learning, consider a simple example of predicting a stock's future price based on historical prices and trading volumes. The input features could include the stock's past prices over a certain time window and corresponding trading volumes, while the target variable could be the stock price at the next time step. By training a supervised learning model on historical data, we aim to predict future stock prices with reasonable accuracy.

Supervised learning offers a powerful framework for tackling a wide range of predictive modeling tasks in finance. However, it is not without challenges. Overfitting, where a model performs well on training data but poorly on unseen data, is a common issue that requires careful mitigation through techniques such as regularization and cross-validation.

In summary, supervised learning forms the backbone of many predictive analytics and decision-making systems in quantitative finance. By mastering the principles and techniques of supervised learning, traders and quants can develop models that provide valuable insights and drive strategic financial decisions. As we progress through this chapter, we will delve deeper into specific supervised learning algorithms and explore their applications in finance, building on the foundational understanding established in this section.

## 5.2 Linear Regression

Linear regression is one of the foundational techniques in supervised learning, especially suited for predicting a continuous response variable. Its simplicity and interpretability make it a popular choice among quantitative analysts and data scientists in finance. This section delves into the mechanics of linear regression, its mathematical formulation, assumptions, and practical applications in financial markets.

At its core, linear regression aims to model the relationship between a dependent variable $y$ and one or more independent variables $X$. The simplest form, simple linear regression, considers a single predictor variable, while multiple linear regression extends this to encompass multiple predictors.

Mathematically, the linear regression model can be expressed as:

$$y_i = \beta_0 + \beta_1 x_{i1} + \beta_2 x_{i2} + \cdots + \beta_p x_{ip} + \epsilon_i$$

where:

- $y_i$ represents the dependent variable for the $i$-th observation.
- $\beta_0$ is the intercept term, indicating the value of $y$ when all $x$ variables are zero.
- $\beta_1, \beta_2, \ldots, \beta_p$ are the coefficients representing the relationship between the predictors and the response.
- $x_{i1}, x_{i2}, \ldots, x_{ip}$ are the independent variables or predictors.
- $\epsilon_i$ is the error term, capturing the variability in $y$ not explained by the linear relationship.

The primary objective in linear regression is to find the best-fitting line through the data points, essentially estimating the coefficients $\beta_0, \beta_1, \ldots, \beta_p$. This is achieved by minimizing the sum of the squared residuals (the differences between the observed and predicted values of $y$). The estimation process typically utilizes the Ordinary Least Squares (OLS) method.

$$\hat{\boldsymbol{\beta}} = \arg\min_{\boldsymbol{\beta}} \sum_{i=1}^{n} (y_i - \boldsymbol{x}_i^\top \boldsymbol{\beta})^2$$

where $\boldsymbol{x}_i$ is the vector of predictor values for observation $i$, and $\boldsymbol{\beta}$ is the vector of coefficients.

For the OLS estimators to be the best linear unbiased estimators (BLUE), certain assumptions need to be satisfied:

- **Linearity:** The relationship between the predictors and the response is linear.

- **Independence:** The residuals (errors) are independent of each other.
- **Homoscedasticity:** The variance of the residuals is constant across all levels of the independent variables.
- **Normality:** For hypothesis tests and confidence intervals to be valid, the residuals should be approximately normally distributed.

Violations of these assumptions can lead to biased or inefficient estimates, making model diagnostics crucial in practice.

In the realm of finance, linear regression is widely used for predicting stock prices, assessing the impact of macroeconomic indicators, and managing portfolio risk. Let's consider a scenario involving the Capital Asset Pricing Model (CAPM), a cornerstone of modern portfolio theory.

The CAPM describes the relationship between the expected return of an asset and its market risk, represented by beta ($\beta$). The model is expressed as:

$$E(R_i) = R_f + \beta_i(E(R_m) - R_f)$$

Here, $E(R_i)$ is the expected return of the asset, $R_f$ is the risk-free rate, $E(R_m)$ is the expected market return, and $\beta_i$ measures the asset's sensitivity to market movements.

To estimate $\beta_i$, historical returns of the asset ($R_i$) are regressed against the market returns ($R_m$), providing us with actionable insights into how the asset is likely to perform relative to the market.

$$R_i = \alpha + \beta_i R_m + \epsilon$$

where $\alpha$ represents the abnormal return not explained by market movements.

Once a linear regression model is fitted, it's essential to evaluate its performance. Key metrics include:

- **R-squared ($R^2$):** This statistic measures the proportion of variance in the dependent variable explained by the independent variables. An $R^2$ close to 1 indicates a model that explains a large portion of the variance.

- **Adjusted R-squared:** Adjusted for the number of predictors in the model, providing a more accurate measure of model performance, especially with multiple predictors.
- **Residual Standard Error (RSE):** Provides an estimate of the standard deviation of the residuals.
- **p-values:** Assess the significance of each predictor, enabling the identification of variables that significantly contribute to the model.

In addition to these metrics, visual diagnostic tools such as residual plots, Q-Q plots, and leverage plots are invaluable for assessing the assumptions and identifying potential issues like heteroscedasticity or influential outliers.

By thoroughly understanding and effectively applying linear regression, financial analysts can glean critical insights and make informed decisions, whether for forecasting prices, managing risk, or unlocking other complex market dynamics. As we progress through this chapter, we'll build upon the fundamental concepts introduced here, exploring more advanced supervised learning techniques that further enhance our predictive capabilities in the realm of quantitative finance.

## 5.3 Logistic Regression

Logistic regression is a powerful statistical method used for binary classification problems, where the outcome variable is categorical and has two possible values. In quantitative finance, logistic regression is commonly applied to predict the probability of a particular event occurring, such as whether a stock price will go up or down.

The logistic regression model predicts the probability $P$ that a given input variable $x$ belongs to a particular category. The model can be expressed as follows:

$$P(Y = 1|\boldsymbol{x}) = \sigma(\boldsymbol{w}^T\boldsymbol{x} + b)$$

where $Y$ is the binary outcome, $\boldsymbol{w}$ is the vector of weights, $\boldsymbol{x}$ is the input feature vector, $b$ is the bias term, and $\sigma$ represents the sigmoid function, defined as:

$$\sigma(z) = \frac{1}{1 + e^{-z}}$$

The sigmoid function ensures that the output of the logistic regression model is a probability value between 0 and 1.

**Training the Logistic Regression Model**

Training a logistic regression model involves estimating the parameters $\boldsymbol{w}$ and $b$ that best fit the data. This is typically done using the maximum likelihood estimation (MLE) method. The likelihood function measures how well the model's predictions align with the actual outcomes in the training data. For logistic regression, the likelihood function for $n$ training examples is:

$$L(\boldsymbol{w}, b) = \prod_{i=1}^{n} P(y^{(i)}|\boldsymbol{x}^{(i)}) = \prod_{i=1}^{n} \sigma(\boldsymbol{w}^T\boldsymbol{x}^{(i)}+b)^{y^{(i)}}(1-\sigma(\boldsymbol{w}^T\boldsymbol{x}^{(i)}+b))^{1-y^{(i)}}$$

To simplify the optimization problem, it is common to maximize the log-likelihood, given by:

$$\log L(\boldsymbol{w}, b) = \sum_{i=1}^{n} \left[ y^{(i)} \log \sigma(\boldsymbol{w}^T\boldsymbol{x}^{(i)} + b) + (1 - y^{(i)}) \log(1 - \sigma(\boldsymbol{w}^T\boldsymbol{x}^{(i)} + b)) \right]$$

Optimizing the log-likelihood function requires gradient ascent or more commonly, gradient descent when minimizing the negative log-likelihood.

$$\mathcal{J}(\boldsymbol{w}, b) = -\log L(\boldsymbol{w}, b)$$

We minimize the cost function $\mathcal{J}(\boldsymbol{w}, b)$ using gradient descent, updating the parameters $\boldsymbol{w}$ and $b$ iteratively:

$$w_j := w_j - \alpha \frac{\partial \mathcal{J}(\boldsymbol{w}, b)}{\partial w_j}$$

$$b := b - \alpha \frac{\partial \mathcal{J}(\boldsymbol{w}, b)}{\partial b}$$

where $\alpha$ is the learning rate.

**Evaluating Model Performance**

Assessing the performance of a logistic regression model in financial applications requires appropriate metrics, given the binary nature of the prediction task. Common evaluation metrics include accuracy, precision, recall, F1 score, and the Area Under the Receiver Operating Characteristic curve (ROC AUC).

- **Accuracy**: Measures the proportion of correct predictions out of the total number of predictions.
- **Precision**: The ratio of true positive predictions to the sum of true and false positive predictions.
- **Recall**: The ratio of true positive predictions to the sum of true positives and false negatives.
- **F1 Score**: The harmonic mean of precision and recall, providing a single metric that balances both.
- **ROC AUC**: Evaluates the performance of the classifier across different threshold values, offering a summary measure of the trade-off between true positive and false positive rates.

Each metric offers unique insights into the model's performance, allowing investors and traders to fine-tune their strategies based on the specific goals of their analysis.

Logistic regression is favored for its simplicity, interpretability, and effectiveness in scenarios where the relationship between the input features and the probability of the outcome is approximately linear. By converting predictions into probabilities, it enables more nuanced trading decisions and risk management strategies. When applied judiciously, it can form the foundation for more advanced machine learning models used in financial forecasting.

## 5.4 Decision Trees

Decision Trees are a powerful and intuitive method for both regression and classification tasks in supervised learning. Employing a tree-like structure, they partition the dataset into subsets based on the input feature values, ultimately generating a series of decision rules that lead to final predictions.

At the core of a decision tree is the concept of *nodes* and *branches*. Each internal node represents a *decision point* based on a specific feature, while each leaf node represents an *outcome*. Branches, on the other hand, correspond to the decision outcomes, guiding the flow from the root node to the leaf nodes. The path from the root to a leaf node encapsulates the rules used in the prediction process.

The construction process of a decision tree involves the recursive splitting of data, maximizing the purity of the resultant subsets at each step. A primary metric used to measure this purity or impurity is the Gini index for classification tasks and variance reduction for regression tasks.

The Gini index, for a given split, measures the amount of mixture within the nodes, mathematically defined as follows:

$$\text{Gini}(D) = 1 - \sum_{i=1}^{m} p_i^2$$

where $D$ is the dataset, $m$ represents the number of classes, and $p_i$ is the probability of selecting the $i$-th class.

For regression trees, a common objective is to reduce the variance of predicted values within each node:

$$\text{Var}(D) = \frac{1}{N} \sum_{i=1}^{N} (y_i - \bar{y})^2$$

where $N$ is the number of observations in dataset $D$, $y_i$ is the actual value, and $\bar{y}$ is the mean of these observed values.

The algorithm for building a decision tree can be summarized through the following steps:

1. **Choose the best feature and threshold for splitting the data.** This involves evaluating all potential splits and selecting the one that results in the highest information gain (or greatest impurity reduction).

2. **Split the dataset into two subsets.** Based on the chosen feature and threshold, the data is divided.

3. **Repeat recursively for each subset.** The above steps are recursively applied to each subset, creating a tree structure.

4. **Stop under predefined conditions.** The recursion can be halted once certain criteria are met, such as reaching a maximum tree depth, obtaining pure nodes, or having a minimal number of samples in a node.

One of the key advantages of decision trees is their interpretability. The hierarchical structure allows investors to readily understand the logic behind the model's predictions, which is especially valuable in finance where transparency is crucial.

However, decision trees are prone to overfitting, particularly when dealing with noisy data or data with many features. To counteract this, techniques such as *pruning* are employed. Pruning involves reducing the size of the tree by removing nodes that contribute little to the predictive power of the model, thus enhancing its generalization capabilities. Two common pruning methods are *pre-pruning*, where the construction halts early based on set criteria, and *post-pruning*, where a fully grown tree is trimmed back.

In quantitative finance, decision trees can be particularly effective for modeling decision-making processes under uncertainty. For instance, they can be used to predict stock price movements, classify trading signals, or even construct fundamental indicators. The clear decision pathways aid in back-testing strategies, providing a robust framework for evaluating historical performance and theoretical scenarios.

Decision trees also serve as foundational components in more complex ensemble methods, such as Random Forests and Gradient Boosting Machines, which address some of the inherent limitations of a single decision tree by combining multiple trees to improve robustness and accuracy.

## 5.5 Random Forests

Random Forests represent a significant advancement in ensemble learning techniques utilized in quantitative finance for predicting market movements. Building on the concept of decision trees, Random Forests enhance predictive accuracy and robustness by combining multiple tree predictors. Each tree is grown on a randomly selected subset of the data, introducing diversity and reducing overfitting—a common issue in individual decision trees.

At its core, a Random Forest is a collection of decision trees, each constructed using a different bootstrap sample of the data. The process of bootstrapping involves randomly sampling the dataset with replacement, ensuring each tree sees a unique subset during its training. This technique contributes to the model's robustness and generalization capability by mitigating variance.

To delve into Random Forests, it is instrumental to comprehend the random selection mechanism applied both to the data and features. When constructing each tree, not only is the training data randomized through bootstrapping, but Random Forests also introduce randomness in the feature selection process. At each node of a tree, a subset of features is randomly chosen, and the best split is found only within this subset. This approach ensures a diverse set of trees as different trees might use different sets of features for splits, contributing to an ensemble model that leverages the 'wisdom of the crowd'.

The power of Random Forests lies in their ability to amalgamate the predictions from multiple trees. For regression tasks, the final prediction is the average of individual tree predictions, mathematically represented as:

$$\hat{y} = \frac{1}{B} \sum_{b=1}^{B} \hat{y}^{(b)}$$

where $\hat{y}$ is the aggregated prediction, $B$ is the total number of trees, and $\hat{y}^{(b)}$ is the prediction from the $b$-th tree. For classification tasks, the final class prediction is determined by majority vote amongst the trees:

$$\hat{C} = \text{mode}\{\hat{C}^{(1)}, \hat{C}^{(2)}, \ldots, \hat{C}^{(B)}\}$$

where $\hat{C}$ is the final class prediction and $\hat{C}^{(b)}$ is the prediction from the $b$-th tree.

The principal advantages of Random Forests are their high accuracy and ease of implementation. These models are also highly interpretable compared to other ensemble methods such as gradient boosting machines. The inherent randomness helps in ensuring that the model is not too sensitive to noise in the training data, which enhances its generalization capability.

However, the flexibility of Random Forests is not without downside. They can become computationally expensive with large datasets, both in terms of time and memory. The training phase, involving the construction of numerous trees, and the prediction phase, where predictions from several trees are aggregated, can demand substantial computational resources. Additionally, although interpretability is generally higher than some other ensemble methods, it can still be challenging to understand the decisions of highly complex Random Forests fully.

For financial applications, Random Forests are particularly valuable in scenarios requiring robust and accurate predictions amidst noisy market data. Their ability to handle various data types (whether categorical or continuous) and their resilience against overfitting make them ideal candidates for tasks such as stock price prediction, credit scoring, and risk assessment.

To implement a Random Forest in Python, the 'scikit-learn' library provides a straightforward interface. The following code snippet demonstrates how to train a Random Forest model for a regression task:

```
from sklearn.ensemble import RandomForestRegressor
from sklearn.model_selection import train_test_split
from sklearn.metrics import mean_squared_error

# Assume we have features X and target variable y
X_train, X_test, y_train, y_test = train_test_split(X, y, test_size=0.2,
     random_state=42)

# Instantiate the RandomForestRegressor
rf = RandomForestRegressor(n_estimators=100, random_state=42)

# Fit the model
rf.fit(X_train, y_train)

# Make predictions
y_pred = rf.predict(X_test)

# Evaluate the model
mse = mean_squared_error(y_test, y_pred)
print(f'Mean Squared Error: {mse}')
```

In this example, 'n_estimators' specifies the number of trees in the forest. The 'RandomForestRegressor' object is fitted on the training data, and predictions are made on the test set. The performance is then evaluated using mean squared error (MSE), a common metric for regression tasks.

When employing Random Forests in trading and investing contexts, hyperparameter tuning is crucial to optimize model performance. Parameters such as the number of trees ('n_estimators'), the maximum depth of each tree ('max_depth'), and the number of features considered for splitting ('max_features') can significantly affect the model's accuracy and efficiency. Cross-validation methods are typically applied to identify the optimal set of hyperparameters. This topic will be further discussed in the section dedicated to hyperparameter tuning.

Embracing Random Forests in quantitative finance necessitates balancing between model complexity and interpretability, striving to maintain accurate predictions without incurring excessive computational costs. As a robust and versatile ensemble method, Random Forests continue to be a staple in the toolkit of quants and financial analysts.

## 5.6 Support Vector Machines (SVM)

Support Vector Machines (SVM) represent a powerful class of supervised learning algorithms that are extensively used in quantitative finance for classification and regression tasks. Their robust performance in high-dimensional spaces makes them particularly valuable for predicting market movements, identifying trading signals, and optimizing investment strategies.

At its core, the SVM algorithm aims to find the optimal hyperplane that separates different classes of data with the maximum margin. This margin serves as a buffer zone, minimizing the risk of misclassification and enhancing the model's generalizability to unseen data.

Given a training dataset $\{(x_i, y_i)\}_{i=1}^n$, where $x_i \in \mathbb{R}^d$ represents the feature vectors and $y_i \in \{-1, 1\}$ the class labels, the primary objective of SVM in a binary classification scenario is to find a hyperplane defined by $w \cdot x + b = 0$ that maximizes the margin between the two classes. Mathematically, this can be formulated as an optimization problem:

$$\min_{w,b} \quad \frac{1}{2}\|w\|^2$$
$$\text{subject to} \quad y_i(w \cdot x_i + b) \geq 1, \quad \forall i = 1, 2, \ldots, n$$

Here, $w$ is the weight vector perpendicular to the hyperplane, and $b$ is the bias term.

To handle non-linearly separable data, SVMs employ the kernel trick, which maps the original features into a higher-dimensional space where a linear separator can be more easily found. Commonly used kernels include:

- **Linear Kernel**:

$$K(x_i, x_j) = x_i \cdot x_j$$

- **Polynomial Kernel**:

$$K(x_i, x_j) = (\gamma x_i \cdot x_j + r)^d$$

where $\gamma$, $r$, and $d$ are kernel parameters.

- **Radial Basis Function (RBF) Kernel**:

$$K(x_i, x_j) = \exp\left(-\gamma \|x_i - x_j\|^2\right)$$

where $\gamma > 0$ is a kernel parameter.

- **Sigmoid Kernel**:

$$K(x_i, x_j) = \tanh(\gamma x_i \cdot x_j + r)$$

where $\gamma$ and $r$ are kernel parameters.

Selecting the appropriate kernel and tuning its parameters are critical steps in constructing an effective SVM model. Cross-validation techniques, such as k-fold cross-validation, can be employed to identify the optimal kernel and its parameters by evaluating the model's performance across different subsets of the training data.

The application of SVMs in quantitative finance often involves feature engineering and selection, ensuring the model ingests the most relevant and predictive input data. Key financial features typically include technical indicators (e.g., moving averages, volatility measures, momentum oscillators), fundamental factors (e.g., earnings growth, P/E ratios), and macroeconomic indicators (e.g., interest rates, inflation rates).

In addition to binary classification, SVMs can be extended to handle multi-class classification problems through techniques such as one-vs-one (OvO) and one-vs-all (OvA) approaches. For regression tasks, the Support Vector Regression (SVR) algorithm is employed, where the objective is to determine a function that deviates from the actual target values by a margin $\epsilon$ at most, while ensuring the model complexity is controlled.

```
from sklearn.svm import SVC
from sklearn.preprocessing import StandardScaler
from sklearn.pipeline import make_pipeline

# Example: Predicting stock price movement
X_train = ... # Feature matrix
y_train = ... # Binary labels

# Pipeline: Standardize features and train SVM with RBF kernel
model = make_pipeline(StandardScaler(), SVC(kernel='rbf', C=1, gamma='scale'))
model.fit(X_train, y_train)

# Predict and evaluate
X_test = ... # Feature matrix for test data
y_test = ... # True labels for test data

y_pred = model.predict(X_test)
```

When evaluating the performance of an SVM model, key metrics such as accuracy, precision, recall, F1-score, and Area Under the Receiver Operating Characteristic Curve (AUC-ROC) should be considered. These metrics provide a comprehensive understanding of how well the model distinguishes between different classes and its overall predictive power.

Support Vector Machines offer a robust and versatile framework for tackling various financial prediction tasks, blending theoretical elegance with practical efficacy to analyze and navigate the complexities of financial markets. By leveraging the extensive modeling capabilities of SVMs, traders and investors can enhance their decision-making processes, uncovering valuable insights and achieving more consistent and profitable outcomes.

## 5.7 Neural Networks

Neural networks, inspired by the human brain, are a pivotal element in modern machine learning, particularly within the realm of supervised learning for quantitative finance. They excel in capturing complex, non-linear relationships in data, making them indispensable for predicting market movements where traditional models might fall short.

A neural network is structured in layers: an input layer, one or more hidden layers, and an output layer. Each layer comprises units known as neurons, which process input signals and propagate them through the network. The power of neural networks lies in their ability to learn intricate patterns through backpropagation and stochastic gradient descent.

**Architecture of Neural Networks**

Consider a simple neural network with an input layer, a single hidden layer, and an output layer. For financial data, the input layer might consist of features such as stock prices, trading volumes, and various technical indicators. Each neuron in the hidden layer computes a weighted sum of the inputs, passes this sum through an activation function, and sends the output to the subsequent layer.

Mathematically, the output $a_j$ of neuron $j$ in the hidden layer can be expressed as:

$$a_j = f\left(\sum_{i=1}^{n} w_{ij}x_i + b_j\right)$$

where:

- $x_i$ represents the inputs,
- $w_{ij}$ denotes the weights connecting input $i$ to neuron $j$,
- $b_j$ is the bias term for neuron $j$,
- $f(\cdot)$ is the activation function.

Common activation functions include the sigmoid function, hyperbolic tangent (tanh), and the Rectified Linear Unit (ReLU). ReLU, given by $f(x) = \max(0, x)$, is particularly popular due to its simplicity and effectiveness in mitigating the vanishing gradient problem.

**Training Neural Networks**

Training a neural network involves optimizing the weights and biases to minimize the prediction error. This is achieved through the backpropagation algorithm, which efficiently computes the gradient of the loss function with respect to each weight by applying the chain rule.

Suppose $L$ represents the loss (or cost) function measuring the discrepancy between the predicted and actual values. The goal is to minimize $L$ using gradient descent. For a given weight $w$, the update rule is:

$$w := w - \eta\frac{\partial L}{\partial w}$$

where $\eta$ is the learning rate, a hyperparameter dictating the step size in the process of weight adjustment.

**Overfitting and Regularization**

Neural networks are prone to overfitting, especially with small training datasets. Overfitting occurs when the network learns not only the underlying patterns but also the noise in the training data, leading to poor generalization on unseen data. To combat overfitting, several regularization techniques can be employed:

- **L2 Regularization** (Ridge): Adds a penalty proportional to the sum of the squares of the weights to the loss function.

$$L_{\text{ridge}} = L + \lambda \sum_j w_j^2$$

- **Dropout**: During training, randomly deactivates a fraction of neurons in each layer, forcing the network to learn redundant representations.
- **Early Stopping**: Monitors the performance on a validation set and halts training when performance ceases to improve, preventing over-training.
- **Data Augmentation**: Enhances the training dataset with artificial samples generated by slight modifications of existing data, improving network robustness.

### Application in Quantitative Finance

Neural networks can be utilized in numerous financial tasks, such as:

- **Price Prediction**: Predicting future stock prices based on historical data and technical indicators.
- **Sentiment Analysis**: Interpreting market sentiment by analyzing news articles, social media, and other text sources.
- **Algorithmic Trading**: Developing trading strategies that adapt to evolving market conditions.
- **Risk Management**: Identifying and mitigating potential financial risks through predictive analytics.

### A Practical Example

Consider a neural network aimed at predicting stock prices. The input features might include historical prices, trade volumes, moving averages, and momentum indicators. A simple network architecture could consist of an input layer with 10 neurons (one for each feature), two hidden layers with 64 and 32 neurons respectively, and an output layer with a single neuron representing the predicted price.

Implementing this in code might look like:

```
import tensorflow as tf
from tensorflow.keras.models import Sequential
```

```
from tensorflow.keras.layers import Dense

# Define the model
model = Sequential([
    Dense(64, activation='relu', input_shape=(10,)),
    Dense(32, activation='relu'),
    Dense(1)
])

# Compile the model
model.compile(optimizer='adam', loss='mean_squared_error')

# Train the model
model.fit(X_train, y_train, epochs=100, validation_split=0.2)
```

For this example, X_train and y_train represent the training features and labels, respectively.

Integrating neural networks into your quantitative finance toolkit provides a powerful method to harness historical data and identify predictive patterns in financial markets. The key is to balance model complexity and regularization to ensure robust performance on real-world data.

## 5.8 Gradient Boosting Machines

Gradient Boosting Machines (GBMs) are a powerful ensemble learning technique that have gained significant popularity in quantitative finance for their high predictive accuracy and ability to handle a variety of data types and structures. GBMs build models sequentially, where each new model attempts to correct the errors made by the previous models. This iterative approach makes them highly effective in capturing complex patterns within the data, leading to remarkable improvements in model performance.

The core idea behind gradient boosting revolves around constructing a strong predictive model by combining many weaker models, typically decision trees. Unlike bagging methods like Random Forests, where trees are built independently, gradient boosting builds trees in a sequential manner with each tree aiming to reduce the residual errors of the preceding tree.

Let us delve deeper into the working mechanism of GBMs and consider their mathematical formulation. Given a dataset $\{(x_i, y_i)\}_{i=1}^{N}$, where $x_i$ represents the feature vector and $y_i$ represents the target variable, the objective is to minimize a loss function $L(y, f(x))$ that measures the discrepancy between the true value and the predicted value.

Initially, GBMs start with a simple model, usually the mean of the target variable for regression tasks:

$$f_0(x) = \arg\min_c \sum_{i=1}^{N} L(y_i, c)$$

For each subsequent iteration $m$, GBMs fit a new model $h_m(x)$ to the residual errors from the previous model. The residuals $r_i^{(m-1)}$ are calculated as follows:

$$r_i^{(m-1)} = -\left[\frac{\partial L(y_i, f(x_i)^{(m-1)})}{\partial f(x_i)^{(m-1)}}\right]$$

Here, $r_i^{(m-1)}$ represents the pseudo-residuals, which are essentially the negative gradients of the loss function with respect to the current model's predictions. These gradients guide the subsequent model in reducing the error more effectively.

The new model $h_m(x)$ is then trained to predict these residuals. The original model is updated by adding this new model, scaled by a learning rate $\eta$, to the previous ensemble:

$$f_m(x) = f_{m-1}(x) + \eta h_m(x)$$

Here, $\eta$ is a hyperparameter that controls the contribution of the new model to the overall prediction. A smaller $\eta$ generally yields better generalization but requires more iterations.

The process continues for a pre-defined number of iterations $M$, resulting in the final model:

$$f_M(x) = f_0(x) + \eta \sum_{m=1}^{M} h_m(x)$$

One of the main strengths of GBMs lies in their ability to handle various types of loss functions, making them versatile for different kinds of tasks, including regression and classification. For example, in regression tasks, a common choice is the squared loss, whereas, in classification tasks, the logistic loss or exponential loss can be used.

GBMs also include mechanisms for regularization to prevent overfitting. Some common regularization techniques include:

- **Tree constraints**: Limiting the depth of individual trees to control the complexity of each weak learner.
- **Tree subsampling**: Using only a subset of the training data to build each tree, similar to bagging, which introduces randomness and reduces overfitting.
- **Learning rate**: A lower learning rate requires more trees but can lead to more robust models.

In finance, GBMs are particularly useful for tasks such as stock price prediction, risk management, and portfolio optimization due to their flexibility and high accuracy. They can capture non-linear dependencies and interactions among features that single models might miss.

Furthermore, GBMs are inherently interpretable to some extent because the underlying models are decision trees, which provide insights through feature importance measures and tree structures. This interpretability is valuable for understanding the factors driving market movements and making informed trading decisions.

Moving forward, it is essential to fine-tune GBMs for optimal performance in financial applications. This involves careful hyperparameter tuning, which we will discuss in the next section. By understanding the intricacies of GBMs and their application in finance, investors and traders can leverage this powerful technique to enhance their predictive models and achieve better trading outcomes.

## 5.9 Hyperparameter Tuning

In the realm of supervised learning, hyperparameter tuning is a critical process that significantly affects the performance and robustness of predictive models. Unlike model parameters, which are learned from the training data during model fitting, hyperparameters are set before the learning process begins and determine the structure and behavior of the model. Effective hyperparameter tuning can transform a mediocre model into an exceptional one, making this step indispensable in quantitative finance applications.

To set the stage, let's define what hyperparameters are. Hyperparameters are external configurations to a model that cannot be estimated from the data. Examples include the learning rate for gradient-based algorithms, the number of trees in a random forest, or the number of layers in a neural network. Selecting optimal hyperparameters requires careful experimentation and validation, as poor choices can lead to overfitting, underfitting, or suboptimal performance.

A powerful approach to hyperparameter tuning involves the use of grid search, where a comprehensive set of hyperparameter combinations is exhaustedly evaluated. Grid search works by specifying a finite set of values for each hyperparameter, creating a grid of possible configurations. Each point in the grid represents a unique set of hyperparameters, and the goal is to identify the combination that yields the best performance on a validation dataset. While grid search is methodical, it can be computationally expensive, especially when dealing with a large number of hyperparameters and possible values.

A more efficient alternative is random search, which randomly samples a predefined number of hyperparameter configurations from the search space. Random search can often find equally good or better solutions in less time compared to grid search. This method is particularly advantageous when only a subset of the hyperparameter space significantly influences model performance, as the randomness increases the chance of focusing computations on the more impactful regions.

Another sophisticated strategy is the use of Bayesian optimization, which models the hyperparameter search space probabilistically and iteratively updates this model to find the optimum. Bayesian methods consider past evaluation results to make informed decisions about the next set of hyperparameters to explore, selecting configurations that promise better outcomes based on a surrogate model. The process maximizes a utility function, often focusing on areas of the search space that balance exploration (evaluating uncertain configurations) and exploitation (testing promising configurations). This approach can be significantly more efficient than grid or random search, especially for complex models with many hyperparameters.

When employing any of these methods, cross-validation becomes an indispensable tool. Cross-validation involves splitting the training data into several subsets and iteratively training and validating the model across these subsets, ensuring that hyperparameter choices generalize well to unseen data. The k-fold cross-validation technique, where data is divided into k subsets, is widely used. The model is trained on k-1 of these subsets and validated on the remaining one, with the process repeated k times. The overall performance metric is averaged over the k iterations, providing a robust estimate of model performance.

For a quantitative finance practitioner, specific considerations become important when tuning hyperparameters. Financial data often presents challenges such as non-stationarity, high dimensionality, and volatility clustering. As such, hyperparameters should be tuned with careful attention to stability and adaptability, striving to strike a balance between responsiveness to market changes and robustness against noise and outliers.

Consider the example of tuning hyperparameters for a Random Forest model in a trading strategy. Crucial hyperparameters might include the number of trees, the maximum depth of each tree, and the minimum number of samples required to split an internal node. Grid or random search could begin with broad ranges - for instance, evaluating the number of trees between 50 and 500, depths from 1 to 20, and minimum sample splits from 2 to 10. Once narrower optimal ranges are identified, the focus could shift to more granular searches within these ranges using Bayesian optimization for fine-tuning.

In practice, the penultimate step is validating the tuned model on an out-of-sample test set or through backtesting on historical data to ensure that the chosen hyperparameters yield robust, real-world performance. Finally, continuous monitoring and periodic re-tuning are often necessary, especially in the fast-paced world of trading, to maintain the model's efficacy as market conditions evolve.

By dedicating time and computational resources to meticulous hyperparameter tuning, quantitative finance professionals can significantly enhance model precision, reduce prediction error, and improve the overall profitability of trading strategies. This stage, while sometimes arduous, is integral to developing robust, reliable financial models that withstand the complexities and challenges of real-world financial markets.

# 5.10 Model Evaluation Metrics in Supervised Learning

In quantitative finance, the accurate evaluation of predictive models is crucial for making informed investment decisions. Without proper evaluation metrics, even well-constructed models can lead to suboptimal trading strategies. This section delves into the key metrics used to gauge the performance of supervised learning models, ensuring that the insights derived are both robust and reliable.

Evaluating a model's performance involves comparing its predictions against actual outcomes using a variety of metrics. These metrics can broadly be categorized into those used for regression tasks and those used for classification tasks.

**Regression Metrics**

For regression models, which predict continuous outcomes such as stock prices or returns, it is essential to measure both the accuracy and the precision of the predictions. Common metrics include:

$$\text{Mean Squared Error (MSE)} = \frac{1}{n}\sum_{i=1}^{n}(y_i - \hat{y}_i)^2$$

MSE measures the average of the squares of the errors—that is, the average squared difference between the actual and predicted values. It penalizes larger errors more severely, making it sensitive to outliers.

$$\text{Root Mean Squared Error (RMSE)} = \sqrt{\text{MSE}}$$

RMSE is the square root of MSE and provides a measure of the error in the same units as the predicted value, making it easier to interpret in the context of financial data.

$$\text{Mean Absolute Error (MAE)} = \frac{1}{n}\sum_{i=1}^{n}|y_i - \hat{y}_i|$$

MAE measures the average magnitude of errors in a set of predictions, without considering their direction. It is less sensitive to outliers compared to MSE.

$$R^2 \text{ (Coefficient of Determination)} = 1 - \frac{\sum_{i=1}^{n}(y_i - \hat{y_i})^2}{\sum_{i=1}^{n}(y_i - \bar{y})^2}$$

$R^2$ represents the proportion of variance in the dependent variable that is predictable from the independent variables. An $R^2$ closer to 1 indicates a model explains a large portion of the variance.

**Classification Metrics**

For classification models, which predict categorical outcomes such as market movements (up or down), evaluating their discriminative power is critical. Key metrics include:

$$\text{Accuracy} = \frac{\text{Number of Correct Predictions}}{\text{Total Number of Predictions}}$$

Accuracy indicates the proportion of true results (both true positives and true negatives) among the total observations. However, it may be misleading in imbalanced datasets.

$$\text{Precision} = \frac{\text{True Positives}}{\text{True Positives + False Positives}}$$

Precision measures the accuracy of the positive predictions. It is particularly important in trading where a high false positive rate might lead to unwarranted transactions.

$$\text{Recall (Sensitivity)} = \frac{\text{True Positives}}{\text{True Positives + False Negatives}}$$

Recall, or sensitivity, measures the ability of a model to identify all relevant instances, which translates to capturing all profitable trades in financial applications.

$$F_1\text{-score} = 2 \cdot \frac{\text{Precision} \cdot \text{Recall}}{\text{Precision + Recall}}$$

The $F_1$-score provides a harmonic mean of precision and recall, offering a single metric that balances the two. It is especially useful when dealing with imbalanced datasets.

Area Under the ROC Curve (AUC-ROC)

AUC-ROC quantifies the overall ability of the model to discriminate between the positive and negative classes. An AUC score closer to 1 indicates better performance.

**Confusion Matrix**

A confusion matrix offers a comprehensive table that illustrates the performance of a classification algorithm:

| | Predicted Positive | Predicted Negative |
|---|---|---|
| Actual Positive | True Positive (TP) | False Negative (FN) |
| Actual Negative | False Positive (FP) | True Negative (TN) |

This matrix allows the identification of both correct and incorrect classifications, providing a granular view of the model's performance across different classes.

Effectively using these metrics provides traders and quants with a nuanced understanding of model performance, informing decisions to tweak models for achieving greater predictive accuracy and reliability in financial markets.

# Chapter 6

# Unsupervised Learning

**This chapter delves into unsupervised learning methods and their applications in finance. It begins by explaining the core concept of unsupervised learning and then explores various clustering techniques, such as K-means and hierarchical clustering, and dimensionality reduction methods like PCA and t-SNE. The chapter also covers association rule learning, anomaly detection, and Gaussian mixture models. Further topics include self-organizing maps (SOM) and the application of unsupervised learning in financial contexts, along with appropriate evaluation metrics for these models.**

## 6.1 What is Unsupervised Learning?

Unsupervised learning is a branch of machine learning that focuses on identifying patterns and structures within data without the need for labeled responses. Unlike supervised learning, where the model is trained using input-output pairs, unsupervised learning works with data that consists solely of input variables $X$. Its goal is to infer the natural structure present within a set of data points. This form of learning is particularly valuable in exploratory data analysis, revealing hidden insights that can inform trading strategies and investment decisions.

The essence of unsupervised learning can be distilled into two primary tasks: clustering and dimensionality reduction. Clustering involves grouping data points into distinct clusters based on their similarities, while dimensionality reduction focuses on reducing the number of random variables under consideration to simplify the data without losing significant information.

One common application of unsupervised learning in finance is the identification of underlying factors that influence stock prices. By clustering stocks that exhibit similar behavior, financial analysts can detect industry sectors, uncover correlations, and manage diversified portfolios more effectively. Dimensionality reduction techniques, on the other hand, assist in simplifying complex market data, making it easier to visualize and analyze trends.

To grasp the utility of unsupervised learning, consider a dataset of historical stock prices. A trader might use clustering algorithms to group stocks with similar price movements, which could suggest a common market influence or sectoral performance. This information is invaluable in constructing hedging strategies or identifying arbitrage opportunities.

At the heart of these tasks lies a range of algorithms designed to capture the intrinsic structure of the data. Clustering algorithms such as K-means and hierarchical clustering partition the data into groups based on proximity metrics, while algorithms like Principal Component Analysis (PCA) and t-Distributed Stochastic Neighbor Embedding (t-SNE) reduce the dimensionality of data, making it easier to manage and interpret.

Consider K-means clustering, which aims to partition observations into $k$ clusters, where each observation belongs to the cluster with the nearest mean. Formally, given a set of observations $\boldsymbol{X} = \{x_1, x_2, \ldots, x_n\}$, K-means clustering seeks to minimize the sum of squared distances between the observations and the corresponding cluster centroids $\mu_k$:

$$\arg\min_{S} \sum_{k=1}^{K} \sum_{x \in S_k} \|x - \mu_k\|^2$$

where $S$ denotes the set of clusters. This method is particularly effective for market segmentation, identifying similar trading patterns, and deducing customer behavior.

Dimensionality reduction techniques like PCA are equally powerful. PCA seeks to transform the data to a new coordinate system such that the greatest variances lie on the first coordinates (principal components). Mathematically, PCA solves the eigenvalue decomposition of the covariance matrix $\Sigma$ of the data $\boldsymbol{X}$:

$$\Sigma \boldsymbol{v}_i = \lambda_i \boldsymbol{v}_i$$

where $\boldsymbol{v}_i$ are the eigenvectors and $\lambda_i$ are the corresponding eigenvalues. The eigenvectors corresponding to the largest eigenvalues form the basis of the reduced dimensional space. In financial analysis, PCA can uncover the underlying risk factors in asset returns, simplifying portfolio optimization.

Unsupervised learning also includes methods like association rule learning, which is used to discover interesting relations between variables in large datasets. This is particularly relevant for market basket analysis – a common technique in retail finance to analyze customer purchasing patterns.

Through this chapter, we will explore these methods in greater detail, elucidating their mathematical foundations and examining their real-world applications in financial trading and investment. By understanding and leveraging unsupervised learning, financial analysts and traders can unveil hidden market structures and enhance their decision-making processes.

## 6.2 Clustering Techniques: K-Means, Hierarchical Clustering

Clustering is a fundamental technique in unsupervised learning where the objective is to partition a set of data points into distinct groups or clusters. These methods prove invaluable in finance for customer segmentation, portfolio clustering, and identifying market regimes. This section focuses on two prominent clustering techniques: K-means and hierarchical clustering, explaining their mechanisms and practical applications.

**K-means Clustering**

K-means clustering aims to divide a dataset into $K$ clusters, where each data point belongs to the cluster with the nearest mean. The overall process involves three main steps:

- **Initialization**: The algorithm begins by randomly selecting $K$ initial centroids.

- **Assignment**: Each data point is assigned to the nearest centroid based on Euclidean distance.
- **Update**: The centroids are recalculated as the mean of the data points assigned to each cluster.

This process iterates between the assignment and update steps until the centroids converge or a predetermined number of iterations is reached. The objective function minimized in K-means clustering is the within-cluster sum of squares (WCSS):

$$\min_{\mathbf{c}} \sum_{i=1}^{K} \sum_{\boldsymbol{x} \in C_i} \|\boldsymbol{x} - \boldsymbol{\mu}_i\|^2$$

where $c$ denotes the cluster assignments, $x$ represents data points, $C_i$ is the $i$-th cluster, and $\boldsymbol{\mu}_i$ is the centroid of cluster $C_i$.

**Practical Application in Finance**

In financial contexts, K-means clustering can be utilized to segment stocks based on performance metrics, trading volumes, or volatility. For instance, clustering stocks by their risk-return profile helps in identifying groups with similar characteristics, aiding in portfolio diversification and risk management.

Consider an example where we aim to cluster a selection of stocks based on their annual returns and standard deviations. Using K-means clustering, we can effectively group stocks into different risk classes, thereby enabling better-informed investment decisions.

**Hierarchical Clustering**

Hierarchical clustering seeks to build a hierarchy of clusters, typically represented in a tree-like structure called a dendrogram. The two primary types of hierarchical clustering are:

- **Agglomerative (Bottom-Up)**: Starts with each data point as an individual cluster and merges the closest pairs of clusters iteratively until a single cluster remains.
- **Divisive (Top-Down)**: Begins with the entire dataset in one cluster and recursively splits it into smaller clusters.

The agglomerative approach is more common and involves the following steps:

- **Calculate Distance Matrix**: Compute the distance between every pair of data points.

- **Merge Clusters**: At each step, merge the two clusters with the minimum distance. Update the distance matrix accordingly.

- **Update Distances**: Depending on the linkage criterion (single, complete, or average linkage), update the distances between the newly formed cluster and remaining clusters.

The linkage criteria determine how the distances between clusters are calculated:

- **Single Linkage**: Distance between the closest points of the clusters.

- **Complete Linkage**: Distance between the farthest points of the clusters.

- **Average Linkage**: Average distance between all points in the clusters.

**Application and Insights in Finance**

Hierarchical clustering is particularly useful in analyzing the structural relationship between financial assets. For example, it can help visualize correlations among a set of stocks, offering insights into market sectors and investment strategies.

Consider a scenario where we analyze the correlation matrix of various financial instruments. Applying hierarchical clustering can reveal hidden structures, such as groups of highly correlated assets. This information is essential for constructing diversified portfolios and identifying potential hedging opportunities.

Furthermore, the dendrogram visualization assists in understanding the hierarchy and nested clustering of financial assets. It provides a clear view of how different assets group together at varying levels of similarity, thus aiding in comprehensive market analysis.

In both K-means and hierarchical clustering, the choice of the number of clusters and the linkage criteria significantly influence the outcomes. Hence, it's crucial to experiment with different configurations and validate the clustering results against financial and economic rationale.

Together, K-means and hierarchical clustering offer robust tools for uncovering patterns and insights from financial data, enhancing the decision-making process in trading and investing.

## 6.3 Dimensionality Reduction Techniques: PCA, t-SNE

Dimensionality reduction is a crucial technique in the realm of unsupervised learning, particularly in financial applications where datasets often comprise numerous variables. The primary goal is to simplify these datasets while retaining as much variance — that is, significant information — as possible. Two widely-used methods for this purpose are Principal Component Analysis (PCA) and t-distributed Stochastic Neighbor Embedding (t-SNE). These techniques help in reducing computational complexity, mitigating the curse of dimensionality, and facilitating better data visualization.

Principal Component Analysis (PCA) is a linear dimensionality reduction technique. It projects the data onto a lower-dimensional space by identifying the directions (principal components) in which the variance of the data is maximized. Here's a detailed look at the step-by-step process of PCA:

1. **Standardize the Data:** Standardization is crucial because PCA is affected by the scale of the variables. This means transforming the data so that each feature has a mean of zero and a variance of one.

2. **Compute the Covariance Matrix:** The covariance matrix captures the covariance (linear relationship) between pairs of features in the dataset.

3. **Calculate the Eigenvalues and Eigenvectors:** By solving the covariance matrix, we obtain the eigenvalues and their corresponding eigenvectors. The eigenvectors represent the direction of the principal components, while the eigenvalues quantify the amount of variance carried in each direction.

4. **Sort the Eigenvalues and Select Principal Components:** Arrange the eigenvalues in descending order. The corresponding eigenvectors of the top $k$ eigenvalues form the new feature space.

5. **Transform the Data:** Project the original standardized data onto the new feature space formed by the top $k$ eigenvectors.

Mathematically, if $\boldsymbol{X}$ is the standardized data matrix, the transformation can be represented as:

$$\boldsymbol{Y} = \boldsymbol{X}\boldsymbol{W}$$

where $\boldsymbol{W}$ is the matrix of selected eigenvectors, and $\boldsymbol{Y}$ is the transformed data in the reduced space.

PCA is particularly useful in finance for various applications, such as portfolio optimization and risk management. For instance, PCA can be employed to decompose the covariance structure of asset returns, isolating the most influential factors driving market movements.

Unlike PCA, t-distributed Stochastic Neighbor Embedding (t-SNE) is a nonlinear dimensionality reduction technique primarily used for data visualization. t-SNE is designed to model the probability distribution of distances between data points in high-dimensional space and attempts to preserve these relationships in a lower-dimensional map. Here is the detailed process involved in t-SNE:

1. **Compute Pairwise Similarities:** In high-dimensional space, compute the pairwise similarities between data points using a Gaussian distribution. The similarity $p_{ij}$ between data points $i$ and $j$ is given by:

$$p_{ij} = \frac{\exp(-\|\boldsymbol{x}_i - \boldsymbol{x}_j\|^2 / 2\sigma_i^2)}{\sum_{k \neq i} \exp(-\|\boldsymbol{x}_i - \boldsymbol{x}_k\|^2 / 2\sigma_i^2)}$$

where $\boldsymbol{x}_i$ and $\boldsymbol{x}_j$ are data points in the high-dimensional space, and $\sigma_i$ is the perplexity parameter controlling the neighborhood size for point $i$.

2. **Define Low-Dimensional Similarities:** In the low-dimensional map, define the similarities $q_{ij}$ by a Student's t-distribution:

$$q_{ij} = \frac{(1 + \|\boldsymbol{y}_i - \boldsymbol{y}_j\|^2)^{-1}}{\sum_{k \neq l} (1 + \|\boldsymbol{y}_k - \boldsymbol{y}_l\|^2)^{-1}}$$

where $\boldsymbol{y}_i$ and $\boldsymbol{y}_j$ are points in the lower-dimensional space.

3. **Minimize the Kullback-Leibler (KL) Divergence:** Minimize the KL divergence between the high-dimensional and low-dimensional similarities:

$$KL(P\|Q) = \sum_{i \neq j} p_{ij} \log \frac{p_{ij}}{q_{ij}}$$

This optimization ensures that the low-dimensional representation preserves the structure of the high-dimensional data as much as possible.

t-SNE is particularly valuable for visualizing complex financial datasets, such as clustering similar stocks or detecting anomalies. Due to its emphasis on preserving local structures, t-SNE often reveals insightful patterns that linear techniques might miss. However, it is essential to note that t-SNE is computationally intensive and more suited for visualization rather than feature extraction for downstream tasks.

Both PCA and t-SNE offer different strengths that make them indispensable tools in the arsenal of a quant, each addressing unique aspects of dimensionality reduction and data interpretation. Proper implementation of these techniques can significantly enhance the analytical capabilities in financial data analysis, enabling more informed and effective decision-making.

## 6.4 Association Rule Learning

Association rule learning is a powerful technique in unsupervised learning that aims to uncover interesting relationships, patterns, or associations among a set of items in large datasets. This method is frequently used in market basket analysis to identify associations between items purchased together. Understanding these associations can provide valuable insights for decision-making in various financial contexts, including portfolio management, trading strategies, and risk management.

At its core, association rule learning involves finding rules in the form $\{A\} \rightarrow \{B\}$, where $\{A\}$ and $\{B\}$ represent disjoint sets of items. The rule implies that the presence of item set $\{A\}$ in a dataset suggests the presence of item set $\{B\}$. Several metrics are crucial for evaluating the quality and usefulness of these rules:

- **Support**: This indicates how frequently an item set appears in the dataset. The support of an item set $I$ is defined as:

$$\text{Support}(I) = \frac{\text{Number of transactions containing } I}{\text{Total number of transactions}}$$

- **Confidence**: This measures the reliability of the inference made by the rule. The confidence of a rule $\{A\} \rightarrow \{B\}$ is defined as:

$$\text{Confidence}(\{A\} \rightarrow \{B\}) = \frac{\text{Support}(\{A\} \cup \{B\})}{\text{Support}(\{A\})}$$

- **Lift**: This indicates how much the presence of $\{A\}$ increases the probability of $\{B\}$. The lift of a rule $\{A\} \rightarrow \{B\}$ is defined as:

$$\text{Lift}(\{A\} \rightarrow \{B\}) = \frac{\text{Support}(\{A\} \cup \{B\})}{\text{Support}(\{A\}) \times \text{Support}(\{B\})}$$

The process of mining association rules involves two main steps: the identification of frequent item sets using a minimum support threshold and the generation of strong rules that meet a minimum confidence threshold. One of the most well-known algorithms for this purpose is the Apriori algorithm.

**The Apriori Algorithm**

The Apriori algorithm operates on the principle that any subset of a frequent item set must also be frequent. It employs a breadth-first search strategy, iteratively identifying frequent item sets and extending them by one item at a time. The algorithm's efficiency hinges on two key steps:

1. **Join Step**: Generate candidate item sets of length $k+1$ by joining frequent item sets of length $k$.
2. **Prune Step**: Eliminate candidate item sets that have any invalid (infrequent) subset.

The iterative process halts once no further candidate item sets can be generated that meet the minimum support threshold.

In the context of finance, association rule learning can be applied to uncover patterns in trading behavior, transaction records, and financial events. For example, analyzing the co-occurrence of certain financial instruments in trading portfolios can help in understanding market dynamics, optimizing portfolio diversification, and identifying new investment opportunities.

**Example: Market Basket Analysis in Finance**

Consider a dataset containing transactions of financial instruments such as stocks, bonds, and derivatives. By applying association rule learning, we might discover rules like $\{\text{Stock A}, \text{Bond B}\} \rightarrow \{\text{Derivative C}\}$, indicating that the concurrent presence of Stock A and Bond B in a portfolio often leads to the inclusion of Derivative C. Such insights can inform portfolio construction strategies and risk assessment models.

Furthermore, association rule learning can be instrumental in detecting market anomalies. Unusual associations may signal underlying issues, such as hidden market manipulations or emergent market trends. By monitoring these associations over time, financial analysts can proactively respond to potential risks and opportunities.

Finally, it is essential to evaluate the discovered association rules within the appropriate financial context. Metrics like support, confidence, and lift must be scrutinized to ensure that the identified patterns are not only statistically significant but also economically meaningful.

Through association rule learning, traders and financial analysts can mine vast datasets for hidden correlations, enhancing their understanding of market behavior and ultimately supporting more informed, data-driven decision-making.

## 6.5 Anomaly Detection

Detecting anomalies, or outliers, in financial data is crucial for identifying unusual or potentially fraudulent activities, market shifts, and other irregular patterns that could signal important investment opportunities or risks. Anomaly detection encompasses a range of techniques designed to pinpoint data points that deviate significantly from the norm. These deviations, though sometimes subtle, can offer valuable insights into market dynamics.

At the heart of anomaly detection is the concept of understanding what constitutes "normal" behavior within a dataset. In financial contexts, normalcy might be defined by the historical price movements of a stock, trading volumes over a period, or even the typical patterns of financial ratios. Establishing this baseline is the first step toward identifying anomalies.

One fundamental approach to anomaly detection is leveraging statistical methods. Consider, for instance, the use of z-scores, which measure how many standard deviations a data point is from the mean of a distribution:

$$z = \frac{X - \mu}{\sigma}$$

where $X$ represents the value being assessed, $\mu$ is the mean of the data, and $\sigma$ is the standard deviation. Data points with a z-score greater than a certain threshold (often set around 3 or -3) are typically flagged as anomalies.

Another common statistical method involves the use of the IQR (Interquartile Range). The IQR method defines data points as outliers if they fall below $Q1 - 1.5 \cdot IQR$ or above $Q3 + 1.5 \cdot IQR$, where $Q1$ and $Q3$ are the first and third quartiles, respectively.

Moreover, financial time series data often exhibit non-linear and complex patterns, making traditional statistical methods less effective. This necessitates the use of machine learning algorithms for anomaly detection. Algorithms such as Isolation Forests, One-Class SVMs (Support Vector Machines), and Autoencoders have proven particularly adept at identifying anomalies in financial datasets.

Isolation Forests operate on the principle of isolating anomalies rather than profiling normal data points. The algorithm randomly selects a feature and then a random split value between the maximum and minimum values of the selected feature. Since anomalies are few and different, they are more susceptible to isolation and thus require fewer splits.

For instance, if we consider a simplified anomaly detection code using Isolation Forests in Python:

```
from sklearn.ensemble import IsolationForest

# Assuming data is our financial time series dataset
isolation_forest = IsolationForest(contamination=0.05)
isolation_forest.fit(data)
anomalies = isolation_forest.predict(data)

# Anomalies indicated by -1 in the results
anomalous_data = data[anomalies == -1]
```

Another advanced method is the use of Autoencoders within a deep learning framework. Autoencoders are a type of artificial neural network used to learn efficient codings of data. For anomaly detection, an autoencoder is trained to minimize the reconstruction error. When presented with a new data point, if the reconstruction error exceeds a certain threshold, it is flagged as an anomaly.

The architecture typically involves an encoder that compresses the data and a decoder that reconstructs it. During the training phase, the model learns to reconstruct normal data patterns with minimal error. Anomalies, which diverge from these patterns, yield higher reconstruction errors.

For instance, the loss function used to train an autoencoder may look like this:

$$\mathcal{L}(X, \hat{X}) = \sum_{i=1}^{n} (X_i - \hat{X}_i)^2$$

where $X$ is the original data input, $\hat{X}$ is the reconstructed data output, and $n$ is the number of data points.

The practical application of these methods in finance includes fraud detection in transaction data, detecting abnormal trading volumes, and identifying sudden shifts in market sentiment. For example, an unusually high trading volume coupled with a minor price change may indicate manipulation or insider trading.

Anomaly detection does not solely rely on the past but frequently involves real-time analysis. Financial markets are dynamic, and continually updating models to incorporate the latest data is essential for maintaining their efficacy. Techniques such as online learning adaptations of these algorithms enable continuous learning and adaptation to recent data changes.

The effectiveness of an anomaly detection model is often evaluated through metrics such as precision, recall, and F1-score, where:

$$\text{Precision} = \frac{\text{True Positives}}{\text{True Positives} + \text{False Positives}}$$

$$\text{Recall} = \frac{\text{True Positives}}{\text{True Positives} + \text{False Negatives}}$$

$$\text{F1-score} = 2 \cdot \frac{\text{Precision} \cdot \text{Recall}}{\text{Precision} + \text{Recall}}$$

These metrics help quantify the model's ability to correctly identify anomalies while minimizing false alarms, which is crucial in high-stakes financial environments.

By utilizing these diverse techniques, financial professionals can enhance their strategies, safeguard assets, and capitalize on emerging trends, thereby optimizing their trading and investment decisions.

## 6.6 Gaussian Mixture Models

Gaussian Mixture Models (GMMs) represent one of the most powerful and flexible probabilistic models for unsupervised learning. These models are used to identify underlying subpopulations or clusters in a given dataset. Unlike the more traditional clustering techniques such as K-means, which assign data points to clusters with a hard boundary, GMMs offer a probabilistic approach to clustering, assigning data points to clusters based on the likelihood of them belonging to each cluster. This soft clustering mechanism is particularly advantageous in financial applications where market behaviors are often influenced by overlapping factors.

At its core, a GMM assumes that the data points are generated from a mixture of several Gaussian distributions with unknown parameters. Each Gaussian distribution represents a cluster. The underlying principle is that each data point $\boldsymbol{x}_i$ is generated with a certain probability $\pi_k$ from a Gaussian distribution with a mean $\mu_k$ and a covariance matrix $\Sigma_k$. The objective is to estimate these parameters, typically using an iterative optimization algorithm called Expectation-Maximization (EM).

Let us formalize this concept mathematically. The probability density function of a GMM for a single data point $\boldsymbol{x}$ can be expressed as:

$$p(\boldsymbol{x}) = \sum_{k=1}^{K} \pi_k \mathcal{N}(\boldsymbol{x}|\mu_k, \Sigma_k)$$

Where:

- $\pi_k$ is the mixing coefficient for the $k$-th Gaussian component and $\sum_{k=1}^{K} \pi_k = 1$.
- $\mathcal{N}(\boldsymbol{x}|\mu_k, \Sigma_k)$ represents the Gaussian distribution with mean $\mu_k$ and covariance matrix $\Sigma_k$.

- $K$ is the number of Gaussian components in the mixture.

The EM algorithm iteratively performs two key steps: Expectation (E-step) and Maximization (M-step).

**E-step:** In the expectation step, the algorithm computes the probability (called the responsibility) that each data point $\boldsymbol{x}_i$ was generated by the $k$-th Gaussian component. This is given by:

$$r_{ik} = \frac{\pi_k \mathcal{N}(\boldsymbol{x}_i | \mu_k, \Sigma_k)}{\sum_{j=1}^{K} \pi_j \mathcal{N}(\boldsymbol{x}_i | \mu_j, \Sigma_j)}$$

**M-step:** In the maximization step, the algorithm updates the parameters (means, covariances, and mixing coefficients) to maximize the likelihood of the observed data given the responsibilities calculated in the E-step. The updated parameters are computed as follows:

$$\mu_k = \frac{\sum_{i=1}^{N} r_{ik} \boldsymbol{x}_i}{\sum_{i=1}^{N} r_{ik}}$$

$$\Sigma_k = \frac{\sum_{i=1}^{N} r_{ik} (\boldsymbol{x}_i - \mu_k)(\boldsymbol{x}_i - \mu_k)^T}{\sum_{i=1}^{N} r_{ik}}$$

$$\pi_k = \frac{1}{N} \sum_{i=1}^{N} r_{ik}$$

where $N$ is the number of data points.

The EM algorithm iterates between these two steps until convergence, typically when the change in the log-likelihood function is below a predefined threshold.

In financial contexts, GMMs have a broad range of applications. For instance, they can be used to model the distribution of asset returns, identify different regimes or states in market data (such as bullish, bearish, or stagnant periods), and cluster financial instruments based on their risk-return profiles. Furthermore, the probabilistic nature of GMMs allows for more nuanced interpretations compared to hard clustering techniques. For example, when assessing the risk associated with a portfolio, GMMs can provide insights into the probability of certain extreme events (tail risks) by modeling the joint distribution of asset returns more accurately.

To illustrate the application of GMMs in finance, let's consider a dataset of daily returns for a range of stocks. By fitting a GMM to this dataset, we can identify clusters of stocks that exhibit similar return distributions. This clustering can help in constructing diversified portfolios by selecting stocks from different clusters, thus reducing the overall portfolio risk.

Another practical example is regime detection. Financial markets are known to exhibit distinct regimes characterized by different volatility levels and correlations. By applying GMMs to historical return data, we can identify and model these regimes. Each Gaussian component can represent a different market regime, enabling traders and portfolio managers to adapt their strategies dynamically based on the prevailing regime's characteristics.

Gaussian Mixture Models, with their capacity to provide a probabilistic framework for clustering, offer significant advantages over traditional methods in capturing the complex and often overlapping structures in financial data. Whether used for risk management, portfolio diversification, or market regime detection, GMMs enhance the analytic capabilities of quantitative analysts, ushering in more sophisticated and adaptable trading and investing strategies.

## 6.7 Self-Organizing Maps (SOM)

Self-Organizing Maps (SOM), also known as Kohonen maps, are a type of artificial neural network introduced by Teuvo Kohonen in the 1980s. They are designed to produce a low-dimensional, discretized representation of the input space of the training samples, preserving the topological properties of the input space. SOMs are an essential tool in exploratory data analysis and visualization, particularly useful in finance for identifying patterns and trends in high-dimensional data sets.

The core idea behind SOM is to map high-dimensional data into a two-dimensional grid while preserving the inherent similarities between data points. This mapping process is achieved through competitive learning, where neurons in the map compete to respond to input signals. The winning neuron and its neighbors are adjusted to become more similar to the input vector, gradually transforming the map into a meaningful representation of the data.

Mathematically, a SOM consists of a grid of neurons, each associated with a weight vector $\boldsymbol{w}_i$ of the same dimensionality as the input data $\boldsymbol{x}$. The training process involves the following steps:

- **Initialization**: Initialize the weight vectors $\boldsymbol{w}_i$ either randomly or by sampling from the input data.

- **Competition**: For each input vector $\boldsymbol{x}$, identify the best matching unit (BMU), which is the neuron with the weight vector closest to $\boldsymbol{x}$. This is typically done using Euclidean distance:

$$\text{BMU} = \arg\min_i \|\boldsymbol{x} - \boldsymbol{w}_i\|$$

- **Adaptation**: Adjust the weight vectors of the BMU and its neighbors to make them more similar to $\boldsymbol{x}$. The degree of adjustment depends on the learning rate $\eta(t)$ and the neighborhood function $h_{ci}(t)$:

$$\boldsymbol{w}_i(t+1) = \boldsymbol{w}_i(t) + \eta(t) \cdot h_{ci}(t) \cdot (\boldsymbol{x} - \boldsymbol{w}_i(t))$$

  The neighborhood function $h_{ci}(t)$ typically decreases over time and with distance from the BMU, ensuring that neurons closer to the BMU are adjusted more than those further away.

- **Iteration**: Repeat the competition and adaptation steps for a specified number of iterations or until convergence.

One of the critical strengths of SOMs is their ability to visualize complex financial data in a two-dimensional grid, which can reveal hidden structures and relationships. For example, in the context of stock market analysis, SOMs can be used to cluster stocks with similar price movements, providing insights into market segments and potential correlation patterns.

To further illustrate the use of SOMs in finance, consider a portfolio management scenario. By applying SOM to a set of historical financial metrics, such as price-to-earnings ratios, dividend yields, and volatility measures, one can visualize and identify clusters of similar stocks. These clusters can then inform investment decisions, risk management strategies, and portfolio diversification efforts.

Another significant application of SOMs in finance is anomaly detection. By training a SOM on historical trading data, one can detect unusual patterns that deviate from the norm, potentially signaling fraudulent activities or market anomalies. The ability of SOMs to preserve topological relationships makes them particularly well-suited for this task, as anomalies often exhibit distinct characteristics that can be effectively isolated in the low-dimensional map.

Despite their advantages, SOMs also have some limitations. One challenge is the need to predefine the map size and topology, which may require domain expertise and experimentation. Additionally, the convergence of SOMs can be sensitive to the initial weight vectors and learning rate schedule, necessitating careful tuning.

Overall, Self-Organizing Maps offer a powerful and versatile approach to understanding and visualizing high-dimensional financial data. By preserving topological properties and enabling intuitive visual exploration, SOMs can uncover valuable insights that support informed trading and investment decisions.

## 6.8 Principal Component Analysis for Feature Extraction

Principal Component Analysis (PCA) is a powerful statistical technique used extensively in the field of machine learning, including in financial applications, for dimensionality reduction and feature extraction. Its primary objective is to transform a large set of variables into a smaller one while retaining the fundamental structure and variability present in the original dataset. This reduction aids in simplifying models, reducing computational load, and eliminating multicollinearity.

At its core, PCA identifies the directions (principal components) along which the variation in the data is maximized. These principal components are orthogonal to each other, which means they are uncorrelated, providing a succinct representation of the original data.

To understand PCA in a financial context, consider a stock market dataset containing multiple features such as trading volume, open price, close price, daily high, daily low, and other factors. This high-dimensional data can be transformed into a lower-dimensional space, capturing the most critical patterns that underline the movements in the stock prices.

The process of PCA involves several key steps, which we will now delve into:

**1. Data Standardization:** Before applying PCA, it is crucial to standardize the data, ensuring that each variable contributes equally to the analysis. This step involves subtracting the mean and dividing by the standard deviation for each feature, resulting in a dataset with zero mean and unit variance. The standardization formula is:

$$X_{std} = \frac{X - \mu}{\sigma}$$

where $X$ is the original data, $\mu$ is the mean, and $\sigma$ is the standard deviation of the data.

**2. Covariance Matrix Computation:** Once the data is standardized, the next step is to compute the covariance matrix. The covariance matrix $\Sigma$ provides insights into how the features vary with respect to each other:

$$\Sigma = \frac{1}{n-1} \sum_{i=1}^{n} (X_i - \bar{X})(X_i - \bar{X})^T$$

where $\bar{X}$ is the mean vector of the standardized variables, and $n$ is the number of observations.

**3. Eigenvalues and Eigenvectors:** The covariance matrix is then decomposed into its eigenvalues and eigenvectors. The eigenvalues indicate the magnitude of variance captured by each principal component, while the eigenvectors determine the direction of these components. Mathematically, this is represented as:

$$\Sigma \boldsymbol{v} = \lambda \boldsymbol{v}$$

where $\boldsymbol{v}$ is an eigenvector and $\lambda$ is the corresponding eigenvalue.

**4. Principal Components Selection:** The principal components are selected based on the eigenvalues. Components with the largest eigenvalues account for the most significant variation. Typically, a threshold is set (e.g., retaining components that capture 95% of the total variance) to decide the number of principal components to keep.

**5. Projection onto the Principal Components:** Finally, the original data is projected onto the selected principal components, resulting in a transformed dataset with reduced dimensions. This projection is carried out as follows:

$$\boldsymbol{Y} = \boldsymbol{X}\boldsymbol{V}$$

where $Y$ is the matrix of the transformed data, $X$ is the standardized data matrix, and $V$ is the matrix of the selected eigenvectors.

Applying PCA in financial contexts can yield significant benefits. For instance, when constructing a portfolio, reducing the dimensionality of the asset features can reveal the underlying factors that drive asset returns. This reduced set of features simplifies the modeling process while retaining essential information for making informed investment decisions.

Moreover, PCA can be used to remove noise from the data, enhancing the predictive performance of machine learning models. In algorithmic trading, identifying the principal components of market data helps in constructing trading signals that are robust and less prone to overfitting.

It is also noteworthy to mention the limitations of PCA. While PCA is effective in capturing linear relationships, it may not be suitable for datasets with intricate nonlinear structures. In such cases, alternative methods like kernel PCA, which extends PCA to nonlinear mappings, may be more appropriate.

PCA remains a cornerstone in the toolbox of quants and financial analysts, providing a means to distill complex, high-dimensional datasets into actionable insight. By transforming and reducing the data, PCA helps in uncovering hidden patterns and relationships, which are invaluable for decision-making in fast-paced financial markets. Through hands-on application and interpretation, PCA allows for the formulation of more streamlined, efficient, and insightful financial models.

## 6.9 Application of Unsupervised Learning in Finance

Unsupervised learning techniques offer a diverse range of applications in the financial domain, enhancing the decision-making process by uncovering hidden patterns and relationships within data. This section delves into the practical uses of unsupervised learning in various financial contexts, including market segmentation, portfolio optimization, anomaly detection, and feature extraction for predictive modeling.

One prominent application of unsupervised learning in finance is market segmentation. By employing clustering methods such as K-means or hierarchical clustering, financial analysts can categorize financial instruments, customers, or markets into distinct segments based on their characteristics and behaviors. For instance, clustering stock returns can reveal groups of stocks that behave similarly under certain market conditions, aiding in the creation of sector-specific trading strategies. Similarly, clustering customers based on their transaction histories and financial behaviors enables personalized marketing strategies and tailored financial products.

Consider the use of K-means clustering for segmenting stocks. Assume we have daily returns data for a set of stocks. Using the K-means algorithm, we can group these stocks into $k$ clusters where each stock belongs to the cluster with the nearest mean return vector. This categorization assists in identifying sectoral trends and potential pairs trading opportunities. The implementation can be illustrated with the following pseudo-code snippet:

```
# Pseudo-code for K-means clustering of stocks
initialize centroids for each cluster
repeat until convergence:
    assign each stock to the closest centroid
    update centroids based on the mean of assigned stocks
```

Another significant application is portfolio optimization. Dimensionality reduction techniques such as Principal Component Analysis (PCA) can be employed to reduce the complexity of financial datasets while preserving essential information. By transforming a high-dimensional dataset of asset returns into a lower-dimensional space, PCA identifies the principal components that capture the most variance. These components can be used to construct diversified portfolios that minimize risk. For example, instead of building a portfolio based on all available asset returns, one can use the principal components as inputs, thus reducing the risk of overfitting and improving the robustness of the portfolio.

Unsupervised learning is also invaluable in anomaly detection, particularly in fraud detection and risk management. Techniques like Gaussian Mixture Models (GMM) and clustering can identify unusual transactions or outliers that deviate significantly from the normal behavior. These anomalies often indicate potential fraudulent activities or emerging risks. For instance, by training a GMM on historical transaction data, we can estimate the probability distribution of normal transactions. Transactions that fall in low-probability regions can be flagged for further investigation:

$$P(x \mid \theta) = \sum_{k=1}^{K} \pi_k \mathcal{N}(x \mid \mu_k, \Sigma_k) \tag{6.1}$$

where $\mathcal{N}(x \mid \mu_k, \Sigma_k)$ is the Gaussian distribution with mean $\mu_k$ and covariance $\Sigma_k$, and $\pi_k$ are the mixing coefficients.

Furthermore, unsupervised learning facilitates feature extraction for predictive modeling. Techniques such as self-organizing maps (SOM) and PCA can generate new features that capture the underlying structure of the data. These features often lead to more accurate predictions when used in supervised learning algorithms. For instance, SOM can project high-dimensional financial data onto a lower-dimensional grid, preserving topology and revealing latent patterns, which can then be used to enhance machine learning models for tasks like stock price prediction or credit scoring.

Finally, unsupervised learning methods enhance the capabilities of algorithmic trading by preprocessing and organizing financial data. Clustering algorithms, for instance, can segment historical price data into different regimes or market states, allowing trading algorithms to adapt their strategies accordingly. This adaptability improves the performance and resilience of trading strategies in different market conditions.

Incorporating these techniques into the financial toolkit not only improves analytical capabilities but also provides a competitive edge by leveraging the full potential of data-driven insights. As financial markets continue to evolve, the applications of unsupervised learning will undoubtedly expand, driving innovation and efficiency in the industry.
'''

This section comprehensively explores the applications of unsupervised learning in the financial domain, emphasizing practical uses, illustrative examples, and implementation insights. The detailed explanations ensure clarity and accessibility, fostering a deeper understanding of how these techniques can enhance financial decision-making.

## 6.10 Evaluation Metrics for Unsupervised Learning

In the context of unsupervised learning, evaluating the accuracy and effectiveness of models presents unique challenges. Unlike supervised learning, where ground truth labels are available for validation, unsupervised learning algorithms operate without predefined categories, making conventional evaluation methods inapplicable. This section will provide an in-depth exploration of evaluation metrics specifically tailored for unsupervised learning methodologies deployed in financial domains.

Clustering forms a significant part of unsupervised learning in finance, organizing data into meaningful groups without labeled classifications. The evaluation of clustering techniques like K-means or hierarchical clustering relies heavily on both internal and external metrics.

**Internal Metrics** evaluate the clustering structure without reference to external information. These include:

- **Silhouette Score:** Measures how similar each point is to its own cluster compared to other clusters. Mathematically, the silhouette value $s(i)$ for a data point $i$ is defined as:

$$s(i) = \frac{b(i) - a(i)}{\max\{a(i), b(i)\}}$$

  where $a(i)$ is the average intra-cluster distance and $b(i)$ is the average nearest-cluster distance. The silhouette score ranges from -1 to 1, with higher values indicating better clustering.

- **Davies-Bouldin Index:** Indicates the average similarity ratio of each cluster with its most similar cluster, where a lower Davies-Bouldin index signifies better clustering. Given clusters $C_1, C_2, \ldots, C_k$, the Davies-Bouldin index $DB$ is calculated as:

$$DB = \frac{1}{k} \sum_{i=1}^{k} \max_{j \neq i} \left( \frac{\sigma_i + \sigma_j}{d_{ij}} \right)$$

  Here, $d_{ij}$ is the distance between cluster centroids $i$ and $j$, and $\sigma_i$ is the average distance between points in cluster $i$ to its centroid.

- **Calinski-Harabasz Index:** Also known as the Variance Ratio Criterion, it evaluates the ratio of the sum of between-cluster dispersion and within-cluster dispersion. The index $CH$ is calculated as:

$$CH = \frac{\text{trace}(B_k)/(k-1)}{\text{trace}(W_k)/(n-k)}$$

where $B_k$ is the between-cluster dispersion matrix, $W_k$ is the within-cluster dispersion matrix, $n$ is the number of data points, and $k$ is the number of clusters.

**External Metrics**, while not always applicable in a purely unsupervised setting, can be used when some form of external validation data, such as labeled datasets, is available. These include:

- **Adjusted Rand Index (ARI):** Measures the similarity between predicted clusters and true labels, adjusted for chance. It is particularly useful in scenarios where ground truth clusters are known for a subset of the data.

- **Normalized Mutual Information (NMI):** Measures the amount of information gained about one cluster by knowing the other. Defined as:

  $$NMI(U, V) = \frac{2 \cdot I(U;V)}{H(U) + H(V)}$$

  where $I(U;V)$ is the mutual information between clusterings $U$ and $V$, and $H(U)$ and $H(V)$ are the entropies of $U$ and $V$ respectively.

Assessing dimensionality reduction techniques like PCA and t-SNE requires different approaches, as these methods transform high-dimensional data into lower dimensions, aiming to preserve significant structures in the data.

- **Explained Variance Ratio:** For PCA, it indicates the proportion of data variance captured by each principal component. If $\lambda_i$ are the eigenvalues, the explained variance ratio for the i-th component is:

  $$\text{Explained Variance Ratio} = \frac{\lambda_i}{\sum_j \lambda_j}$$

  Summing the explained variance ratios for the principal components used elucidates how much of the data's variance is retained.

- **Reconstruction Error:** Evaluates how well a lower-dimensional representation reconstructs the original data. For PCA, the reconstruction error for the dataset $X$ is:

$$\text{Reconstruction Error} = \left\| X - \hat{X} \right\|_F$$

where $\hat{X}$ is the reconstructed data matrix and $\|\cdot\|_F$ is the Frobenius norm.

- **Pairwise Distance Preservation:** For methods like t-SNE, which focus on preserving local structures, pairwise distance preservation evaluates how well the distances between data points are maintained in the lower-dimensional representation. The measure can be computed using:

$$\text{Distance Preservation} = \frac{1}{n(n-1)} \sum_{i \neq j} \left| d_{ij}^{(high)} - d_{ij}^{(low)} \right|$$

where $d_{ij}^{(high)}$ and $d_{ij}^{(low)}$ denote the distances between points $i$ and $j$ in the high-dimensional and low-dimensional spaces, respectively.

When applying unsupervised techniques to financial data, domain-specific considerations become pertinent. The evaluation often hinges not only on statistical metrics but also on actionable insights and practical utility.

- **Cluster Cohesion and Separation:** For clustering algorithms applied to financial portfolios, evaluating both cohesion (within-cluster similarity) and separation (between-cluster dissimilarity) aids in ensuring that clusters represent distinct market segments or asset groups. This can be directly related to risk-adjusted return metrics.
- **Risk-Return Tradeoffs:** Dimensionality reduction techniques in finance are often evaluated based on their ability to unravel latent factors that accurately capture risk-return tradeoffs. This can lead to more robust portfolio optimization strategies. Metrics like the Sharpe ratio could be recalculated in the reduced dimension space to verify that key financial relationships are preserved.
- **Regulatory Compliance and Anomalous Behavior Detection:** For anomaly detection models, which might flag unusual trading

patterns, precision and recall become critical. Anomaly detection must be fine-tuned to minimize false positives (normal activities flagged as anomalies) and false negatives (true anomalies going undetected). This ensures alignment with regulatory compliance and strengthens fraud detection mechanisms.

Utilizing these evaluation metrics ensures that unsupervised learning models remain effective, robust, and aligned with financial industry standards, providing deep insights and practical benefits to traders and investors. The discussed metrics provide a comprehensive toolkit to gauge the performance of models without relying on labeled data, thus maintaining the quintessential unsupervised learning paradigm.

# Chapter 7

# Time Series Analysis

**This chapter focuses on the analysis of time series data in financial markets. It begins by explaining the characteristics and components of time series data, such as trend, seasonality, and noise. Topics include stationarity, autocorrelation, and partial autocorrelation. The chapter covers time series decomposition, moving averages, and smoothing techniques. Advanced models such as ARIMA, SARIMA, and GARCH are discussed, as well as the application of LSTM and recurrent neural networks for time series forecasting. Evaluation methods specific to time series models are also reviewed.**

## 7.1 What is Time Series Data?

Time series data is a sequence of data points collected or recorded at successive points in time, typically at equally spaced intervals. Unlike cross-sectional data, which captures a snapshot at a single point in time, time series data allows us to observe how variables evolve over a period. This temporal dimension is crucial in finance, where the past behavior of securities, indices, or economic indicators can give insights into future movements and help in creating robust trading strategies.

A fundamental characteristic of time series data is its sequential nature, making the order of data points essential for analysis. This sequential nature introduces complexity, as patterns, trends, and periodic behaviors can emerge over time. Comprehensive time series analysis, therefore, aims to identify, model, and exploit these characteristics to predict future values.

The key components of time series data include trend, seasonality, and noise, each of which contributes to the overall structure observed in the data.

A **trend** is the long-term progression of the series. It represents the long-direction movement and is usually attributed to systematic factors such as economic growth or technological advancements. Trends can be upward, indicating growth, or downward, indicating decline, and can often be linear or nonlinear.

**Seasonality** refers to periodic fluctuations that repeat at regular intervals, such as daily, monthly, or yearly. These fluctuations are often driven by predictable events or cycles. For instance, retail sales often increase during the holiday season, and energy consumption might peak in summer and winter due to heating and cooling demands.

**Noise**, or random variation, encompasses the irregular or unpredictable movements in the series that do not exhibit a discernable pattern. Noise is inherent in all real-world data and can result from a myriad of factors such as sudden market news, economic shocks, or data recording errors. While it is generally challenging to model noise directly, understanding its presence is vital as it affects the precision of forecasts and models.

To formally define a time series, let $\{ X_t \}$ be a time series where $X_t$ represents the value at time $t$. A simple example of a time series dataset might look like:

| Time (t) | Value (X_t) |
|---|---|
| 1 | 55 |
| 2 | 57 |
| 3 | 58 |
| 4 | 60 |
| 5 | 63 |
| 6 | 65 |

In this table, we observe that the data is measured at consecutive time intervals, and one can infer potential trends by further analyzing the series.

Additionally, when dealing with financial time series data, it is often represented in different forms such as daily closing prices of a stock, quarterly earnings reports, or even high-frequency trading data captured at millisecond intervals. Each of these forms can reveal unique patterns and insights depending on the temporal granularity involved.

Furthermore, recognizing the importance of the stationarity property in time series is imperative. Stationarity implies that a time series has statistical properties, such as mean and variance, which are constant over time. Non-stationary data, being more challenging to forecast, often requires transformation methods such as differencing or detrending to make it stationary, improving model accuracy.

Understanding the intricate nature of time series data, its components, and the fundamental principles of its analysis are the foundational steps in leveraging time series methodologies. These principles will enable us to build sophisticated financial models that can better predict market movements and improve trading strategies.

## 7.2 Components of Time Series

A time series is a sequence of data points collected or recorded at successive points in time, usually at equally spaced intervals. Understanding the various components of time series data is paramount for effective analysis and forecasting. These components help in identifying patterns, making predictions, and constructing appropriate models. The primary components of time series data include trend, seasonality, and noise.

**Trend:** The trend represents the long-term movement or direction in the data over a prolonged period. It signifies the general tendency of the data to increase, decrease, or remain stable over time. Mathematically, a trend can be expressed as a linear or nonlinear function.

For a linear trend, the relationship is typically modeled as:

$$Y_t = \beta_0 + \beta_1 t + \epsilon_t$$

where $Y_t$ is the value of the time series at time $t$, $\beta_0$ is the intercept, $\beta_1$ is the slope of the trend line, and $\epsilon_t$ is the error term.

In some situations, a nonlinear trend, such as a quadratic trend, might better describe the long-term movement of the data:

$$Y_t = \beta_0 + \beta_1 t + \beta_2 t^2 + \epsilon_t$$

Understanding the trend component can be crucial for long-term investment strategies as it reflects the underlying progression of the market or economic variable under study.

**Seasonality:** Seasonality refers to the recurring short-term cycle in the data that repeats at regular intervals, typically within a year. These patterns are often linked to calendar-related events such as fiscal quarters, months, or days of the week. Seasonality is characterized by systematic, predictable variations.

A simple way to model seasonality is through the inclusion of seasonal dummy variables or sine and cosine terms in regression models. For instance, in monthly data, seasonality can be represented by adding twelve dummy variables (one for each month) or by using Fourier terms:

$$Y_t = \alpha + \sum_{k=1}^{K} \left( \gamma_k \cos\left(\frac{2\pi kt}{s}\right) + \delta_k \sin\left(\frac{2\pi kt}{s}\right) \right) + \epsilon_t$$

where $s$ is the periodicity (e.g., $s = 12$ for monthly data), and $K$ is the number of harmonics included.

Seasonal decomposition techniques, such as the additive or multiplicative decomposition models, can also be used to separate seasonality from other components in the series.

**Noise:** Noise, or the random component, encompasses the irregular, unpredictable variations in the time series data that cannot be attributed to the trend or seasonality. Noise is often considered to be the residual or error term after removing all identifiable components from the data.

Mathematically, noise can be represented as:

$$Y_t = T_t + S_t + \epsilon_t$$

or

$$Y_t = T_t \times S_t \times \epsilon_t$$

for additive and multiplicative models, respectively, where $Y_t$ is the observed value, $T_t$ is the trend component, $S_t$ is the seasonality component, and $\epsilon_t$ is the noise component.

Noise is critical to consider because it can significantly affect the accuracy of time series models and forecasts. Techniques such as moving averages, exponential smoothing, and filtering can help mitigate the impact of noise.

Recognizing these essential components—trend, seasonality, and noise—is foundational for any time series analysis. Analyzing these components individually allows for more accurate modeling and forecasting by tailoring approaches to each distinct behavior observed in the data. By decomposing time series data into its fundamental elements, financial analysts and traders are better equipped to understand market dynamics and make informed decisions based on clearer insights into past and present trends.

## 7.3 Stationarity in Time Series

Understanding the concept of stationarity is fundamental in time series analysis since many forecasting and modeling techniques rely on this property. Intuitively, a time series is considered stationary if its statistical properties, such as mean and variance, remain constant over time. Conversely, a non-stationary series exhibits changing statistical properties, making it more challenging to model and predict.

Mathematically, a time series $\{X_t\}$ is said to be strictly stationary if for any set of time points $t_1, t_2, \ldots, t_k$, the joint distribution of $(X_{t_1}, X_{t_2}, \ldots, X_{t_k})$ is the same as the joint distribution of $(X_{t_1+h}, X_{t_2+h}, \ldots, X_{t_k+h})$ for all $t_1, t_2, \ldots, t_k$, and all $h$. In practice, a weaker form of stationarity known as weak or wide-sense stationarity is often used. A time series $\{X_t\}$ is weakly stationary if the following conditions are met:

- The mean function $E(X_t) = \mu$ is constant and does not depend on $t$.
- The variance function Var$(X_t) = \sigma^2$ is constant and does not depend on $t$.
- The autocovariance function $\gamma(t, t+h)$ depends only on the lag $h$ and not on the specific time points $t$ and $t+h$. This can be expressed as $\gamma(h) = E[(X_t - \mu)(X_{t+h} - \mu)]$.

Ensuring that a time series is stationary simplifies the modeling process, as many time series models, such as ARIMA, assume stationarity. Non-stationary data often require transformation to achieve stationarity.

Common methods include differencing, detrending, and seasonal adjustment.

**Differencing:** This technique involves subtracting a previous observation from the current observation. For instance, the first-order differenced series is given by

$$Y_t = X_t - X_{t-1} \tag{7.1}$$

This method effectively removes trends and can help stabilize the mean. Higher-order differencing $Y_t = \Delta^d X_t$ may be necessary for more complex trends.

**Detrending:** Another approach to achieve stationarity is to remove the trend component from the series. This can be done by fitting a regression model with time as an independent variable and subtracting the fitted trend values from the original series. For example, if the trend is linear, we might fit

$$X_t = \beta_0 + \beta_1 t + \epsilon_t \tag{7.2}$$

and then use the residuals $\epsilon_t = X_t - (\beta_0 + \beta_1 t)$ as the detrended series.

**Seasonal Adjustment:** For time series with seasonal patterns, seasonal differencing is used. This process involves subtracting the value from the same season in the previous cycle, effectively removing seasonal effects. For example, monthly data might be seasonally differenced as follows:

$$Y_t = X_t - X_{t-12} \tag{7.3}$$

Once a time series is made stationary, it becomes feasible to apply various models such as ARIMA. Determining stationarity can be done visually via plots or using statistical tests such as the Augmented Dickey-Fuller (ADF) test and the Kwiatkowski-Phillips-Schmidt-Shin (KPSS) test.

In practice, a combination of visual inspection and formal testing provides a robust method for assessing stationarity. A time series plot can reveal obvious trends or seasonal patterns, while the ADF test helps to statistically confirm the presence of a unit root, indicating non-stationarity. If the ADF test's p-value is low, it suggests the series is stationary. Contrarily, the KPSS test assesses the null hypothesis of stationarity, where a higher p-value indicates stationarity.

Achieving and confirming stationarity is crucial for effective time series analysis and forecasting. By applying the appropriate transformations and tests, traders and investors can ensure that their models are built on solid foundations, paving the way for more accurate and reliable market predictions.

## 7.4 Autocorrelation and Partial Autocorrelation

Understanding the dependencies and relationships within time series data is paramount for effective modeling and forecasting. Two essential concepts that help unravel these relationships are autocorrelation and partial autocorrelation. Grasping these concepts enables traders and investors to identify patterns and structures in time series data, facilitating better predictive models and more informed trading strategies.

Autocorrelation, also known as serial correlation, refers to the correlation of a time series with a lagged version of itself. It measures the degree of similarity between observations as a function of the time lag between them. Formally, for a time series $Y_t$, the autocorrelation function (ACF) at lag $k$ is defined as:

$$\rho_k = \frac{\sum_{t=1}^{T-k}(Y_t - \bar{Y})(Y_{t+k} - \bar{Y})}{\sum_{t=1}^{T}(Y_t - \bar{Y})^2}$$

where $\bar{Y}$ is the mean of the time series, $T$ is the total number of observations, and $k$ is the lag.

When inspecting the ACF, patterns can indicate underlying data properties. For instance, a slow decay in the ACF graph suggests a trend, while seasonal patterns in the data often manifest as periodic spikes at corresponding lags.

While autocorrelation shows the overall correlation between the values at different lags, it can sometimes be misleading due to the indirect correlations introduced by intermediate lags. This is where partial autocorrelation becomes critical. Partial autocorrelation measures the correlation between the time series and its lagged values after removing the effects of intervening lags. The partial autocorrelation function (PACF) at lag $k$ can be interpreted as the correlation between $Y_t$ and $Y_{t+k}$, with the linear influence of $Y_{t+1}, \ldots, Y_{t+k-1}$ removed.

The mathematical definition of the PACF can be derived using the Yule-Walker equations. For a time series $Y_t$, the PACF $\phi_k$ at lag $k$ can be estimated by fitting a $k$-th order autoregressive (AR) model and examining the coefficient of the $k$-th lag. In simplest form, the AR($k$) model is expressed as:

$$Y_t = \phi_1 Y_{t-1} + \phi_2 Y_{t-2} + \cdots + \phi_k Y_{t-k} + \varepsilon_t$$

where $\phi_i$ are the parameters and $\varepsilon_t$ is white noise. The partial autocorrelation at lag $k$, $\phi_k$, is precisely the coefficient of $Y_{t-k}$ in this regression.

In practice, both ACF and PACF are used to choose appropriate models. For instance, the ACF and PACF plots help in selecting the order of autoregressive (AR) and moving average (MA) components in ARIMA models. A typical guideline is:

- An AR($p$) process exhibits a PACF that cuts off sharply after lag $p$, while the ACF tails off.
- An MA($q$) process, conversely, has an ACF that cuts off after lag $q$, with the PACF tailing off.

To visualize and interpret these concepts, traders and analysts often rely on ACF and PACF plots. An ACF plot displays $\rho_k$ for different lags $k$, typically with dashed lines representing confidence intervals around zero. Values exceeding these lines suggest significant autocorrelation at corresponding lags. The PACF plot, on the other hand, displays $\phi_k$, again with confidence intervals to highlight significant lags.

The following example code snippet in Python demonstrates how to generate and interpret ACF and PACF plots using the 'statsmodels' library:

```
import pandas as pd
import numpy as np
import matplotlib.pyplot as plt
from statsmodels.graphics.tsaplots import plot_acf, plot_pacf

# Generate a sample time series data
np.random.seed(42)
data = np.random.randn(100)
ts = pd.Series(data)

# Plot the ACF and PACF
fig, axes = plt.subplots(1, 2, figsize=(16, 4))
plot_acf(ts, lags=20, ax=axes[0])
plot_pacf(ts, lags=20, ax=axes[1])
plt.show()
```

The generated plots provide visual tools to identify the presence and extent of autocorrelation and partial autocorrelation. Significant bars at specific lags in these plots guide model selection, revealing whether an

AR, MA, or mixed ARIMA model is likely to capture the underlying data structure effectively.

Having a firm grasp on autocorrelation and partial autocorrelation enhances the toolkit of any quantitative analyst or trader, equipping them with the insights needed to model time series data accurately and make data-driven investment decisions.

## 7.5 Time Series Decomposition

Time series decomposition is a fundamental technique in the analysis of financial time series data, allowing us to dissect and understand its underlying structure. By breaking down a time series into its constituent components, we can gain insights into the pattern and behavior of asset prices, aiding in more accurate forecasting and strategic decision-making. This section delves into the key elements of time series decomposition: trend, seasonality, and residual (noise).

A time series $y_t$ can be expressed as the sum or product of these components:

$$y_t = T_t + S_t + R_t \qquad \text{(Additive Model)}$$

$$y_t = T_t \times S_t \times R_t \qquad \text{(Multiplicative Model)}$$

where $T_t$ represents the trend component, $S_t$ the seasonal component, and $R_t$ the random or residual component.

**Trend Component**

The trend component $T_t$ captures the long-term movement in the data. It is the part of the series that shows the general direction in which the series is moving over a substantial period, representing the underlying growth or decline. This can be due to economic factors, long-term market trends, or changes in the industry. Trend extraction can be achieved using various methods such as moving averages or polynomial fitting.

$$T_t = \frac{1}{2k+1} \sum_{j=-k}^{k} y_{t+j} \qquad \text{(Centered Moving Average)}$$

By applying centered moving averages, we can smooth out short-term fluctuations, allowing the long-term trend to emerge more clearly.

**Seasonal Component**

The seasonal component $S_t$ captures repetitive and predictable patterns that occur at regular intervals within the time series. This is common in financial markets where certain assets may exhibit quarterly earnings patterns, or commodities might show cyclical behavior due to seasonal demand variations.

Seasonality can be isolated by:

- Estimating the trend component $T_t$.
- Removing the trend from the original series to focus on the periodic fluctuations.
- Averaging the detrended series over the seasonal cycle.

Mathematically:

$$S_t = y_t - T_t \qquad \text{(Additive Seasonality)}$$

$$S_t = \frac{y_t}{T_t} \qquad \text{(Multiplicative Seasonality)}$$

The periodicity $p$ of the seasonality needs to be known or estimated, representing the number of periods after which the seasonal pattern repeats.

**Residual Component**

The residual component $R_t$, often called noise, encompasses the irregularities and random variation in the series after the trend and seasonality components have been removed. These residuals do not exhibit any systematic pattern and are generally considered noise within the context of the model. Understanding the residuals is crucial because they can indicate the limits of predictability in the series.

For effective modeling, the residuals should ideally resemble white noise, meaning they have a constant mean and variance, with no discernible autocorrelation. This can be formally expressed as:

$$R_t = y_t - T_t - S_t \qquad \text{(Additive Model Residuals)}$$

$$R_t = \frac{y_t}{T_t \times S_t} \qquad \text{(Multiplicative Model Residuals)}$$

Once the components are isolated, they provide a comprehensive view of the underlying patterns in the financial time series. This decomposition aids in more accurate forecasting by allowing models like ARIMA to handle the residuals while the trend and seasonality are modeled separately.

By understanding and implementing time series decomposition, traders and investors can better interpret their data, identify patterns, and make informed decisions based on a clearer understanding of the intrinsic components driving market behaviors. This holistic approach is invaluable, particularly when applied to crafting robust forecasting models and enhancing predictive accuracy.

## 7.6 Moving Averages and Smoothing Techniques

In the realm of time series analysis, various techniques are employed to discern patterns and mitigate noise within financial data. Among these techniques, moving averages and smoothing methods are fundamental. They serve to generate clearer signals by filtering out short-term fluctuations and highlighting underlying trends. Understanding and applying these methods can significantly enhance the predictive power of time series models, ultimately aiding in more informed trading and investment decisions.

The concept of a moving average involves calculating the mean of a fixed subset of data points within a time series. This subset progresses through the series, yielding a sequence of averages. Consider a time series $\{y_t\}$. The simple moving average (SMA) of order $n$ is defined as:

$$SMA_t = \frac{1}{n} \sum_{i=t-n+1}^{t} y_i$$

where $t$ is the current time period, and $n$ is the number of periods over which the average is calculated. The choice of $n$ is crucial, balancing the trade-off between smoothness and responsiveness. Smaller $n$ values make the moving average more sensitive to recent changes, while larger $n$ values provide a smoother series at the expense of lagging behind actual movements.

Expanding upon this, the exponential moving average (EMA) assigns exponentially decreasing weights to older observations, giving more importance to recent data points. The EMA at time $t$, with a smoothing factor $\alpha$ (where $0 < \alpha < 1$), is computed as:

$$EMA_t = \alpha y_t + (1 - \alpha) EMA_{t-1}$$

The smoothing factor $\alpha$ governs the rate of weight decay. Typically, $\alpha$ is derived from the number of periods $n$ through the relation $\alpha = \frac{2}{n+1}$. The recursive nature of the EMA makes it particularly useful for continuous updating as new data arrives.

Beyond simple and exponential moving averages, more advanced smoothing techniques are employed to reveal different aspects of time series dynamics. One such technique is the weighted moving average (WMA), which assigns specific weights to each data point within the moving window. Mathematically, the WMA is expressed as:

$$WMA_t = \frac{\sum_{i=0}^{n-1} w_i y_{t-i}}{\sum_{i=0}^{n-1} w_i}$$

where $w_i$ denotes the weight assigned to observation $y_{t-i}$. Weights can be adapted to emphasize particular segments of the data, enabling tailored smoothing according to specific analytical requirements.

Another sophisticated method is kernel smoothing, which utilizes a kernel function to weight observations within the moving window. Common kernel functions include Gaussian and Epanechnikov kernels, which offer flexibility in managing the shape of the smoothing window. The smoothed value at time $t$ using kernel $K$ and bandwidth parameter $h$ is given by:

$$K(t, y_i, h) = \sum_{i=0}^{n-1} K\left(\frac{t-i}{h}\right) y_{t-i}$$

The choice of kernel and bandwidth impacts the level of smoothness and the ability to preserve underlying data characteristics.

Smoothing techniques extend beyond simple moving windows. The Hodrick-Prescott (HP) filter, for instance, is a widely used tool to separate cyclical components from the trend component of a time series. The HP filter minimizes the following objective function:

$$\min_{\{y_t^*\}} \sum_{t=1}^{T} (y_t - y_t^*)^2 + \lambda \sum_{t=2}^{T-1} ((y_{t+1}^* - y_t^*) - (y_t^* - y_{t-1}^*))^2$$

Here, $y_t$ is the observed value, $y_t^*$ the trend component, and $\lambda$ a smoothing parameter. Choosing an appropriate $\lambda$ value is essential; higher values extract smoother trends, while lower values capture more detailed fluctuations.

In financial applications, these smoothing techniques aid in various tasks such as trend detection, momentum calculation, and volatility estimation. For instance, moving averages can signal potential buy or sell points when shorter-term averages cross longer-term averages—commonly known as moving average crossovers. Additionally, smoothed time series data often serve as inputs for more advanced predictive models, including ARIMA and LSTM networks, providing a cleaner representation of underlying market movements.

Engaging effectively with moving averages and smoothing techniques requires both understanding their mathematical foundations and appreciating their practical applications. By integrating these methods into a broader analytical framework, investors can derive deeper insights and improve their decision-making processes within the financial markets.

## 7.7 ARIMA and SARIMA Models

The task of modeling and forecasting time series data introduces both challenges and opportunities. Among the most reputable and widely adopted methodologies are ARIMA (AutoRegressive Integrated Moving Average) and its seasonal counterpart, SARIMA (Seasonal AutoRegressive Integrated Moving Average). In this section, we will delve into the core principles of these models, their components, and their practical applications.

ARIMA models are defined by three primary parameters: $p$, $d$, and $q$. These parameters govern the autoregressive (AR), integrated (I), and moving average (MA) components of the model, respectively.

The general form of an ARIMA model can be expressed as:

$$ARIMA(p, d, q)$$

To understand ARIMA models, let's break down each component:

- **Autoregressive (AR) Component**: This involves regressing the variable on its own lagged values. The parameter $p$ represents the number of lagged terms included in the model. The mathematical expression for an AR(p) model is:

$$Y_t = \phi_1 Y_{t-1} + \phi_2 Y_{t-2} + \ldots + \phi_p Y_{t-p} + \epsilon_t$$

Here, $\phi$ denotes the coefficients of the lagged terms, and $\epsilon_t$ represents a white noise error term.

- **Integrated (I) Component**: This refers to the differencing of observations to make the time series stationary, denoted by $d$. For example, a first-order differencing ($d = 1$) transforms the series $Y_t$ into $Y_t - Y_{t-1}$.
- **Moving Average (MA) Component**: This comprises the dependency between an observation and a residual error from a moving average model applied to lagged observations. The parameter $q$ indicates the number of lagged forecast errors in the prediction model:

$$Y_t = \epsilon_t + \theta_1 \epsilon_{t-1} + \theta_2 \epsilon_{t-2} + \ldots + \theta_q \epsilon_{t-q}$$

Here, $\theta$ denotes the coefficients of the lagged error terms.

Combining these components, an ARIMA(p, d, q) model can be represented as:

$$\Delta^d Y_t = \phi_1 \Delta^d Y_{t-1} + \phi_2 \Delta^d Y_{t-2} + \ldots + \phi_p \Delta^d Y_{t-p} + \epsilon_t + \theta_1 \epsilon_{t-1} + \theta_2 \epsilon_{t-2} + \ldots + \theta_q \epsilon_{t-q}$$

The selection of $p$, $d$, and $q$ plays a crucial role in accurately capturing the patterns in the time series data. Various techniques, such as the Autocorrelation Function (ACF) and the Partial Autocorrelation Function (PACF), assist in determining these parameters.

When seasonality is present in the time series, the ARIMA model is extended to account for seasonal variations using SARIMA. The SARIMA model incorporates additional seasonal parameters: $P$, $D$, $Q$, and $s$, where:

- $P$ is the seasonal autoregressive order.
- $D$ is the seasonal differencing order.
- $Q$ is the seasonal moving average order.

- $s$ is the length of the seasonal cycle.

The SARIMA model is formally denoted as $SARIMA(p,d,q) \times (P,D,Q)_s$. Its general form can be written as:

$$\Phi(L^s)\Delta_s^D Y_t = \Theta(L^s)(\Delta^d Y_t - \phi(L)\Delta^d Y_{t-1} - \epsilon_t - \theta(L)\epsilon_{t-1})$$

In this equation: - $\Phi(L^s)$ and $\Theta(L^s)$ are the seasonal components of the model. - $\phi(L)$ and $\theta(L)$ represent the non-seasonal components. - $\Delta_s^D$ is the seasonal differencing operator.

When implementing SARIMA, the same principles for determining $p$, $d$, and $q$ apply, albeit with an additional focus on capturing the seasonal patterns via $P$, $D$, $Q$, and $s$.

The practical application of ARIMA and SARIMA involves iterative model fitting and validation. Tools like the Akaike Information Criterion (AIC) or the Bayesian Information Criterion (BIC) are often employed to select the optimal model. Once the appropriate model is identified, it can be used for forecasting future values of the time series, providing insights and aiding strategic financial decisions.

Thus, mastering ARIMA and SARIMA models equips traders and investors with robust tools to predict and analyze market movements, helping them navigate and capitalize on financial markets with increased precision.

## 7.8 GARCH Models

In the realm of financial time series analysis, volatility modeling plays a crucial role, especially for risk management and derivative pricing. A popular model used for capturing volatility dynamics is the Generalized Autoregressive Conditional Heteroskedasticity (GARCH) model, introduced by Tim Bollerslev in 1986. Concretely, the GARCH model is an extension of the Autoregressive Conditional Heteroskedasticity (ARCH) model, which was developed by Robert Engle in 1982. The GARCH model elegantly incorporates both short-term and long-term memory in volatility, making it particularly adept at modeling the volatility clustering observed in financial markets.

To begin understanding the GARCH model, let's introduce the foundational ARCH($q$) model, which describes the conditional variance $\sigma_t^2$ of a time series. The model can be expressed as:

$$\sigma_t^2 = \alpha_0 + \sum_{i=1}^{q} \alpha_i \epsilon_{t-i}^2 \tag{7.4}$$

Here, $\sigma_t^2$ represents the conditional variance at time $t$, $\alpha_0$ is a constant term, and $\alpha_i$ are parameters that capture the influence of past squared errors $\epsilon_{t-i}^2$.

Building on this, the GARCH($p, q$) model adds further lags of the conditional variance $\sigma_{t-j}^2$ to the equation:

$$\sigma_t^2 = \alpha_0 + \sum_{i=1}^{q} \alpha_i \epsilon_{t-i}^2 + \sum_{j=1}^{p} \beta_j \sigma_{t-j}^2 \tag{7.5}$$

In this representation:

- $\alpha_0$ is the constant term.
- $\alpha_i$ are the coefficients for the lagged squared residuals $\epsilon_{t-i}^2$ (ARCH terms).
- $\beta_j$ are the coefficients for the lagged conditional variances $\sigma_{t-j}^2$ (GARCH terms).

The inclusion of past variances $\sigma_{t-j}^2$ allows the model to account for long-term patterns in volatility, thereby addressing the characteristic "volatility clustering" in financial returns, where periods of high volatility tend to be followed by high volatility and periods of low volatility tend to be followed by low volatility.

An essential aspect of fitting GARCH models involves maximum likelihood estimation (MLE), where the parameters $\alpha_0$, $\alpha_i$, and $\beta_j$ are estimated by maximizing the likelihood of the observed series under the assumed distribution. This distribution is often taken to be normal, but heavy-tailed alternatives like the Student's $t$ distribution can be used to better capture the properties of financial return series.

To implement and evaluate a GARCH model, one can follow these general steps:

- **Model Specification**: Define the order of the GARCH($p, q$) model. Common choices are GARCH(1,1), which balances model complexity with parameter parsimony.

- **Parameter Estimation**: Using historical data, estimate the model parameters via MLE.

- **Model Diagnostics**: Examine residuals and conditional variances to check model fit. Standard diagnostics include inspecting autocorrelation function (ACF) of the residuals and standardized residuals, as well as conducting Ljung-Box tests.

Let's consider an illustrative example of implementing a GARCH(1,1) model using Python's 'arch' package:

```
import pandas as pd
from arch import arch_model

# Load financial time series data
data = pd.read_csv('financial_data.csv')
returns = data['Returns']

# Specify and fit the GARCH(1,1) model
model = arch_model(returns, vol='Garch', p=1, q=1)
garch_fit = model.fit()

# Print model summary
print(garch_fit.summary())
```

In this code snippet, we load the financial returns data, specify a GARCH(1,1) model, fit the model to the data, and print the summary of the model estimation results.

The GARCH model can be extended to address various practical issues in volatility modeling. For example, the Exponential GARCH (EGARCH) model accounts for asymmetries in volatility response to positive and negative shocks, acknowledging that financial markets often react differently to good and bad news. The GJR-GARCH model, another variant, introduces leverage effects where negative returns increase future volatility more than positive returns of the same magnitude.

Understanding and applying GARCH models allow investors and financial analysts to better anticipate market volatility, essential for tasks such as portfolio optimization, risk management, and derivative pricing. They provide a robust framework for modeling and forecasting volatility across different asset classes, making them indispensable tools in the quantitative finance toolkit.

## 7.9 LSTM and Recurrent Neural Networks for Time Series

In the domain of financial markets, predicting future prices and trends based on historical data is a paramount task for any quantitative analyst. Traditional statistical methods often fall short in capturing intricate temporal dependencies inherent in time series data. This is where Recurrent Neural Networks (RNNs) and their more advanced variant, Long Short-Term Memory networks (LSTMs), come into play, offering an unparalleled edge in time series forecasting through their superior capacity for learning long-term dependencies.

RNNs are designed to recognize patterns across sequences by maintaining a hidden state that operates as a memory, enabling the network to process sequences of arbitrary length. Unlike traditional feedforward neural networks, an RNN can leverage information from previous steps in the sequence, making it particularly suited for time series data.

While RNNs are structurally powerful, they suffer from the vanishing and exploding gradient problems, which hamper their ability to effectively learn long-term dependencies. This intrinsic limitation led to the development of LSTMs, which are specifically engineered to counter these issues by incorporating a more sophisticated architecture.

LSTMs contain a set of gates: the input gate, forget gate, and output gate, that precisely regulate the flow of information through the cell state. This gating mechanism allows LSTMs to efficiently promote, retain, and discard information, making them highly effective for tasks involving long sequences of data.

To illustrate the implementation of LSTM networks for time series forecasting, consider the following example in Python using the popular Keras library, which builds on top of TensorFlow:

LSTM implementation in Keras

```
import numpy as np
import pandas as pd
from sklearn.preprocessing import MinMaxScaler
from keras.models import Sequential
from keras.layers import LSTM, Dense

# Load and preprocess data
data = pd.read_csv('financial_timeseries.csv', date_parser=True)
data = data[['Close']] # Select the relevant column for forecasting

scaler = MinMaxScaler(feature_range=(0, 1))
scaled_data = scaler.fit_transform(data)
```

```
# Create training and testing datasets
train_size = int(len(scaled_data) * 0.75)
train_data, test_data = scaled_data[:train_size], scaled_data[train_size:]

# Convert data into sequences
def create_sequences(data, seq_length):
    x, y = [], []
    for i in range(len(data) - seq_length):
        x.append(data[i:i+seq_length])
        y.append(data[i+seq_length])
    return np.array(x), np.array(y)

seq_length = 50
x_train, y_train = create_sequences(train_data, seq_length)
x_test, y_test = create_sequences(test_data, seq_length)

# Reshape data to fit LSTM input
x_train = x_train.reshape((x_train.shape[0], x_train.shape[1], 1))
x_test = x_test.reshape((x_test.shape[0], x_test.shape[1], 1))

# Build LSTM model
model = Sequential()
model.add(LSTM(50, return_sequences=True, input_shape=(seq_length, 1)))
model.add(LSTM(50))
model.add(Dense(1))

model.compile(optimizer='adam', loss='mean_squared_error')
model.fit(x_train, y_train, epochs=25, batch_size=32)

# Make predictions
predictions = model.predict(x_test)
predictions = scaler.inverse_transform(predictions)

# Evaluation
import matplotlib.pyplot as plt

plt.figure(figsize=(10,6))
plt.plot(data.index[train_size:], scaler.inverse_transform(test_data), color='blue', label
    ='Actual Prices')
plt.plot(data.index[train_size:], predictions, color='red', label='Predicted Prices')
plt.xlabel('Date')
plt.ylabel('Price')
plt.title('LSTM Time Series Forecasting')
plt.legend()
plt.show()
```

This example demonstrates a practical application of an LSTM network for financial time series forecasting. Here, we start by loading and scaling the data, transforming it to suit the input requirements of an LSTM network. We then build a sequential model with two LSTM layers and a dense output layer, fitting it to the training data before making predictions on the testing data.

The performance of LSTM networks can be further enhanced by tuning hyperparameters, employing dropout regularization to prevent overfitting, and integrating other sophisticated techniques like attention mechanisms to focus on relevant parts of the sequence.

Recurrent Neural Networks and their advanced counterparts, LSTMs, represent a significant leap forward in the analysis and forecasting of time series data. Their ability to capture and learn from vast temporal dependencies and patterns makes them invaluable tools for quants aiming to gain deeper insights and predictive capabilities in the financial markets.

## 7.10 Evaluating Time Series Models

Evaluating time series models is a crucial step in the analysis process, ensuring that the models we develop are robust, accurate, and appropriate for the intended applications. Given the dynamic and often unpredictable nature of financial markets, it is imperative to utilize rigorous evaluation techniques to assess model performance. This section explores various metrics and methods used to evaluate the efficacy of time series models.

To begin with, we need to understand that unlike traditional statistical models, time series models inherently account for the temporal ordering of data points. This distinctive characteristic requires tailored evaluation methods, which we will delve into below.

**1. Train-Test Split:**

A fundamental step in evaluating any predictive model is to split the dataset into a training set and a test set. The training set is used to fit the model, while the test set is reserved for evaluating its performance. In time series analysis, it is critical to ensure that the training data precedes the test data temporally to maintain the chronological consistency.

$$\text{Train data set} = \{X_1, X_2, \ldots, X_t\}$$

$$\text{Test data set} = \{X_{t+1}, X_{t+2}, \ldots, X_n\}$$

**2. Walk-Forward Validation:**

To get a more robust evaluation, we use walk-forward validation, which involves re-training and testing the model at each step. This method simulates real-time prediction by evaluating the model as new data becomes available.

Consider the following process:

- Fit the model on $\{X_1, X_2, \ldots, X_t\}$, and predict $X_{t+1}$
- Fit the model on $\{X_1, X_2, \ldots, X_{t+1}\}$, and predict $X_{t+2}$
- Continue this process until the end of the time series.

**3. Error Metrics:**

Different error metrics help to quantify the accuracy of predictions in various aspects. Commonly used metrics include:

*Mean Absolute Error (MAE)*:

$$\text{MAE} = \frac{1}{n}\sum_{i=1}^{n} |y_i - \hat{y}_i|$$

where $y_i$ is the actual value and $\hat{y}_i$ is the predicted value. MAE provides a straightforward measure of average error magnitude.

*Mean Squared Error (MSE)*:

$$\text{MSE} = \frac{1}{n}\sum_{i=1}^{n} (y_i - \hat{y}_i)^2$$

MSE penalizes larger errors more severely, making it useful for highlighting significant discrepancies between actual and predicted values.

*Root Mean Squared Error (RMSE)*:

$$\text{RMSE} = \sqrt{\frac{1}{n}\sum_{i=1}^{n} (y_i - \hat{y}_i)^2}$$

RMSE is the square root of MSE, providing an error metric in the same units as the original data, which aids in interpretability.

*Mean Absolute Percentage Error (MAPE)*:

$$\text{MAPE} = \frac{100}{n}\sum_{i=1}^{n} \left|\frac{y_i - \hat{y}_i}{y_i}\right|$$

MAPE illustrates the average percentage error, but it can be problematic if the actual values are very close to zero.

**4. AIC and BIC:**

The Akaike Information Criterion (AIC) and the Bayesian Information Criterion (BIC) are critical in comparing different time series models. Both criteria aim to balance model fit and complexity.

*Akaike Information Criterion (AIC)*:

$$\text{AIC} = 2k - 2\ln(L)$$

where $k$ is the number of parameters in the model, and $L$ is the likelihood of the model.

*Bayesian Information Criterion (BIC)*:

$$\text{BIC} = \ln(n)k - 2\ln(L)$$

BIC introduces a stronger penalty for models with more parameters, offering a more conservative approach than AIC.

**5. Residual Diagnostics:**

Beyond numerical metrics, examining residuals (the difference between observed and predicted values) provides deep insights into a model's performance. Key aspects of residual diagnostics include:

- *Autocorrelation of Residuals*: Ensuring residuals are uncorrelated helps validate the model's assumption that any remaining signal in residuals does not provide predictive power.

$$\rho_k = \frac{\sum_{t=k+1}^{n}(e_t - \bar{e})(e_{t-k} - \bar{e})}{\sum_{t=1}^{n}(e_t - \bar{e})^2}$$

  where $\bar{e}$ is the mean of the residuals $e_t$.

- *Histogram of Residuals*: Verifying that residuals approximate a normal distribution supports the validity of model assumptions, particularly for linear models.

- *Q-Q Plot*: Comparing the quantiles of residuals against a standard normal distribution can visually highlight deviations from normality.

**6. Rolling Forecast Origin Evaluation:**

In sophisticated analysis, rolling forecast origin evaluation replicates real-world usage by continuously updating model parameters and testing on an expanding test set. This method highlights how model performance evolves over time and adjusts to new data patterns.

### 7. Comparing Models:

Finally, it can be beneficial to compare multiple models to select the best-performing one. Statistical tests like the Diebold-Mariano test evaluate the predictive accuracy of two competing models, ensuring that model selection is based on robust statistical evidence.

$$DM = \frac{\bar{d}}{\sigma_{\bar{d}}}$$

where $\bar{d}$ is the mean of the loss differential series, and $\sigma_{\bar{d}}$ is its standard deviation.

Ultimately, evaluating time series models requires a multifaceted approach, incorporating both quantitative metrics and qualitative diagnostics. By meticulously assessing models on these dimensions, we can ensure that our predictions are both accurate and reliable, paving the way for informed financial decision-making and robust investment strategies.

# Chapter 8

# Model Evaluation and Validation

**This chapter emphasizes the importance of proper model evaluation and validation in machine learning for finance. It starts by discussing the roles of training, validation, and test sets and introduces cross-validation techniques. Key evaluation metrics such as confusion matrix, ROC, AUC, precision, recall, F1 score, MAE, MSE, and R-squared are covered. The chapter also explores model selection criteria including AIC and BIC, and presents techniques for validating models in a financial context to ensure robustness and reliability.**

## 8.1 Importance of Model Evaluation

In the realm of financial machine learning, developing a predictive model is only part of the journey. The ultimate goal is to ensure that the model is both accurate and robust when applied to unseen data, particularly in the volatile and unpredictable financial markets. This is where model evaluation steps in as an indispensable process. Through rigorous evaluation, traders and quantitative analysts can ascertain the performance, reliability, and potential pitfalls of their models before deploying them in real-world scenarios.

Model evaluation encompasses a series of well-defined steps aimed at determining how well a model generalizes to an independent dataset. Here, understanding the significance of various segments of the data—specifically, the training, validation, and test sets—forms the bedrock of sound evaluation practices. Evaluating a model's performance on the training data alone can yield misleadingly optimistic results since the model has optimized its parameters specifically for that dataset. Conversely, a model evaluated solely on out-of-sample data can reveal its true predictive power.

The approach of separating data into distinct training, validation, and test sets is foundational. The training set is utilized to build the model, aiming to capture the underlying patterns within this dataset. The validation set serves as an intermediary to fine-tune model parameters, ensuring that model optimization does not lead to overfitting—where the model performs well on training data but poorly on new, unseen data. The test set, completely isolated during model building and validation, acts as the final yardstick for assessing model performance under real-world conditions.

Cross-validation techniques, particularly k-fold cross-validation, further enhance the robustness of this evaluation process. By partitioning the data into $k$ subsets and alternately training and validating the model across these subsets, one can achieve a more comprehensive understanding of model performance. This method mitigates the risk of overfitting and ensures that the evaluation is not unduly influenced by any particular data split.

Beyond splitting the data, various evaluation metrics provide quantifiable measures of model effectiveness. Metrics such as precision, recall, F1 score, and the area under the ROC curve (AUC) are pivotal in assessing classification models, which are often used in predicting market directions. For regression tasks, common in predicting asset prices or returns, metrics like mean absolute error (MAE), mean squared error (MSE), and R-squared are invaluable. Each metric offers a unique lens through which to view model performance, allowing traders to balance different aspects such as accuracy, sensitivity, and predictive power.

Moreover, selecting the right model involves more than just performance metrics; it also requires considering model complexity and avoiding overfitting. Information criteria such as Akaike Information Criterion (AIC) and Bayesian Information Criterion (BIC) provide additional tools for model selection by penalizing overly complex models, thus promoting simplicity and generalizability.

Lastly, validating models in a financial context demands considering the unique nature of financial data. Market conditions change, future prices are influenced by myriad unpredictable factors, and models must be resilient to these shifts. Techniques such as rolling window analysis and backtesting against historical data enable deeper validation, reflecting the temporal nature of financial markets.

In finance, the stakes are high. A model that seems promising in theory but fails under real market conditions can lead to significant financial loss. Therefore, a rigorous and thorough model evaluation process is not merely an academic exercise but a critical component of successful trading and investing strategies. By committing to a comprehensive evaluation, traders can move forward with confidence, armed with models that have been meticulously vetted and validated against the challenges of the financial markets.

## 8.2 Training, Validation, and Test Sets

In the realm of machine learning, especially within financial contexts, the importance of appropriately partitioning data into training, validation, and test sets cannot be overstated. This practice forms the cornerstone of developing robust and reliable predictive models, ensuring that our algorithms generalize well to unseen data, which is particularly crucial in volatile markets.

When we speak of these three distinct subsets of data, we refer to their specific roles in the model development pipeline. Each subset serves a unique purpose, contributing to the overall effectiveness and resilience of the model.

**Training Set**: The training set is used to train the machine learning model. It consists of historical data that the model learns from, capturing underlying patterns and relationships. For instance, when predicting future stock returns, the training set might include historical price movements, trading volumes, and other relevant features. The model iterates over this data, adjusting its parameters to minimize error. One key point to note is that the training set should be sufficiently large and representative of the problem space to avoid the model underfitting, where it fails to capture the complexity of the data.

$$y = f(\boldsymbol{x}; \boldsymbol{\theta})$$

where $x$ represents the input features, $\boldsymbol{\theta}$ the model parameters, and $y$

the output. The model optimizes $\boldsymbol{\theta}$ using the training set to find the best possible fit.

**Validation Set**: The validation set is employed for model tuning, including hyperparameter optimization. Unlike the training set, it is not used to adjust the model's internal parameters but rather to evaluate its performance on data not seen during training. This evaluation helps in preventing overfitting, where the model performs exceptionally well on the training data but poorly on unseen data. For instance, in a machine learning model for algorithmic trading, one might use cross-validation techniques on the validation set to select optimal parameters such as learning rate, depth of decision trees, or the number of layers in a neural network.

$$\text{Validation Error} = \frac{1}{n_v} \sum_{i=1}^{n_v} L(y_i, \hat{y}_i)$$

Here, $n_v$ is the number of validation samples, $y_i$ are the actual values, $\hat{y}_i$ are the predicted values, and $L$ denotes the loss function used to assess model performance. Performing cross-validation involves splitting the training data into multiple folds and ensuring that each fold serves as a validation set once, hence giving a robust estimate of model performance.

**Test Set**: Once the model has been fine-tuned using the validation set, its ultimate performance is evaluated using the test set. This set comprises data that has not been touched during any phase of the model building and is meant to provide an unbiased assessment of how well the model generalizes to new data. In financial applications, the test set could include recent market data not involved in training or validation processes. The error rate on the test set is a crucial metric, as it reflects the model's real-world predictive power.

$$\text{Test Error} = \frac{1}{n_t} \sum_{i=1}^{n_t} L(y_i, \hat{y}_i)$$

Again, $n_t$ refers to the number of test samples. The test error helps to gauge whether the model can perform well beyond the data it was trained on and tuned with.

To illustrate the importance of these data partitions, consider a scenario where an algorithmic trading model is designed to predict market uptrends and downtrends. If the model is trained and validated properly but performs poorly on the test set, it indicates that the model is overfitting or underfitting, necessitating revisiting the training procedures, data preprocessing, or even rethinking the features used.

Balancing the sizes of these datasets is essential. A common split might be 70%-80% for training, 10%-15% for validation, and 10%-15% for testing, though this can vary based on the total amount of data available and specific project requirements. In financial contexts, ensuring temporal separation between training, validation, and test sets maintains the chronological order of events, thereby preserving the causality and real-time dynamics of the market.

By meticulously structuring data into training, validation, and test sets, traders and investors can develop machine learning models that are robust, reliable, and able to withstand the unpredictable nature of financial markets. This process lays the groundwork for achieving more accurate predictions and making more informed trading decisions.

## 8.3 Cross-Validation Techniques

Cross-validation is an essential technique in the toolbox of quants, enabling robust model evaluation and validation. The primary goal of cross-validation is to mitigate the risk of overfitting and ensure that the model generalizes well to unseen data. Here, we will explore various cross-validation techniques, understand their advantages and limitations, and examine their applications in financial modeling.

**Holdout Method**: The holdout method is the simplest form of cross-validation. The dataset is randomly split into two disjoint sets: a training set and a test set. Typically, a common split is 70% for training and 30% for testing, but these ratios can vary. The model is trained on the training set and evaluated on the test set. While straightforward, this method can be susceptible to high variance since the evaluation depends solely on a single train-test split.

$$\text{Training Set} : 70\%$$
$$\text{Test Set} : 30\%$$

**K-Fold Cross-Validation**: K-fold cross-validation is a more sophisticated approach. The dataset is divided into $K$ equally sized folds. The model is trained $K$ times, each time using $K - 1$ folds for training and the remaining fold for testing. This process is repeated $K$ times with each fold used exactly once as the test set. The evaluation metric is then averaged over the $K$ iterations, providing a more stable estimate of model performance. A common choice is $K = 5$ or $K = 10$.

$$\text{Evaluate} = \frac{1}{K}\sum_{i=1}^{K}\text{Metric}_i$$

This method helps in reducing both bias and variance compared to the holdout method.

**Leave-One-Out Cross-Validation (LOOCV)**: LOOCV is a special case of K-fold cross-validation where $K$ equals the number of data points $N$. Each sample is used once as the test set while the remaining $N - 1$ samples form the training set. This method provides an exhaustive evaluation but can be computationally expensive, especially for large datasets. LOOCV is highly useful when the dataset is very small.

$$\text{Evaluate} = \frac{1}{N}\sum_{i=1}^{N}\text{Metric}_i$$

**Stratified K-Fold Cross-Validation**: Stratified K-fold cross-validation aims to address the issue of class imbalance by ensuring that each fold maintains the proportion of classes similar to the entire dataset. This is particularly important in financial applications for classification problems where certain outcomes might be rare. The procedure is similar to K-fold cross-validation, but the dataset is split in a way that preserves the relative class frequencies in each fold.

$$\text{Class Distribution} : \text{Maintained across all folds}$$

**Time Series Cross-Validation**: Traditional cross-validation techniques assume that data points are independently and identically distributed, which often does not hold in time series data found in financial markets. Time series cross-validation, such as rolling-window or expanding-window cross-validation, respects the temporal ordering of observations.

*Rolling-Window Cross-Validation*: The data is divided into an initial training set and several subsequent evaluation windows. In each iteration, the model is trained on a window that rolls forward in time and evaluated on the subsequent time window.

$$\begin{aligned}\text{Train}_1 &: [1, 2, \ldots, t_1] \\ \text{Test}_1 &: [t_1 + 1, t_1 + 2, \ldots, t_2] \\ \text{Train}_2 &: [2, 3, \ldots, t_2] \\ \text{Test}_2 &: [t_2 + 1, t_2 + 2, \ldots, t_3]\end{aligned}$$

*Expanding-Window Cross-Validation*: Similar to rolling-window, but the training set expands with each iteration by including all previous data points.

$$\begin{aligned}\text{Train}_1 &: [1, 2, \ldots, t_1] \\ \text{Test}_1 &: [t_1 + 1, t_1 + 2, \ldots, t_2] \\ \text{Train}_2 &: [1, 2, \ldots, t_2] \\ \text{Test}_2 &: [t_2 + 1, t_2 + 2, \ldots, t_3]\end{aligned}$$

Both approaches ensure that the test data is always in the future relative to the training data, which is crucial for time series prediction accuracy.

**Bootstrapping**: Bootstrapping involves repeatedly sampling with replacement from the dataset to create multiple training datasets, allowing for the estimation of the accuracy of the model. It can be particularly useful when the original dataset is small or when an estimation of the variance of the model is needed.

$$\text{Bootstrap Estimate} = \frac{1}{B} \sum_{i=1}^{B} \text{Metric}_{\text{bootstrap}_i}$$

With $B$ denoting the number of bootstrap samples.

Incorporating these cross-validation techniques will significantly improve model evaluation. Selecting the appropriate method depends on the specifics of the dataset and the financial problem at hand. Utilizing these techniques offers a rigorous framework to assess model performance, and thereby enhances the predictive power and reliability of financial algorithms.

## 8.4 Confusion Matrix

Understanding the confusion matrix is fundamental for evaluating classification models in machine learning, especially within the context of financial predictions. At its core, a confusion matrix is a tabular representation of the actual versus predicted classifications, which provides a transparent view of a model's performance.

To lay the groundwork, consider a binary classification scenario where the model is tasked with predicting whether a stock price will go up (Positive) or down (Negative). The confusion matrix is a 2x2 matrix with the following cells:

| | **Predicted Positive** | **Predicted Negative** |
|---|---|---|
| **Actual Positive** | True Positive (TP) | False Negative (FN) |
| **Actual Negative** | False Positive (FP) | True Negative (TN) |

Here, the terms are defined as follows:

- **True Positive (TP)**: The number of positive instances correctly predicted by the model.
- **False Negative (FN)**: The number of positive instances incorrectly predicted as negative by the model.
- **False Positive (FP)**: The number of negative instances incorrectly predicted as positive by the model.
- **True Negative (TN)**: The number of negative instances correctly predicted by the model.

The confusion matrix offers valuable insights for various performance metrics that are critical in financial modeling:

**Accuracy:** The ratio of correctly predicted instances (both TP and TN) to the total instances.

$$\text{Accuracy} = \frac{TP + TN}{TP + TN + FP + FN}$$

While accuracy is a widely used metric, it may not be sufficient on its own, especially in cases of imbalanced datasets where the number of positive and negative instances differ significantly.

**Precision:** This metric indicates the proportion of true positive predictions out of the total predicted positives.

$$\text{Precision} = \frac{TP}{TP + FP}$$

Precision is particularly relevant in high-stake financial decisions where false positives can lead to significant fiscal impacts.

**Recall (Sensitivity or True Positive Rate):** This reflects the proportion of actual positives that are correctly identified by the model.

$$\text{Recall} = \frac{TP}{TP + FN}$$

**Specificity (True Negative Rate):** This measures the proportion of actual negatives correctly identified.

$$\text{Specificity} = \frac{TN}{TN + FP}$$

Balancing precision and recall is essential, and a high value in one often comes at the expense of the other. To harmonize these metrics, the F1 Score is used:

**F1 Score:** The harmonic mean of precision and recall, the F1 Score is a composite metric that gives a balanced view of the model performance.

$$\text{F1 Score} = 2 \cdot \frac{\text{Precision} \cdot \text{Recall}}{\text{Precision + Recall}}$$

**Example Calculation:** Assume a financial model yields the following confusion matrix:

| | **Predicted Up** | **Predicted Down** |
|---|---|---|
| **Actual Up** | 40 | 10 |
| **Actual Down** | 15 | 35 |

From this matrix:

$$TP = 40, \quad FN = 10, \quad FP = 15, \quad TN = 35$$

Calculating the metrics:

$$\text{Accuracy} = \frac{40 + 35}{40 + 35 + 15 + 10} = \frac{75}{100} = 0.75$$

$$\text{Precision} = \frac{40}{40+15} = \frac{40}{55} \approx 0.727$$

$$\text{Recall} = \frac{40}{40+10} = \frac{40}{50} = 0.80$$

$$\text{F1 Score} = 2 \cdot \frac{0.727 \cdot 0.80}{0.727 + 0.80} \approx 0.761$$

These metrics collectively offer a nuanced understanding of the financial model's performance. Precision and recall are particularly critical in different financial contexts, such as predicting market booms or busts. Financial analysts must carefully interpret these metrics to ensure model robustness and avoid potential financial pitfalls.

In financial contexts where trade-offs between different types of errors (like Type I and Type II) significantly impact decision-making, the confusion matrix and its derived metrics provide a solid foundation for further analysis and model improvement. Effective use of these tools can lead to more reliable and informed trading strategies.

## 8.5 ROC and AUC

Understanding the Receiver Operating Characteristic (ROC) curve and the Area Under the Curve (AUC) is crucial for evaluating classifier performance, particularly in the financial context where accurate predictions have significant implications. This section will delve into the ROC curve's construction, interpretation, and the calculation and significance of the AUC.

The ROC curve is a graphical representation that illustrates the diagnostic ability of a binary classifier system as its discrimination threshold is varied. It is plotted with the True Positive Rate (TPR) on the Y-axis and the False Positive Rate (FPR) on the X-axis. The True Positive Rate, also known as sensitivity or recall, measures the proportion of actual positives correctly identified by the model. The False Positive Rate, on the other hand, measures the proportion of actual negatives incorrectly classified as positives.

To formulate these concepts mathematically, let us define:

$$TPR = \frac{TP}{TP + FN}$$

$$FPR = \frac{FP}{FP + TN}$$

where $TP$, $FN$, $FP$, and $TN$ denote True Positives, False Negatives, False Positives, and True Negatives, respectively.

To construct the ROC curve, one needs to compute the TPR and FPR for various threshold values. As the threshold changes, the rates fluctuate, providing different points that comprise the ROC curve. A perfect classifier would achieve a point in the upper-left corner of the ROC space, representing 100% sensitivity (no false negatives) and 0% false positive rate.

Mathematically, this curve can be interpreted as follows:

- The ROC curve of a random classifier lies along the diagonal line from (0,0) to (1,1), indicating no discriminative power.
- The performance of different classifiers can be compared via their ROC curves, and those that push closer to the (0,1) point exhibit better performance.

The Area Under the Curve (AUC) quantifies the overall ability of the model to discriminate between positive and negative classes. It ranges from 0 to 1, where a higher value indicates a better performing model. An AUC of 0.5 suggests the model performs no better than random guessing, while an AUC of 1.0 denotes perfect discrimination.

To compute the AUC, one typically employs numerical integration techniques to measure the area under the ROC curve:

$$AUC = \int_0^1 \text{TPR } d(\text{FPR})$$

This integral can be approximated using the trapezoidal rule:

$$AUC \approx \sum_{i=1}^{n-1} \frac{(FPR_{i+1} - FPR_i)(TPR_{i+1} + TPR_i)}{2}$$

where $n$ is the number of distinct thresholds.

From a practical standpoint, the AUC offers several benefits:

- **Threshold Independence**: Unlike single threshold metrics like accuracy, AUC provides a single measure of performance regardless of threshold selection.
- **Class Imbalance Robustness**: AUC is relatively invariant to changes in class distribution, which is particularly useful in financial datasets where events like defaults or fraud are rare.

The ROC and AUC are integral to model performance evaluation in finance due to their ability to provide a comprehensive view of a classifier's discriminative power across all possible thresholds. For example, in credit scoring, an accurate ROC curve can help assess the probability thresholds for accepting or rejecting credit applications, ensuring that the financial institution minimizes defaults while maintaining profitability. Similarly, in fraud detection, a high AUC value would imply that the model effectively distinguishes between fraudulent and legitimate transactions, which is crucial for risk management and loss prevention.

Accurately interpreting the ROC curve and the AUC requires a deep understanding of the contextual significance of true positive and false positive classifications. This foundational knowledge empowers quants and financial analysts to select models that align closely with their strategic objectives, optimizing portfolios and trading algorithms with confidence.

As you evaluate your models, remember that the ROC and AUC are part of a suite of metrics. While they provide invaluable insight, they should be used in conjunction with other performance measures to get a holistic view of model efficacy. In subsequent sections, we will explore additional metrics such as precision, recall, and F1 score, which further aid in fine-tuning and assessing your financial models.

## 8.6 Precision, Recall, and F1 Score

Understanding the metrics of Precision, Recall, and F1 Score is crucial for evaluating classification models, especially in the context of financial predictions, where discerning the correct signals from noise is of paramount importance. These metrics provide more nuanced insights beyond accuracy, particularly in scenarios with class imbalances or when the cost of false positives and false negatives differs significantly.

Precision, recall, and F1 score are derived from the confusion matrix, a tabular representation of actual versus predicted outcomes. Let's start by revisiting the confusion matrix:

| | Predicted Positive | Predicted Negative |
|---|---|---|
| Actual Positive | True Positive (TP) | False Negative (FN) |
| Actual Negative | False Positive (FP) | True Negative (TN) |

Precision, also known as Positive Predictive Value, measures the correctness of positive predictions:

$$\text{Precision} = \frac{TP}{TP + FP}$$

Precision thus quantifies the proportion of true positives among all instances that were predicted as positive. In trading terms, if a model identifies potential profitable trades, precision indicates the percentage of those trades that actually yield a profit.

Recall, or Sensitivity or True Positive Rate, measures the ability of the model to capture all the actual positives:

$$\text{Recall} = \frac{TP}{TP + FN}$$

Recall expresses the ratio of true positives correctly identified by the model out of all actual positives. In financial predictions, recall could represent the model's effectiveness in identifying all profitable trading opportunities.

While precision focuses on the reliability of positive predictions, recall emphasizes the completeness of the prediction of positives. There is often a trade-off between precision and recall; improving one can sometimes deteriorate the other. This leads us to the F1 score, a harmonic mean of precision and recall:

$$\text{F1 Score} = 2 \cdot \frac{\text{Precision} \cdot \text{Recall}}{\text{Precision} + \text{Recall}}$$

The F1 score balances the two metrics, providing a single measure that considers both false positives and false negatives. This is particularly relevant in financial decision-making, where the cost of missed opportunities (false negatives) and erroneous trades (false positives) must both be minimized.

In financial applications, it is essential to tailor the model's optimization to the specific goals and costs associated with false positives and false negatives. For instance, a high recall might be prioritized for detecting rare but highly profitable trades, while high precision could be crucial in environments with high penalties for incorrect trades.

When evaluating models for predicting market movements, it's necessary to consider these metrics' implications in tandem:

- **Precision in Trading Algorithms:** A high precision in trading models means fewer false alarms about profitable trades, translating into more reliable signals for making trades. However, a model with overly high precision but low recall might miss out on many profitable trading opportunities.

- **Recall in Market Predictions:** High recall ensures that the model identifies most profitable trading opportunities, but it might also lead to an increase in false alarms, causing unnecessary trades that could lead to losses.

- **F1 Score for Balanced Performance:** The F1 score is particularly useful when the model needs to maintain a fine balance between precision and recall. It is especially relevant in adaptive trading strategies, where market conditions can change, necessitating a flexible evaluation criterion.

To gain a holistic understanding and ensure that the model performs well under various market conditions, it is advisable to use all three metrics in conjunction. By analyzing precision, recall, and the F1 score, traders can better understand their models' strengths and weaknesses and make more informed adjustments.

Ultimately, integrating precision, recall, and F1 score assessments within the broader model validation framework enables a comprehensive evaluation, ensuring that the trading algorithms are both robust and reliable across different market scenarios.

## 8.7 Mean Absolute Error (MAE) and Mean Squared Error (MSE)

Evaluating the performance of predictive models is crucial in finance, where predictions drive investment decisions and financial strategies. Among the various metrics available, Mean Absolute Error (MAE) and Mean Squared Error (MSE) are two of the most widely used for regression models. Both metrics serve as indicators of the predictive accuracy of a model, but each has its own unique characteristics and applications.

Mean Absolute Error (MAE) measures the average magnitude of the errors in a set of predictions, without considering their direction. It is defined mathematically as:

$$\text{MAE} = \frac{1}{n} \sum_{i=1}^{n} |y_i - \hat{y}_i|$$

where $y_i$ represents the true value, $\hat{y}_i$ denotes the predicted value, and $n$ is the number of observations. MAE provides a clear metric that is easy to interpret: it represents the average absolute deviation of predictions from the actual values. The key advantage of MAE is its straightforwardness and ease of understanding. Because it treats all deviations equally, it provides a balance between positive and negative errors.

Mean Squared Error (MSE) is similar to MAE but squares the errors before averaging them. It is defined as:

$$\text{MSE} = \frac{1}{n} \sum_{i=1}^{n} (y_i - \hat{y}_i)^2$$

The squaring process in MSE amplifies larger errors, making the metric more sensitive to outliers. This characteristic can be advantageous when large errors are particularly undesirable in a financial context, as it imposes a higher penalty on these deviations. However, this also means that MSE can be influenced disproportionately by outliers, potentially skewing the performance evaluation of the predictive model.

Both MAE and MSE have their strengths and weaknesses, and the choice between them depends on the specific context and goals of the model evaluation. To illustrate the differences between MAE and MSE more clearly, we consider the following hypothetical example:

Suppose we have a set of actual and predicted stock prices over five trading days:

| Day | 1 | 2 | 3 | 4 | 5 |
|---|---|---|---|---|---|
| Actual Price ($y_i$) | 100 | 102 | 101 | 103 | 105 |
| Predicted Price ($\hat{y}_i$) | 98 | 105 | 100 | 104 | 106 |

The error for each day is the difference between the actual and predicted prices:

| Day | 1 | 2 | 3 | 4 | 5 |
|---|---|---|---|---|---|
| Error ($y_i - \hat{y}_i$) | 2 | -3 | 1 | -1 | -1 |

For MAE, we take the absolute value of each error and compute the average:

$$\text{MAE} = \frac{|2| + |-3| + |1| + |-1| + |-1|}{5} = \frac{8}{5} = 1.6$$

For MSE, we square each error and then compute the average:

$$\text{MSE} = \frac{2^2 + (-3)^2 + 1^2 + (-1)^2 + (-1)^2}{5} = \frac{4 + 9 + 1 + 1 + 1}{5} = \frac{16}{5} = 3.2$$

From this example, we can see how MAE and MSE provide different perspectives on the error. MAE indicates an average error magnitude of 1.6, while MSE reveals an average squared error of 3.2, highlighting the impact of the larger error on Day 2.

When choosing between these metrics, consider the following points:

- **Interpretability**: MAE is often easier to interpret since it directly represents the average error in the same units as the original data.
- **Outliers**: If large errors are more critical and must be penalized heavily, MSE may be more appropriate because it amplifies these errors.
- **Consistency with Financial Goals**: Align the metric with the specific financial goals and risk tolerance. For instance, in high-frequency trading where precision is paramount, MSE might be favored due to its sensitivity to larger errors.

Ultimately, a comprehensive model evaluation in finance often involves looking at both MAE and MSE in conjunction with other metrics discussed in this chapter, providing a multi-faceted view of model performance. Such an approach ensures that you capture both the general accuracy and sensitivity to significant deviations, aligning model evaluation more closely with practical financial outcomes.

## 8.8 R-squared and Adjusted R-squared

Understanding the goodness-of-fit of a model is crucial in the context of financial data analysis, as it reveals how well our model's predictions align with the actual observed data. In this section, we will delve into two widely-used metrics: R-squared (also known as the coefficient of determination) and Adjusted R-squared. Both metrics are instrumental in assessing the performance of predictive models, particularly in regression analyses, and offer valuable insight into the proportion of variance captured by the model.

The R-squared value, denoted as $R^2$, quantifies the percentage of the dependent variable's variance that is explained by the independent variables in the model. It ranges from 0 to 1, where 0 indicates that the model does not explain any variability in the response data, and 1 implies that the model explains all the variability. The formula for R-squared is:

$$R^2 = 1 - \frac{\sum_{i=1}^{n}(y_i - \hat{y}_i)^2}{\sum_{i=1}^{n}(y_i - \bar{y})^2}$$

In this equation:

- $y_i$ represents the actual values of the dependent variable.
- $\hat{y}_i$ denotes the predicted values from the model.
- $\bar{y}$ is the mean of the actual values.
- $\sum_{i=1}^{n}(y_i - \hat{y}_i)^2$ is the sum of squared residuals (SSR).
- $\sum_{i=1}^{n}(y_i - \bar{y})^2$ is the total sum of squares (TSS).

While a higher R-squared value generally indicates a better fit, it is essential to note that R-squared alone can be misleading, especially in the presence of multiple predictors. One key limitation is that it always increases as more predictors are added to the model, regardless of their actual contribution to the variance explained.

To address this limitation, we use the Adjusted R-squared, denoted as $\bar{R}^2$. Adjusted R-squared adjusts the R-squared value based on the number of predictors in the model and the number of observations, providing a more accurate measure of goodness-of-fit for multiple regression models. The formula for Adjusted R-squared is:

$$\bar{R}^2 = 1 - \left(\frac{(1 - R^2)(n - 1)}{n - k - 1}\right)$$

Here:

- $n$ is the number of observations.
- $k$ is the number of predictors.
- $1 - R^2$ is the unexplained variance.

By introducing the terms $n$ and $k$, Adjusted R-squared penalizes the inclusion of non-contributory predictors, thus preventing the oversimplification that occurs with R-squared. This ensures that only those predictors that genuinely improve the model's explanatory power contribute positively to the metric.

A practical example helps to clarify these concepts. Suppose you are developing a model to predict the daily return of a stock based on historical data of various influencing factors like market indices, interest rates, and macroeconomic indicators. After fitting the model, you obtain an R-squared value of 0.85, implying that 85% of the variability in daily returns is explained by the model.

However, upon adding additional factors, the R-squared value might increase slightly to 0.87. Upon calculating the Adjusted R-squared, you might observe a different scenario: it increases to 0.86 from an initial 0.84, reflecting the true improvement of the model by considering the penalty for each additional predictor. This evaluation clearly indicates that the new predictors have indeed added value.

Thus, in financial modeling and prediction, it is imperative to prioritize Adjusted R-squared over R-squared when dealing with multiple regressors. While R-squared provides an optimistic view of model performance, Adjusted R-squared offers a grounded and holistic perspective by accounting for model complexity. This comprehensive understanding assists in creating robust and reliable predictive models, ultimately fostering sound investment decisions.

Through exploring R-squared and Adjusted R-squared, we gain invaluable insights into the explanatory power of our models. By judiciously applying these metrics, financial analysts and traders can enhance the efficacy of their predictive algorithms, ensuring that they derive meaningful, actionable intelligence from their data.

## 8.9 Model Selection Criteria: AIC and BIC

In the realm of model evaluation, the selection of an appropriate model is critical for ensuring predictive accuracy and interpretability. Two criteria that serve as essential tools in this selection process are the Akaike Information Criterion (AIC) and the Bayesian Information Criterion (BIC). Both these criteria balance goodness-of-fit with model complexity, mitigating the risk of overfitting. This section delves into the underlying mathematics, practical implications, and application of AIC and BIC in financial modeling.

The Akaike Information Criterion (AIC) is rooted in the principle of information theory. It estimates the relative quality of statistical models for a given dataset, providing a means to compare models even when they are not nested. The formula for AIC is given by

$$\text{AIC} = 2k - 2\ln(\hat{L})$$

where $k$ represents the number of estimated parameters in the model and $\hat{L}$ is the maximum likelihood of the model. The term $2k$ serves as a penalty for the number of parameters, thus accounting for model complexity, while $-2\ln(\hat{L})$ measures the goodness-of-fit. A lower AIC value typically indicates a better model, as it suggests a good balance between accuracy and simplicity.

The Bayesian Information Criterion (BIC), sometimes referred to as the Schwarz criterion, extends this approach by incorporating the sample size into its complexity penalty. The BIC is formulated as

$$\text{BIC} = k\ln(n) - 2\ln(\hat{L})$$

where $n$ is the sample size. The term $k\ln(n)$ imposes a more stringent penalty for models with more parameters, particularly when the sample size is large. Consequently, BIC tends to favor simpler models compared to AIC. Like AIC, a lower BIC value indicates a preferable model.

To illustrate their use in a financial context, consider the task of selecting between multiple autoregressive integrated moving average (ARIMA) models to forecast stock prices. Suppose we have several ARIMA models with different orders. By calculating the AIC and BIC for each model, we can systematically compare their performance. Here is an example of how such a comparison might appear:

In this example, the ARIMA(2,1,2) model has the lowest AIC and BIC values, suggesting it as the optimal model under both criteria.

It is essential to understand that AIC and BIC serve as relative rather than absolute measures. They do not test the accuracy of a model

| Model | AIC | BIC |
|---|---|---|
| ARIMA(1,1,1) | 230.56 | 240.84 |
| ARIMA(2,1,1) | 225.34 | 238.63 |
| ARIMA(1,1,2) | 228.45 | 241.74 |
| ARIMA(2,1,2) | 223.22 | 239.52 |

Table 8.1: AIC and BIC values for different ARIMA models

in isolation but rather indicate which of a set of models is more likely to be the best given the observed data. Consequently, these criteria should be used in conjunction with other evaluation metrics and domain knowledge to make informed decisions.

While AIC is generally preferred for smaller sample sizes or when the goal is purely predictive accuracy, BIC is often favored in contexts where penalizing complexity is crucial, such as when dealing with large datasets. In financial applications, where the balance between complexity and overfitting can be delicate, choosing the appropriate criterion is pivotal.

The application of AIC and BIC in machine learning models, particularly in algorithmic trading, underscores their versatility. When selecting features for a predictive model, such as a Random Forest or Gradient Boosting Machine in predicting future stock returns, these criteria can hierarchically prioritize features that contribute to predictive power without inflating model complexity.

By integrating AIC and BIC into the model evaluation and selection process, we ensure a methodical, data-driven approach that enhances model robustness and generalizability. These criteria thus play a vital role in refining algorithms tailored for the nuanced and dynamic landscape of financial markets.

## 8.10 Techniques for Model Validation in Finance

Effective model validation is a cornerstone of reliable algorithmic trading and financial analysis. Given the complexity and dynamism of financial markets, rigorous validation techniques are paramount to ensure that the predictive power of a model is both robust and resilient across various market conditions. This section delves into several advanced techniques for validating models in a financial context, focusing particularly on methods that address the unique challenges and requirements of financial datasets.

One key aspect in financial model validation is addressing the temporal dependency and non-stationary nature of financial data. Unlike typical machine learning datasets, financial data is characterized by time-series properties where observations are not independent and identically distributed (i.i.d.). To account for this, specific validation techniques have been developed to mimic the realistic trading environment and to avoid the pitfalls of overfitting.

A commonly used method in finance is the rolling window cross-validation. This technique involves splitting the timeline into multiple training and validation sets, ensuring each validation set simulates a future period that had not been seen by the model during training. Formally, suppose we have a time-series dataset of length $T$. The data is divided into $n$ rolling windows, each of length $w$, with a step size $s$. At each step $i$, the model is trained on data from time $t_i$ to $t_i + w$ and validated on data from $t_i + w + 1$ to $t_i + w + v$. Mathematically, this can be visualized as:

$$\text{Training set: } [t_i, t_i + w],$$
$$\text{Validation set: } [t_i + w + 1, t_i + w + v],$$
$$\text{where } t_i = 1, s, 2s, \ldots, (n-1)s.$$

Another critical validation technique particularly suited for financial models is the backtesting framework. Backtesting is a historical analysis where the model's predictions are applied to past data to simulate trade execution and strategy performance. This involves reconstructing the trading strategy's outcomes by using historical market data to calculate returns, drawdowns, and other performance metrics. It is essential to ensure that backtesting is performed with high-fidelity market simulation techniques to account for transaction costs, slippage, and market impact.

Furthermore, the walk-forward optimization is a variant of the rolling window approach that is especially popular in trading strategy development. Here, the model is continually updated as new data becomes available, similar to a live trading environment. The process involves training the model on an initial in-sample period, validating on a following out-of-sample period, then moving the training window forward, and repeating the process. This method helps in assessing how adaptive the model is to changing market regimes and ensures that the model employs up-to-date market information while being tested on genuinely unseen data.

To address the issue of overfitting, regularization techniques play a crucial role, particularly when combined with cross-validation. Regularization techniques, such as L1 (Lasso) and L2 (Ridge), add a penalty term to the model's complexity, discouraging overfitting by balancing bias and variance. These can be applied during the cross-validation steps to find the optimal trade-off between model complexity and predictive power.

Another layer of validation is the application of out-of-sample testing. After selecting the best model through cross-validation, it is prudent to hold back a portion of data completely unseen by the model, only to be used for final out-of-sample testing. This final evaluation step on genuinely unseen data is critical for gauging the model's true predictive performance under real-world conditions.

In practical terms, it is also vital to check the model's stability and sensitivity to different market conditions, known as scenario analysis. This includes stress testing the model against extreme market events, such as financial crises or periods of high volatility, to understand how the model performs under adverse conditions. Scenario analysis can be particularly insightful for risk management, helping to identify potential vulnerabilities in the trading strategy.

Finally, ensemble methods can be employed to enhance model robustness. Combining predictions from multiple diverse models, each validated using the previously described techniques, can lead to improved generalization. Techniques like bagging, boosting, and stacking can be used to form a consensus prediction that generally outperforms individual models.

Overall, validating a financial model involves a comprehensive approach that combines temporal cross-validation techniques, rigorous backtesting, regularization, out-of-sample testing, scenario analysis, and potentially ensemble methods. Deploying these techniques effectively ensures that the model is not only predictive but also robust and adaptable to the ever-changing landscape of financial markets. These rigorous validation steps instill confidence in the model's ability to perform reliably in live trading environments, an essential quality for any successful algorithmic trading strategy.

# Chapter 9

# Algorithmic Trading Strategies

**This chapter explores various algorithmic trading strategies used in financial markets. It starts by explaining the concept of algorithmic trading and reviews different types of strategies, including mean reversion, momentum, and statistical arbitrage. The chapter also covers pairs trading, market making, and high-frequency trading. Additionally, it discusses the importance of backtesting trading strategies and provides insights into execution algorithms to optimize trade performance.**

## 9.1 What is Algorithmic Trading?

Algorithmic trading, often referred to as algo trading, is the process of using computer algorithms to perform trading activities in financial markets. These algorithms are sophisticated, rule-based programs designed to execute trades at optimal times and prices, often faster and more efficiently than human traders can achieve. The primary advantage of algorithmic trading lies in its ability to process large datasets, identify patterns, and react to market movements with high precision and speed.

At its core, algorithmic trading leverages mathematical models and statistical analysis to make trading decisions. These models can range from simple moving averages to complex neural networks. The algorithms can autonomously decide the timing, price, and quantity of orders, thus minimizing the influence of emotional or subjective human judgment.

$$P(t) = W_0 + W_1X_1 + W_2X_2 + \cdots + W_nX_n$$

In this equation, $P(t)$ represents the predicted price at time $t$, and $W_i$ are the weights assigned to each of the factors $X_i$.

The efficiency of algorithmic trading is boosted by techniques that include high-frequency trading (HFT) and complex event processing (CEP). High-frequency trading seeks to capitalize on very brief periods of market inefficiencies, whereas complex event processing handles massive streams of information data in real-time, identifying opportunities in microseconds.

Consider a trading strategy rooted in statistical arbitrage. It identifies price discrepancies between correlated financial instruments. The algorithm might execute a trade to capitalize on the mean reversion tendencies of these prices. For instance, if stock A and stock B are historically correlated but diverge due to market noise, the algorithm might short the over-performing stock and go long on the under-performing stock in anticipation of a reversion to the mean.

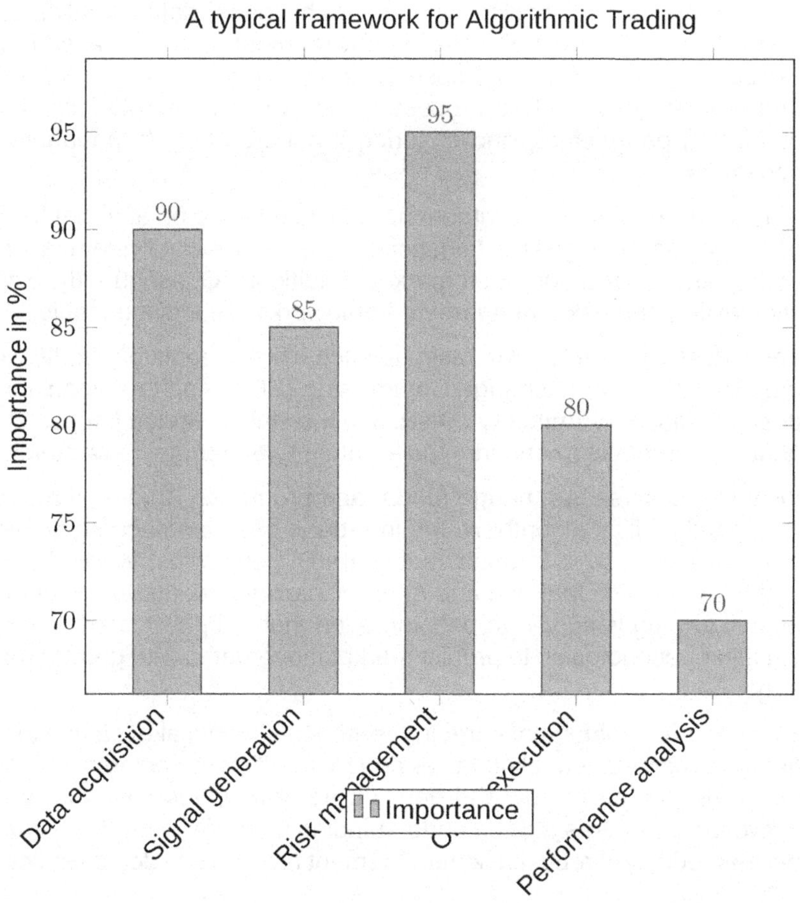


Figure illustrates a typical framework for algorithmic trading. This framework includes components like data acquisition, signal generation, risk management, order execution, and performance analysis. Each of these components plays a crucial role in ensuring that the trading strategy performs efficiently and profitably.

In algorithmic trading, the quality of data is paramount. Financial models are as good as the data fed into them. Historical price data, trading volumes, and economic indicators must be accurate and relevant. Furthermore, real-time market data is essential for executing trades effectively.

Backtesting is another critical aspect. Before deploying an algorithm in live markets, it is backtested against historical data to validate its performance. A robust backtesting environment replicates actual market conditions, including all costs such as slippage, transaction fees, and market impact. This process helps in fine-tuning the algorithm, optimizing parameters, and ensuring it adheres to risk management constraints.

Algorithmic trading is not without risks. The reliance on automated systems can lead to significant financial losses in case of system failures, coding errors, or unforeseen market conditions. Consequently, extensive testing and risk management frameworks are indispensable.

The industry is regulated to mitigate such risks. Regulatory bodies like the Securities and Exchange Commission (SEC) and the Financial Industry Regulatory Authority (FINRA) in the United States impose stringent requirements to ensure market integrity and protect investors.

Institutional investors, hedge funds, and proprietary trading firms predominantly utilize algorithmic trading, but it has also become accessible to retail investors through various trading platforms. With advancements in machine learning and artificial intelligence, the future of algorithmic trading is poised to become even more sophisticated, leveraging these technologies to predict market movements with greater accuracy.

To summarize, algorithmic trading represents a critical evolution in the financial markets, enabling faster and more efficient trading processes, minimizing human error, and opening up new opportunities for profit. However, it requires a deep understanding of financial models, statistical methods, and robust risk management protocols to deploy successfully.

## 9.2 Types of Trading Strategies

In the dynamic world of financial markets, there is no one-size-fits-all approach to maximizing returns. Algorithmic trading leverages computational power to deploy a variety of trading strategies, each with its objectives, methodologies, and suitable market conditions. Understanding the core types of trading strategies is essential for any quant seeking to develop a robust trading algorithm. This section delves into several primary types of trading strategies, providing a foundation for more advanced topics discussed in subsequent sections.

Algorithmic trading strategies can be broadly categorized into several key types: mean reversion, momentum, statistical arbitrage, pairs trading, market making, and high-frequency trading. Each strategy has distinct characteristics and applications, which we will explore in detail.

**Mean Reversion Strategies:** The principle behind mean reversion strategies is that asset prices and returns tend to revert to their historical mean or average level over time. Traders implementing mean reversion strategies identify assets that have deviated from their mean value, anticipating that these prices will eventually move back towards the mean. This approach often involves calculating historical averages, variances, and employing statistical measures such as the Z-score to determine the extent of deviation.

Here, a simple mean reversion strategy might be mathematically expressed as:

$$\text{Z-score} = \frac{P_t - \mu}{\sigma}$$

where $P_t$ is the current price, $\mu$ is the historical mean price, and $\sigma$ is the standard deviation. When the Z-score reaches a certain threshold, it signals a potential reversion opportunity.

**Momentum Strategies:** Contrary to mean reversion, momentum strategies capitalize on the tendency of asset prices to continue in their current direction for some time. Momentum traders seek to exploit continuous trends by buying assets that have shown an upward price movement and selling those with downward movement. This strategy assumes that trends persist over a medium-term horizon.

A popular model used in momentum strategies is the moving average crossover technique, which involves comparing short-term and long-term moving averages:

$$\text{MA}_{\text{short}} = \frac{1}{n}\sum_{i=0}^{n-1} P_{t-i}, \quad \text{MA}_{\text{long}} = \frac{1}{m}\sum_{i=0}^{m-1} P_{t-i}$$

where $n$ and $m$ represent the periods for the short-term and long-term moving averages respectively. A typical signal is generated when the short-term moving average crosses above the long-term moving average, indicating a buy signal, or vice versa for a sell signal.

**Statistical Arbitrage:** This strategy involves identifying and exploiting statistically significant price differences between assets that are expected to revert to a historical relationship. Statistical arbitrage strategies rely heavily on statistical models and sophisticated algorithms. Techniques such as cointegration testing and principal component analysis are used to find pairs or baskets of securities that historically move together.

A simple example is the creation of a spread between two cointegrated stocks $A$ and $B$:

$$\text{Spread} = P_A - \theta P_B$$

where $\theta$ is the hedge ratio determined through regression analysis. By trading the spread, statistical arbitrageurs bet on the mean reversion of this spread to profit from deviations.

**Pairs Trading:** Pairs trading is a specific form of statistical arbitrage where two correlated assets are traded to exploit price divergences. The main idea is to go long on the underperforming asset while going short on the outperforming one, expecting the prices to converge. Traders frequently use statistical tests to ensure the correlation and mean-reversion properties of the pair.

Typically, pairs traders execute trades based on a standardized spread, expressed as:

$$\text{Spread} = \frac{P_A - \beta P_B}{\sigma_{\text{spread}}}$$

where $\beta$ is the correlation ratio and $\sigma_{\text{spread}}$ is the standard deviation of the spread. A normalized spread helps in identifying entry and exit points.

**Market Making:** Market making strategies involve providing liquidity to the market by simultaneously quoting buy and sell prices for assets, thereby earning the bid-ask spread. Market makers aim to profit from the difference between the prices at which they buy and sell securities. These strategies require sophisticated algorithms for order placement, execution, and inventory management to ensure that trades are both profitable and compliant with regulatory constraints.

Market making often requires continuous rebalancing and dynamically adjusting quotes based on market conditions. A simplified profit function for a market maker can be represented as:

$$\text{Profit} = \sum (S_i - B_i) - \text{Transaction Costs}$$

where $S_i$ and $B_i$ represent sell and buy prices respectively.

**High-Frequency Trading (HFT):** High-frequency trading strategies involve executing a large number of orders at extremely high speeds, often in fractions of a second. HFT relies on sophisticated algorithms and latency-sensitive trading systems to capture small price inefficiencies. These strategies encompass various sub-strategies, including market making, arbitrage, and momentum ignition.

The success of HFT strategies often hinges on the speed of execution, data processing, and the ability to co-locate servers close to exchange data centers.

Each of these strategies requires a deep understanding of market dynamics, rigorous quantitative analysis, and robust technological infrastructure. As we proceed to dissect individual strategies in the following sections, the intricacies and implementation nuances will be further elaborated, empowering traders to apply these methodologies effectively.

## 9.3 Mean Reversion Strategies

Mean reversion strategies are a cornerstone of algorithmic trading, predicated on the principle that asset prices tend to revert to their historical average over time. This concept, rooted in the efficient market hypothesis, posits that deviations from the mean are temporary and will correct themselves as equilibrium is restored. By capitalizing on these deviations, traders can potentially exploit profitable opportunities.

The fundamental idea behind mean reversion is that if an asset's price deviates significantly from its historical mean, it is likely to return to this mean over time. This reversion can be driven by factors such as overreaction by market participants, transient supply-demand imbalances, or other short-term anomalies. To implement a mean reversion strategy, traders typically follow these key steps:

**Identify Historical Average:** First, traders must determine the historical mean or average price of the asset. This can be achieved by computing the moving average over a desired lookback period. The length of this period can vary depending on the specific characteristics and volatility of the asset being traded. While shorter periods may capture more recent price trends, longer periods provide a broader historical context.

$$\text{Moving Average}(MA) = \frac{1}{n}\sum_{i=1}^{n} P_i$$

where $P_i$ is the price of the asset at time $i$ and $n$ is the number of periods in the lookback window.

**Detect Deviations:** Once the moving average is established, traders need to monitor the current asset price and identify significant deviations from this mean. This can be done using statistical measures such as standard deviation. A common approach is to set a threshold, often expressed in terms of standard deviations, to determine when the asset is sufficiently deviated to warrant a trade.

$$\text{Z-score} = \frac{P_t - MA}{\sigma}$$

where $P_t$ is the current price, $MA$ is the moving average, and $\sigma$ is the standard deviation of the asset's price.

**Generate Trade Signals:** Trade signals are generated when the asset price crosses predefined thresholds of deviation. For instance, if the price exceeds the moving average by a certain multiple of standard deviations (positive Z-score), it may signal an overbought condition, suggesting a potential sell (short) opportunity. Conversely, if the price falls below the moving average by the same threshold (negative Z-score), it may signal an oversold condition, suggesting a potential buy (long) opportunity.

$$\begin{cases} \text{Go Long if } Z\text{-score} < -\text{Threshold} \\ \text{Go Short if } Z\text{-score} > \text{Threshold} \end{cases}$$

**Position Sizing and Risk Management:** Effective risk management is critical to the success of mean reversion strategies. Traders must determine the appropriate position size based on factors such as the volatility of the asset, account equity, and risk tolerance. Incorporating stop-loss orders and profit targets can help mitigate potential losses and lock in gains.

$$\text{Position Size} = \frac{\text{Account Equity} \times \text{Risk per Trade}}{\text{Distance to Stop-Loss}}$$

**Backtesting and Optimization:** Before deploying any mean reversion strategy in a live trading environment, it is essential to backtest the strategy using historical data. This involves running the strategy on past market data to evaluate its performance, identify any potential issues, and refine its parameters. Metrics such as Sharpe ratio, maximum drawdown, and profit factor provide insight into the strategy's risk-reward profile.

$$\text{Sharpe Ratio} = \frac{\text{Average Return} - \text{Risk-Free Rate}}{\text{Standard Deviation of Return}}$$

Mean reversion strategies can be applied across various asset classes, including equities, commodities, and currencies. One popular example within the equities market is the RSI (Relative Strength Index)-based mean reversion strategy. The RSI measures the speed and change of price movements and can denote overbought or oversold conditions. Traders might go long when the RSI is below 30 (indicating an oversold market) and short when the RSI is above 70 (indicating an overbought market).

**Algorithmic Implementation:** Implementing a mean reversion strategy algorithmically often requires programming skills and familiarity with trading platforms and APIs. Tools such as Python or R, coupled with libraries like Pandas, NumPy, and SciPy, can facilitate data analysis and strategy development. Here's a basic pseudocode outline for a mean reversion algorithm:

```
# Pseudocode for Mean Reversion Strategy

Initialize parameters: lookback_period, threshold, stop_loss, take_profit

while True:
    current_price = get_current_price()
    historical_prices = get_historical_prices(lookback_period)

    moving_average = mean(historical_prices)
    std_deviation = standard_deviation(historical_prices)
    z_score = (current_price - moving_average) / std_deviation

    if z_score > threshold:
        place_short_order(current_price, stop_loss, take_profit)
    elif z_score < -threshold:
        place_long_order(current_price, stop_loss, take_profit)

    sleep(time_interval)
```

The dynamics of mean reversion trading can be profoundly impacted by market conditions, liquidity, and transaction costs. Hence, continuous monitoring and adaptation are pivotal, as what might have been a reliable signal in historical data may not necessarily translate into future profitability. Integrating machine learning models can further enhance these strategies by predicting the likelihood of mean reversion under varying conditions, thus bolstering decision-making processes and improving overall strategy robustness.

By understanding and implementing mean reversion strategies, traders can potentially achieve consistent returns, leveraging the natural tendency of markets to revert to equilibrium. However, it demands rigorous analysis, disciplined risk management, and continuous refinement to remain effective amid the ever-evolving financial landscape.

## 9.4 Momentum Strategies

Momentum strategies leverage the tendency of asset prices to continue moving in the same direction for a specific period. This phenomenon, often discussed in the context of behavioral finance, suggests that assets which have performed well in the past are likely to continue to outperform, while those that have underperformed are likely to continue to do so. This section delves into the theoretical foundations, practical applications, and empirical performance of momentum strategies.

The core principle behind momentum investing can be summarized succinctly: "Buy high, sell higher." By identifying and riding trends, traders aim to capitalize on the persistence in asset price movements. Momentum can be found in various time frames, from intra-day fluctuations to long-term trends spanning months or even years.

To implement a momentum strategy, a trader typically follows a few key steps: measure momentum, establish holding periods, and manage risk. Numerous metrics can be employed to quantify momentum, each offering its unique perspective on price trends. One of the simplest and most widely used measures is the rate of change (ROC) or the relative strength index (RSI), calculated as follows:

$$\text{ROC}_t = \frac{P_t - P_{t-n}}{P_{t-n}}$$

where $P_t$ is the current price and $P_{t-n}$ is the price $n$ periods ago. Similarly, the RSI, introduced by J. Welles Wilder, oscillates between 0 and 100 and compares the magnitude of recent gains to recent losses:

$$\text{RSI}_t = 100 - \left( \frac{100}{1 + \frac{\text{Average Gain over } n \text{ periods}}{\text{Average Loss over } n \text{ periods}}} \right)$$

A common approach involves ranking assets based on these momentum indicators and selecting the top $k$ percent for inclusion in a momentum portfolio. Holding periods for momentum strategies can vary, but monthly or quarterly rebalancing is typical.

Empirical studies have generally demonstrated that momentum strategies yield significant positive returns across various asset classes, including equities, commodities, and foreign exchange. Notably, Jegadeesh and Titman's seminal work in 1993 provided robust evidence supporting the profitability of momentum strategies in the U.S. equity market. Their study revealed that portfolios formed based on past six-month returns and held for six months earned significant abnormal returns.

Despite their historical success, momentum strategies are not without risks. Momentum crashes, periods when the strategy dramatically underperforms, are a notable concern. For instance, during market reversals, momentum strategies can incur substantial losses as prevailing trends abruptly change direction. Risk management techniques such as stop-loss orders, diversification across multiple securities, and blending momentum with other strategies can help mitigate these risks.

Technological advancements have enabled the implementation of sophisticated momentum strategies through algorithmic trading. Modern algorithms can rapidly process large datasets, identify emerging trends, and execute trades with precision. For example, machine learning models like random forests and neural networks can enhance traditional momentum strategies by capturing complex patterns in historical price data.

Consider the following Python code snippet demonstrating a simple implementation of a momentum strategy using a moving average crossover approach:

```
import numpy as np
import pandas as pd

def momentum_strategy(data, short_window, long_window):
    signals = pd.DataFrame(index=data.index)
    signals['price'] = data['Close']
```

```
    signals['short_mavg'] = data['Close'].rolling(window=short_window, min_periods
        =1).mean()
    signals['long_mavg'] = data['Close'].rolling(window=long_window, min_periods=1)
        .mean()
    signals['signal'] = 0
    signals['signal'][short_window:] = np.where(signals['short_mavg'][short_window:] >
         signals['long_mavg'][short_window:], 1, 0)
    signals['positions'] = signals['signal'].diff()
    return signals

# Download historical data and apply the strategy
data = pd.read_csv('historical_stock_prices.csv', index_col='Date', parse_dates=
    True)
signals = momentum_strategy(data, short_window=40, long_window=100)

print(signals.tail())
```

This code defines a simple moving average crossover strategy where a short-term moving average (e.g., 40 days) is compared with a long-term moving average (e.g., 100 days). When the short-term average crosses above the long-term average, a buy signal is generated. Conversely, a sell signal is issued when the short-term average crosses below the long-term average.

Momentum strategies remain a popular choice among traders and investors seeking to capitalize on established price trends. While they require diligent monitoring and robust risk management, their implementation can be highly rewarding with the appropriate tools and knowledge.

## 9.5 Statistical Arbitrage

Statistical arbitrage, often abbreviated as "stat arb," refers to a category of trading strategies that leverage statistical and mathematical models to exploit inefficiencies in the price relationships between financial instruments. Unlike traditional arbitrage, which might involve simultaneous purchases and sales to lock in guaranteed profits, statistical arbitrage strategies are typically based on statistical analysis and often involve taking temporary positions that are expected to revert to a historical or equilibrium relationship.

Stat arb strategies can be applied to a wide range of financial instruments, including stocks, bonds, commodities, derivatives, and exchange-traded funds (ETFs). The core idea is to identify pairs or groups of securities whose historical price relationships deviate from their norm, indicating a trading opportunity.

To develop a statistical arbitrage strategy, a trader generally follows these key steps:

- **Identify Potential Pairs or Groups**: The first step involves selecting financial instruments that exhibit a historical price relationship. This can be done using a variety of techniques, such as correlation analysis, cointegration tests, or clustering algorithms. Pairs trading is a popular form of statistical arbitrage, where two highly correlated stocks are chosen.
- **Model the Price Relationship**: The next step is to model the historical relationship between the selected instruments using statistical techniques such as linear regression, mean reversion models, or cointegration vectors. For instance, if a trader is considering stocks A and B for a pairs trade, they might fit a linear regression model:

  $$P_A(t) = \alpha + \beta P_B(t) + \epsilon(t)$$

  where $P_A(t)$ and $P_B(t)$ are the prices of stocks A and B at time $t$, respectively, $\alpha$ and $\beta$ are the regression coefficients, and $\epsilon(t)$ is the residual error term.
- **Determine Entry and Exit Points**: Based on the model, the trader sets specific criteria for entering and exiting trades. For instance, if the price spread between the two assets deviates significantly from its long-term average, it may signal an entry point. The trader would then short the over-performing asset and go long on the underperforming one, expecting the spread to revert to its mean. Entry and exit thresholds can be expressed in terms of standard deviations from the mean spread:

  $$\text{Enter trade if } |\epsilon(t)| > k \cdot \sigma_\epsilon$$

  where $\sigma_\epsilon$ is the standard deviation of the residuals, and $k$ is a constant determining the threshold level.
- **Backtest the Strategy**: Before deploying the strategy in a live trading environment, it is crucial to backtest it using historical data to evaluate its performance. This involves running the strategy on past data to examine statistics such as profitability, sharp ratio, maximum drawdown, and the frequency and duration of trades. Effective backtesting helps in refining entry and exit rules and adjusting model parameters.

- **Risk Management and Execution**: Managing risk is paramount in statistical arbitrage. Traders may employ stop-loss limits, position size constraints, and leverage controls to contain potential losses. Additionally, execution algorithms are used to minimize market impact and slippage. For instance, VWAP (Volume Weighted Average Price) or TWAP (Time Weighted Average Price) algorithms can be employed to execute trades efficiently.

Example of Linear Regression for Pairs Trade :

```
import numpy as np
import pandas as pd
import statsmodels.api as sm

# Load historical price data
data = pd.read_csv('price_data.csv')
prices_A = data['Stock_A']
prices_B = data['Stock_B']

# Perform linear regression
X = sm.add_constant(prices_B)
model = sm.OLS(prices_A, X).fit()
alpha, beta = model.params

# Calculate residuals (spread)
spread = prices_A - (alpha + beta * prices_B)
spread_std = np.std(spread)

# Signal generation
entry_threshold = 2.0 * spread_std
exit_threshold = 0.5 * spread_std

# Signals
long_signals = spread < -entry_threshold
short_signals = spread > entry_threshold
exit_signals = np.abs(spread) < exit_threshold

# Display model summary
print(model.summary())
```

In this Python code snippet, we load historical price data for two stocks and perform a linear regression analysis to model their relationship. The residuals (spread) between the stocks are calculated and used to generate trading signals based on the defined entry and exit thresholds.

Statistical arbitrage strategies are not without their challenges. They require accurate modeling of price relationships, robust backtesting, and sound risk management practices. Moreover, market conditions and correlations between assets can change over time, necessitating regular review and adjustment of the strategy.

By systematically exploiting deviations from normal trading relationships and rigorously managing risk, statistical arbitrage can be a powerful tool in a trader's arsenal. However, the complexity and computational requirements of such strategies also mean they are best suited to traders with a solid foundation in quantitative analysis and algorithmic trading.

## 9.6 Pairs Trading

Pairs Trading, also known as statistical arbitrage or convergence trading, is a market-neutral strategy that involves the simultaneous buying and selling of two correlated securities. The essence of this strategy is to exploit the price discrepancies between the two securities, betting that they will revert to their historical relationship over time. This trading approach is particularly appealing because it attempts to minimize market risk by hedging – the long and short positions effectively cancel out market trends, focusing on the relative performance of the selected pair.

At its core, pairs trading hinges on the concept of mean reversion. It assumes that the prices of two related assets will deviate from and revert to their long-term equilibrium. Pairs trading can be applied to stocks, indices, commodities, or any assets with a historical price correlation.

To illustrate pairs trading mathematically, consider two securities, $A$ and $B$. Let $P_A(t)$ and $P_B(t)$ denote their respective prices at time $t$. The spread $S(t)$ between these two prices can be defined as:

$$S(t) = P_A(t) - P_B(t)$$

If the spread $S(t)$ deviates significantly from its historical mean $\mu$, it implies a temporary imbalance that provides a trading opportunity. The spread is expected to revert to $\mu$ over time due to mean reversion. The key steps in implementing a pairs trading strategy are detailed below:

- **Selection of Pairs**: Choosing which pairs to trade is crucial for the strategy's success. The selection is typically based on historical correlation and cointegration analysis. Correlation measures the degree to which two securities move in relation to each other. However, high historical correlation alone does not guarantee profitable pairs. Cointegration, on the other hand, is a stronger statistical property indicating that a linear combination of the two non-stationary series (prices) is stationary. In mathematical terms, two time series $X_t$ and $Y_t$ are cointegrated if there exists a coefficient $\beta$ such that the residual $e_t = X_t - \beta Y_t$ is stationary.

To identify suitable pairs, we use econometric tests such as the Engle-Granger two-step method or the Johansen test. If cointegration is established, it suggests that any divergence between the price series is temporary and will converge.

- **Trading Signals**: Once a cointegrated pair is identified, the next step is to generate trading signals based on the spread. The mean $\mu$ and standard deviation $\sigma$ of the spread $S(t)$ over a historical period are calculated. When the spread $S(t)$ deviates from $\mu$ by more than a certain threshold $k\sigma$, trading positions are initiated. Typical thresholds are set at 1 or 2 standard deviations, depending on the desired sensitivity and risk tolerance.

  The trading rules can be summarized as follows:

  - **Enter Long-Short Position**: When the spread $S(t) > \mu + k\sigma$, sell security $A$ and buy security $B$.
  - **Enter Short-Long Position**: When the spread $S(t) < \mu - k\sigma$, buy security $A$ and sell security $B$.
  - **Exit Positions**: Close positions when the spread reverts to the mean, i.e., when $S(t) \approx \mu$.

$$\text{If } S(t) > \mu + k\sigma, \text{ then sell } A \text{ and buy } B$$
$$\text{If } S(t) < \mu - k\sigma, \text{ then buy } A \text{ and sell } B$$
$$\text{Close positions when } S(t) \approx \mu$$

- **Risk Management**: Effective risk management is vital for the success of pairs trading strategies. Key considerations include:

  - **Stop-loss Mechanisms**: Implementing stop-loss orders to limit potential losses when the spread continues to diverge.
  - **Position Sizing**: Properly sizing positions based on the statistical properties of the spread to avoid over-leveraging.
  - **Diversification**: Trading multiple pairs to reduce idiosyncratic risk associated with any single pair.

- **Backtesting**: Backtesting pairs trading strategies on historical data is essential to validate their profitability and robustness. The process involves simulating trades over a historical period to evaluate performance, drawdowns, and the impact of transaction costs. Successful backtesting provides confidence that the identified pairs and the corresponding trading logic will hold in live trading environments.

In summary, pairs trading offers a disciplined approach to exploit temporary price divergences between two correlated assets. By relying on solid statistical foundations such as cointegration and mean reversion, traders can generate potentially profitable opportunities while mitigating overarching market risks.

## 9.7 Market Making

Market making is a fundamental concept in the trading world, serving as a crucial mechanism for providing liquidity and ensuring the smooth functioning of financial markets. Market makers, often large financial institutions or specialized trading firms, continuously quote both buy and sell prices for a specific set of securities, thereby creating a market for those securities. The role of market makers is essential because they ensure that market participants can buy and sell assets without significant delays, and the presence of market makers helps stabilize prices by balancing supply and demand.

Market making operates on the simple principle of profiting from the spread, which is the difference between the bid price (the price at which a market maker is willing to buy a security) and the ask price (the price at which they are willing to sell it). Successful market makers aim to capture this spread consistently while managing the risks associated with holding inventory.

To better understand market making, let's delve into the mechanics and strategies involved.

At the core of market making lies the bid-ask spread. Consider a security with an ask price of $100 and a bid price of $99. The market maker earns a spread of $1 per share traded. However, capturing this spread repeatedly requires sophisticated strategies to manage inventory risk and market fluctuations.

Market makers employ both passive and active strategies:

- **Passive Market Making:** This involves quoting continuous bids and asks while generally not initiating trades actively. The goal is to earn the spread over a large number of transactions. Passive market makers maintain their positions by constantly adjusting their quotes based on market conditions.

- **Active Market Making:** In contrast, active market makers may take a more aggressive approach by reacting swiftly to market changes and actively seeking to manage their inventory. They might employ algorithms that dynamically adjust quotes and even anticipate market movements based on real-time data analysis.

Market making algorithms play an instrumental role in modern financial markets. These sophisticated algorithms continuously analyze a myriad of factors, such as order flow, market depth, and volatility, to optimize quoting strategies. Let's consider a simplified representation of a market-making algorithm:

```
# Pseudocode for a basic market making algorithm

Initialize bid and ask prices

while market is open:
    # Update quotes based on market conditions
    bid_price = get_current_bid() - adjustment_factor
    ask_price = get_current_ask() + adjustment_factor

    # Place buy and sell orders
    place_order(bid_price, "buy")
    place_order(ask_price, "sell")

    # Manage inventory risk
    current_position = get_current_inventory()
    if current_position > max_inventory_threshold:
        reduce_position("sell", excess_amount)
    elif current_position < min_inventory_threshold:
        increase_position("buy", shortfall_amount)

    wait a short interval
```

The algorithm begins by initializing the bid and ask prices. During the market hours, it continuously updates its quotes based on the prevailing market conditions. Adjustments to the bid and ask prices are made to ensure they reflect current market dynamics. It places buy orders at the bid price and sell orders at the ask price, aiming to capture the spread. Additionally, it monitors and manages its inventory levels to avoid unwanted risks.

Moreover, advanced market-making algorithms utilize machine learning techniques to enhance decision-making. They analyze historical data, recognize patterns, and even predict short-term price movements to optimize their quoting and inventory management strategies. For example, reinforcement learning can be employed to adaptively learn the best quoting strategy by maximizing a long-term reward, which is often a combination of captured spread and minimized inventory risk.

Risk management is a critical aspect of market making. Market makers face the risk of adverse price movements in the securities they hold. Effective risk management requires maintaining a balanced inventory and employing hedging strategies when necessary. Market makers often use correlated assets or derivatives to hedge their positions and reduce exposure to market risk.

For instance, consider a market maker dealing in stock options. If they are making markets in a call option, they might hedge their position by taking an offsetting position in the underlying stock or in a put option. This helps mitigate the impact of adverse price movements in the option they are quoting.

Market making plays a pivotal role in the liquidity and efficiency of financial markets. The presence of market makers narrows the bid-ask spread, reduces price volatility, and increases market depth. For traders and investors, this translates to lower transaction costs, better price discovery, and improved market access.

As markets evolve, so do the techniques and technologies employed by market makers. The integration of high-frequency trading (HFT) and algorithmic trading has revolutionized market making, enabling faster and more efficient execution of trades. High-frequency market makers can execute thousands of trades per second, swiftly reacting to market changes and capturing tiny spreads over a massive volume of trades.

Market making is therefore not just about quoting prices; it is about utilizing advanced strategies and technologies to maintain liquidity, manage risks, and ensure the optimal functioning of financial markets. Traders and investors benefit greatly from these activities, experiencing smoother and more efficient markets that enable better trading opportunities and investment outcomes.

## 9.8 High-Frequency Trading

High-Frequency Trading (HFT) represents a specialized subset of algorithmic trading that leverages sophisticated technological infrastructure to execute a large number of orders at extremely high speeds. Typically characterized by low-latency execution, HFT strategies aim to capitalize on minute price discrepancies that exist for only fractions of a second. This practice relies on complex algorithms, high-speed data processing, and proximity to exchange servers to minimize latency—every microsecond can impact profitability.

At its core, HFT focuses on exploiting inefficiencies in the market to facilitate high-speed arbitrage, enhance liquidity, and provide tighter spreads. These micro-second strategies necessitate not just proficiency in financial markets but also in computer science and network engineering.

To better grasp HFT, it's critical to understand the key components and processes involved:

- **1. Low Latency Trading Infrastructure:** The backbone of HFT is its trading infrastructure. This includes high-speed connections to exchange servers, co-location services, and ultra-low latency network components. Co-location allows traders to place their servers within the same data centers as the stock exchanges, drastically reducing the time it takes for their orders to reach the market.

- **2. Data Acquisition and Processing:** HFT firms continuously gather a vast array of data, including market quotes, trade volumes, and order book data. This requires the use of real-time data feeds and sophisticated processing engines capable of analyzing information in microseconds. Accurate and rapid data assessment is crucial for the timely execution of trades.

- **3. Algorithm Development:** The algorithms used in HFT are designed to identify profitable opportunities in milliseconds. These algorithms are developed using advanced statistical and machine learning techniques to predict short-term price movements. Common strategies include market making, statistical arbitrage, and latency arbitrage.

$$P_t = P_{t-1} + \epsilon_t \tag{9.1}$$

Here, $P_t$ represents the price at time $t$, and $\epsilon_t$ represents the error term. High-frequency models often assume that price changes over ultra-short periods are random, relying on high-volume trading to generate profit through the aggregation of minimal gains.

- **4. Execution Algorithms:** Execution algorithms in HFT are optimized to enter and exit positions faster than human capabilities. These algorithms must manage the trade-off between execution speed and market impact—executing trades quickly without significantly distorting market prices.

- **5. Risk Management:** Given the sheer volume of trades executed per second, risk management is paramount. HFT systems incorporate real-time monitoring and rapid response mechanisms to mitigate potential losses. This includes setting strict limits on individual trade sizes, portfolio-wide exposure, and leveraging high-speed risk assessment algorithms.

A crucial aspect to note is the regulatory environment surrounding HFT. Regulatory bodies have increased scrutiny and introduced various measures to ensure fair trading practices. These measures include circuit breakers to pause trading in extreme volatility situations and imposed restrictions on flash orders.

High-Frequency Trading has reshaped market dynamics in significant ways. By providing liquidity and narrowing bid-ask spreads, it enhances market efficiency. However, it also poses challenges, such as exacerbating market volatility and contributing to events like the "Flash Crash" of 2010.

In practice, the effectiveness of HFT strategies hinges on the ability to manage vast computational resources, maintain low-latency communication, and adapt to ever-evolving market conditions. Firms engage in continuous development and refinement of their algorithms to stay ahead in this highly competitive landscape.

Understanding the intricacies of HFT requires not only an analytical mindset but also a considerable investment in technological infrastructure. This convergence of finance and technology epitomizes the future of trading, where speed and precision are paramount.

## 9.9 Backtesting Trading Strategies

Backtesting is a fundamental aspect of developing and refining algorithmic trading strategies. It involves testing a trading strategy using historical market data to evaluate its potential performance. The primary aim of backtesting is to understand how a strategy would have performed in the past, providing an indication of its potential effectiveness in real trading scenarios. This section delves into the key components of backtesting, methodologies, common pitfalls, and best practices to ensure robust and reliable results.

Key Components of Backtesting:

The essential elements of a comprehensive backtesting process include the following:

- **Historical Data:** The foundation of backtesting is accurate and relevant historical market data. This data should include price information (open, high, low, close prices), volume, and if applicable, order book data for more granular strategies. The quality and granularity of the data are critical as they can significantly impact the results of the backtest.
- **Strategy Rules:** Clearly define the rules of your trading strategy. These include entry and exit points, position sizing, risk management protocols, and any other conditions that influence trading decisions. Consistency in these rules is crucial to ensure the reliability of backtest results.
- **Performance Metrics:** Determine the metrics that will be used to evaluate the strategy's performance. Common metrics include net profit, return on investment (ROI), maximum drawdown, Sharpe ratio, and Sortino ratio. These metrics provide insights into the profitability, risk, and efficiency of the strategy.
- **Transaction Costs:** Incorporate realistic transaction costs, including commissions, slippage, and other trading fees. Ignoring transaction costs can lead to overestimating the strategy's profitability, especially in high-frequency trading strategies.

Methodologies:

Backtesting methodologies can vary based on the complexity and nature of the trading strategy. Some common approaches are:

- **Walk-Forward Analysis:** This method involves segmenting historical data into several periods. The strategy is optimized on one period and tested on the subsequent one. This process is repeated across the entire dataset, simulating a more realistic out-of-sample testing environment.

- **Monte Carlo Simulation:** This technique involves running the backtest multiple times with variations in input parameters. It helps to assess the robustness of a strategy by evaluating its performance under different market conditions and random scenarios.
- **Bootstrapping:** Bootstrapping involves resampling the historical price data to generate new datasets. By backtesting the strategy on these resampled datasets, traders can get a sense of its performance variability and statistical significance.

Common Pitfalls:

Despite its advantages, backtesting comes with several pitfalls that traders must avoid:

- **Overfitting:** Overfitting occurs when a strategy is excessively complex and fits the historical data too closely. This can result in excellent backtest performance but poor real-world performance. Keeping the strategy simple and avoiding excessive parameter tuning can mitigate overfitting.
- **Look-Ahead Bias:** This happens when future data is inadvertently used in generating signals. Ensuring that trading decisions are based solely on information available at the time is critical to avoiding look-ahead bias.
- **Survivorship Bias:** Using historical data that only includes current components of the market or index can lead to survivorship bias. For a realistic test, include data for delisted or bankrupt stocks that were part of the market during the historical period.
- **Data Snooping:** Excessive optimization or repeated testing on the same data can lead to data snooping bias, where the strategy becomes tailored to the peculiarities of the historical dataset. Employing out-of-sample testing and walk-forward analysis can reduce this risk.

Best Practices:

Adhering to best practices helps ensure the reliability and validity of backtesting results:

- **Out-of-Sample Testing:** Always divide your historical data into in-sample (training) and out-of-sample (testing) periods. Develop and optimize the strategy on the training dataset, and evaluate its performance on the testing dataset to ensure robustness.

- **Cross-Validation:** Use cross-validation techniques to verify the consistency of the strategy's performance across different data subsets. This helps in identifying any potential overfitting issues.
- **Realistic Assumptions:** Incorporate all realistic trading assumptions, including liquidity constraints, market impact, and bid-ask spreads. This adds realism and robustness to your backtest.
- **Continual Improvement:** Backtesting is an iterative process. Continually refine and improve your strategy based on backtest results. Incorporate new market data as it becomes available to keep the strategy adaptive to changing market conditions.

By adhering to these principles and best practices, traders and investors can leverage backtesting to validate their algorithmic trading strategies effectively. It serves as a vital tool in the development of strategies that not only perform well historically but are also equipped to navigate the uncertainties of live market conditions.

## 9.10 Execution Algorithms

Execution algorithms are specialized algorithms designed to efficiently execute large orders with minimal market impact. Unlike traditional trading strategies that focus on predicting price movements, execution algorithms target the optimal performance of order execution by minimizing slippage, reducing market impact, and ensuring scalability. Execution is a crucial aspect of algorithmic trading, especially when dealing with large volumes or when trading in less liquid markets. This section will elucidate various types of execution algorithms, their key features, and their applications, ensuring a comprehensive understanding for both novice and experienced traders.

One of the most widely used execution algorithms is the *Volume Weighted Average Price* (VWAP) algorithm. VWAP is the ratio of the value traded to the total volume traded over a particular time horizon. Mathematically, VWAP is expressed as:

$$\text{VWAP} = \frac{\sum_{i=1}^{n} P_i \times V_i}{\sum_{i=1}^{n} V_i}$$

where $P_i$ is the price of trade $i$, $V_i$ is the volume of trade $i$, and $n$ is the total number of trades considered. The VWAP algorithm aims to execute orders in line with the market volume profile, thereby reducing market impact and minimizing deviation from this benchmark price.

Another common execution algorithm is the *Time Weighted Average Price* (TWAP) algorithm. TWAP is designed to execute orders evenly over a specified period, thereby avoiding market timing risks. This algorithm breaks down the larger order into smaller slices, executed at regular intervals, ensuring that the execution is spread throughout the trading session. This approach is ideal for assets with significant intraday volatility or when trading in illiquid markets.

The *Implementation Shortfall* (IS) algorithm, also known as the *Arrival Price* algorithm, is designed to minimize the difference between the decision price (the price when the trader decided to execute the order) and the final execution price. This algorithm seeks to balance the trade-off between market impact and opportunity cost by dynamically adjusting the order pace based on real-time market conditions. The IS algorithm incorporates market forecasts and volatility estimates to optimize the execution process.

In high-frequency trading environments, the *Participation Rate* (PR) algorithm is frequently employed. This algorithm aims to execute an order in proportion to the market trading volume, generally targeting a pre-determined percentage of the market volume. The participation rate can be adjusted based on market conditions, liquidity, and the trader's risk appetite. This method ensures that the execution follows the natural liquidity of the market, reducing the risk of significant market impact.

More advanced and dynamic execution algorithms include *Algorithmic Market Participation* (AMP) and *Stealth* algorithms. The AMP algorithm adjusts the execution rate based on real-time price and volume changes, thereby dynamically optimizing the trade execution process. The Stealth algorithm, as its name implies, aims to execute orders without revealing the trader's intentions, using sophisticated techniques to minimize market impact and avoid detection by other market participants.

The choice of execution algorithm depends largely on the trader's objectives, market conditions, and the specific characteristics of the asset being traded. Factors such as liquidity, volatility, and the size of the order relative to the average trading volume play a significant role in determining the appropriate execution strategy.

Execution algorithms are continuously evolving, leveraging advancements in machine learning and artificial intelligence to enhance their capabilities. Modern execution algorithms incorporate predictive analytics, real-time market data, and various optimization techniques to achieve superior execution performance. By understanding and selecting the appropriate execution algorithm, traders can significantly improve trade outcomes, maintain anonymity, and reduce overall trading costs. Mastery of execution algorithms is, thus, a critical component of successful algorithmic trading.

# Chapter 10

# Risk Management

**This chapter covers essential concepts and techniques in risk management for quantitative finance. It begins by defining various types of financial risks and introduces key risk measures such as Value at Risk (VaR) and Expected Shortfall. The chapter discusses stress testing, scenario analysis, and risk-adjusted return metrics. It also delves into portfolio risk management and hedging strategies. Additionally, the chapter addresses regulatory requirements and compliance to ensure adherence to industry standards.**

## 10.1 What is Risk Management?

Risk management is a crucial aspect of quantitative finance that involves identifying, assessing, and prioritizing risks followed by coordinated and economical application of resources to minimize, monitor, and control the probability or impact of unfortunate events. In the context of quantitative trading, risk management strategies are designed to manage potential losses so that a portfolio remains robust under various market conditions.

At its core, risk management aims to balance the potential for gains against the potential for losses. It is the systematic and disciplined approach employed by traders and investors to mitigate losses while optimizing the risk-return trade-off. Effective risk management allows financial professionals to withstand short-term market turmoil and align their portfolios with long-term investment goals.

Risk management begins with the identification of risks, which can come from a variety of sources. These include market risks, such as changes in equity prices or interest rates; credit risks, which pertain to the possibility of a counterparty defaulting on a financial obligation; and operational risks, which arise from failures in internal processes, systems, or human errors. Understanding the different types of risks is the first step toward developing a comprehensive risk management strategy.

Once risks are identified, they need to be assessed to determine their potential impact. This involves quantifying the likelihood and severity of each risk, often using statistical models and historical data. Measures such as Value at Risk (VaR) and Expected Shortfall are commonly used to provide a quantitative assessment of risk levels. These metrics help in understanding the potential maximum loss over a given time frame and the expected value of losses that exceed the VaR threshold, respectively.

The next phase is the prioritization of risks based on their potential impact and likelihood. Not all risks are equal—some may have the potential to cause significant financial distress whereas others might have a minor effect. This prioritization helps in focusing resources on managing the most significant risks.

Risk mitigation involves implementing measures to reduce the likelihood or impact of risks deemed unacceptable. This could include diversifying investments, using hedging strategies, setting stop-loss orders, or buying insurance products like credit default swaps. The implementation of these measures requires a deep understanding of both the financial instruments available and the specific risk profile of the portfolio.

Monitoring and controlling risks is an ongoing process. Financial markets are dynamic, and risk exposures can change rapidly. Continuous monitoring ensures that risk management strategies remain effective and aligned with the investment goals. This involves regular review and adjustment of risk metrics and management strategies in response to changing market conditions and new risk factors.

Risk management is not merely a set of static rules but a dynamic framework that requires continuous learning and adaptation. A proactive risk management culture enables an organization to respond swiftly to emerging risks and opportunities. Advanced tools and techniques such as machine learning and real-time analytics are increasingly being used to enhance risk management capabilities.

In conclusion, risk management in quantitative finance encompasses a series of processes that start with the identification of risks and proceed through the assessment, prioritization, mitigation, and monitoring of these risks. When effectively executed, risk management not only protects against potential losses but also provides a systematic approach to achieving sustainable returns. By understanding and managing the risks associated with financial investments, traders and investors can make more informed decisions, fostering greater confidence and success in their trading strategies.

## 10.2 Types of Financial Risks

Understanding the diverse array of financial risks is fundamental to developing robust risk management strategies. Financial risks can be broadly categorized into several types, each with its unique characteristics and implications. Here, we delve into the primary types of financial risks: market risk, credit risk, liquidity risk, operational risk, and legal and regulatory risk.

Market risk, often considered the most visible and immediate form of financial risk, refers to the potential for financial losses due to movements in market prices. This encompasses a range of elements, including equity risk, interest rate risk, currency risk, and commodity risk.

**Equity risk** involves the volatility in stock prices, affecting the value of stock portfolios. Investors holding equities face the uncertainty of stock price fluctuations, influenced by company performance, market sentiment, and broader economic conditions.

**Interest rate risk** captures the sensitivity of an investment's value to changes in interest rates. Fixed income instruments, such as bonds, are particularly susceptible to interest rate movements. When interest rates rise, bond prices typically fall, leading to potential losses for bondholders.

**Currency risk**, or exchange rate risk, arises from fluctuations in foreign exchange rates. Investors and companies engaged in international trade or investments face the risk that currency movements could erode the value of their foreign-denominated assets or earnings.

**Commodity risk** is related to price changes in raw materials such as oil, gold, or agricultural products. Commodity price volatility can significantly affect companies involved in the production, distribution, or consumption of these materials, impacting their profitability and market valuation.

Credit risk, another critical financial risk, involves the likelihood that a borrower will default on their financial obligations, leading to losses for the lender or investor. Credit risks are prevalent in loans, bonds, and other fixed income securities. This risk is assessed through metrics such as credit ratings and credit spreads, which indicate the perceived probability of default and the risk premium demanded by investors as compensation.

Credit risk can be further dissected into **default risk** and **downgrade risk**. Default risk is the direct risk of non-payment of interest or principal by the borrower. Downgrade risk pertains to the possibility of a deterioration in the credit quality of an issuer, leading to a drop in its credit rating. Such a downgrade can reduce the market value of the issuer's existing debt and increase future borrowing costs.

Liquidity risk emerges from the difficulty of converting assets into cash without a substantial price concession, affecting both market participants' ability to meet short-term financial obligations. This risk bifurcates into **market liquidity risk** and **funding liquidity risk**. Market liquidity risk refers to the possibility that an investor cannot quickly buy or sell an asset without significantly affecting its price, commonly seen in thinly traded markets. Funding liquidity risk, on the other hand, pertains to the risk that a financial institution cannot meet its short-term debt obligations due to an inability to access sufficient funding or liquidate assets promptly.

Operational risk encompasses the risks of loss resulting from inadequate or failed internal processes, people, systems, or external events. It is broad and includes diverse elements such as fraud, human errors, system failures, and natural disasters. Effective management of operational risk involves implementing strong internal controls, regular audits, and contingency planning to mitigate potential vulnerabilities.

Legal and regulatory risk involves the risk of financial loss due to changes in law or regulations or from non-compliance with existing rules. Legal disputes, regulatory fines, or sanctions can have substantial financial repercussions. This type of risk requires constant monitoring of regulatory environments and ensuring compliance through rigorous internal policies and procedures.

By comprehending these various types of financial risks, investors and financial professionals can develop more effective strategies to mitigate their impact. It's essential to recognize that these risks are often interconnected, and a comprehensive risk management approach must consider their interplay to safeguard against potential losses. This detailed understanding forms the backbone of successfully navigating the complexities of financial markets.

## 10.3 Risk Measures: Value at Risk (VaR)

Understanding the quantifiable limits of potential financial losses is a fundamental aspect of risk management. One of the cornerstone tools in this endeavor is the Value at Risk (VaR). VaR provides a probabilistic measure of the maximum potential loss in value of a portfolio over a defined period for a given confidence interval. This section will delve into the intricacies of VaR, exploring its definition, calculation methods, and practical applications in managing financial risk.

The primary appeal of VaR lies in its capacity to condense complex risk assessments into a single, interpretable figure. By defining a worst-case loss boundary that will not be exceeded with a specified level of confidence, VaR gives financial professionals a clear and actionable risk metric. Formally, the VaR of a portfolio can be defined as follows:

- For a given confidence level $\alpha$, the VaR is the threshold value such that the probability of a loss exceeding this value is $(1-\alpha)$. In mathematical terms, if $L$ is the loss, $\text{VaR}_\alpha$ is defined by:

$$P(L > \text{VaR}_\alpha) = 1 - \alpha$$

To improve understanding, let's consider a practical example. Assume we have a portfolio and wish to determine the one-day VaR at the 95% confidence level. If the calculated VaR is $1 million, this implies that there is only a 5% probability that the portfolio will lose more than $1 million in one day.

There are three commonly used methods to calculate VaR, each with its own strengths and limitations:

- **Historical Simulation**: The historical simulation method calculates VaR by analyzing past market data. Specifically, it involves rearranging historical returns of the portfolio and determining the loss percentile that corresponds to the chosen confidence level. This non-parametric method makes no assumptions about the return distribution, making it conceptually straightforward and easy to implement. However, its reliance on historical data can be a limitation, especially if market conditions change or if the historical period used is not representative of future dynamics. Mathematically, one can express this as:

$$\text{VaR}_\alpha = -\text{Percentile}(R, 1 - \alpha)$$

where $R$ represents the vector of historical portfolio returns.

- **Variance-Covariance (Parametric) Method**: This approach assumes that asset returns are normally distributed and leverages the mean-variance framework. First, the portfolio's expected return and standard deviation are calculated. The VaR is then derived from the properties of the normal distribution, using the portfolio's standard deviation as a measure of risk. The formula for VaR in a parametric model at confidence level $\alpha$ is:

$$\text{VaR}_\alpha = \mu + z_\alpha \sigma$$

where $\mu$ is the mean return, $\sigma$ is the standard deviation of returns, and $z_\alpha$ is the quantile of the standard normal distribution corresponding to the confidence level $\alpha$. For example, at $\alpha = 95\%$, $z_\alpha \approx -1.645$. While this method allows for ease of calculation and interpretation, its reliance on the normality assumption can be problematic as financial returns often exhibit fat tails and skewness that the normal distribution does not capture.

- **Monte Carlo Simulation**: The Monte Carlo method involves generating a large number of potential future price paths for the portfolio through random sampling. This method models the evolution of asset prices based on specified probability distributions, enabling the calculation of potential outcomes and the construction of the VaR estimate. The process typically involves:
  - Specifying the statistical properties (mean, variance, correlation) of asset returns.
  - Simulating a large number (e.g., 10,000) of random paths for portfolio returns over the specified time horizon.
  - Determining the loss distribution from these simulations and identifying the VaR at the desired confidence level.

This technique is highly flexible and can accommodate various distributional assumptions and complex dynamics. Its drawback, however, lies in its computational intensity, requiring significant processing power and time, especially for large portfolios or lengthy time horizons.

VaR provides invaluable insights, but it is not without limitations. Crucially, it does not predict the magnitude of extreme losses beyond the confidence level threshold. To address this, financial practitioners often complement VaR with measures such as Expected Shortfall (ES), which estimates the average loss given that the VaR threshold has been exceeded.

Moreover, VaR models can sometimes fail to capture tail risk effectively, particularly in markets experiencing significant turmoil or non-linear interactions among assets. Therefore, incorporating scenario analysis and stress testing into the risk management framework is essential to ensure robust risk assessment.

In practice, financial institutions employ VaR to set risk limits, allocate capital, and satisfy regulatory requirements. Banks, asset managers, and hedge funds use VaR as a standard tool for reporting and monitoring risk exposures, ensuring that they stay within acceptable boundaries. Regulatory bodies, such as the Basel Committee on Banking Supervision, also mandate the use of VaR for determining market risk capital requirements, underpinning its critical role in the financial industry's risk management practices.

Understanding and effectively implementing VaR allows financial professionals to navigate the complexities of risk with clarity and confidence, safeguarding portfolios against potential adverse movements and fostering informed decision-making rooted in quantitative analysis.

## 10.4 Expected Shortfall

Expected Shortfall (ES), also known as Conditional Value at Risk (CVaR), is a sophisticated risk measure that augments the insights provided by Value at Risk (VaR). While VaR quantifies the maximum potential loss over a specified time period with a certain confidence level, it fails to address the severity of losses beyond this threshold. Expected Shortfall, on the other hand, focuses on the tail end of the loss distribution, providing a more comprehensive view of potential extreme losses.

To begin, let's formally define Expected Shortfall. For a given confidence level $\alpha$, Expected Shortfall $\text{ES}_\alpha$ is the expected loss given that the loss is beyond the VaR threshold at $\alpha$. Mathematically, this can be represented as follows:

$$\text{ES}_\alpha = E[L \mid L > \text{VaR}_\alpha]$$

where $L$ represents the loss. This notion of conditioning on the loss exceeding VaR is crucial because it captures the tail risk, which is often a significant concern for portfolio managers and regulatory bodies.

**Calculating Expected Shortfall**

There are several methods to calculate Expected Shortfall, including historical simulation, parametric methods, and Monte Carlo simulation. Each approach has its strengths and practical considerations.

- **Historical Simulation** involves using actual historical data to construct the loss distribution. This method is straightforward and does not assume any specific distribution for losses. The steps are:
  - Gather historical returns data.
  - Calculate the loss percentage for each data point.
  - Determine the $\alpha$ percentile loss (i.e., VaR).
  - Average the losses that exceed this VaR threshold.

  For example, if we consider the worst 5% of the historical losses (for a 95% confidence level), the average of these losses would give us ES at 95%.

- **Parametric Methods** assume a specific probability distribution for losses, commonly a normal distribution. Given the mean $\mu$ and standard deviation $\sigma$ of the distribution, VaR is computed as:

  $$\text{VaR}_\alpha = \mu + \sigma\Phi^{-1}(\alpha)$$

  where $\Phi^{-1}$ is the inverse of the standard normal cumulative distribution function. Expected Shortfall under the normal distribution can then be derived as:

  $$\text{ES}_\alpha = \frac{\sigma \exp\left(-\frac{1}{2}(\Phi^{-1}(\alpha))^2\right)}{\alpha\sqrt{2\pi}} + \mu$$

This method's elegance lies in its simplicity and closed-form solution, though it may not capture tails accurately if the true distribution of returns exhibits fat tails.

- **Monte Carlo Simulation** offers a more flexible approach, especially when dealing with non-normally distributed returns or complex portfolio structures. The process involves:

  - Generating a large number of potential loss scenarios based on the statistical properties of the portfolio's returns.
  - Calculating the loss for each scenario.
  - Determining the VaR and averaging the losses that exceed this VaR threshold.

  Monte Carlo methods are computationally intensive but very powerful, capturing a wide range of possible loss distributions and scenarios.

**Advantages and Disadvantages of Expected Shortfall**

Expected Shortfall offers several advantages over traditional VaR:

- **Greater Sensitivity to Tail Risk:** By focusing on the distribution tail, ES provides a clearer picture of extreme losses, which are critical yet often neglected in VaR analysis.
- **Coherent Risk Measure:** Expected Shortfall satisfies the properties of a coherent risk measure—monotonicity, subadditivity, homogeneity, and translational invariance. This coherence is an essential feature for risk aggregation and diversification analysis across portfolios.

However, despite its benefits, ES has some limitations:

- **Computational Complexity:** Calculating ES, particularly via Monte Carlo simulation, can be computationally demanding, requiring significant processing power and time.
- **Data Dependency:** Like all empirical methods, ES results can be heavily influenced by the quality and quantity of historical data, potentially leading to skewed estimates in times of low data availability or rapidly changing market conditions.

### Practical Application in Portfolio Management

Portfolio managers use Expected Shortfall to enhance their risk assessment frameworks, ensuring that portfolios are resilient against significant downturns. For example, in stress testing scenarios, ES is employed to gauge the impact of extreme but plausible adverse conditions on portfolio values. Integrating ES into the risk management process involves:

- **Routine Calculation:** Regularly computing ES at multiple confidence levels to monitor the portfolio's risk profile over time.
- **Setting Risk Limits:** Establishing policy limits based on ES metrics, thereby enforcing a ceiling on the acceptable level of tail risk.
- **Scenario Analysis:** Using ES to assess potential losses under different stressed market conditions and evaluate the adequacy of risk mitigation strategies.

By adopting Expected Shortfall as a complement to VaR, portfolio managers gain a more holistic view of risk, enabling more informed and strategic decision-making under uncertainty.

In conclusion, Expected Shortfall addresses the limitations of VaR by focusing on the magnitude of losses in the tail of the distribution. Its ability to provide a clearer picture of tail risks makes it an indispensable tool for risk management in quantitative finance. Though it requires careful implementation and computational resources, the insights it offers are invaluable for safeguarding against extreme market downturns and enhancing overall portfolio resilience.

## 10.5 Stress Testing

Stress testing is a fundamental aspect of risk management, designed to evaluate how a portfolio or financial institution might perform under extreme but plausible adverse conditions. This practice helps identify potential vulnerabilities and prepares investors and managers to mitigate risks effectively.

Stress testing begins by modeling hypothetical scenarios that reflect severe market conditions. These scenarios, though unlikely, should be based on historical crises, economic downturns, or other significant disruptive events. The primary objective is to assess the resilience of portfolios and risk management strategies.

To conduct stress testing, the following steps and methodologies are typically employed:

- 1. **Defining Scenarios**: Scenarios can be constructed using historical data or hypothetical constructs. Historical scenarios replicate past events such as the 2008 financial crisis or the Dot-com bubble burst. Hypothetical scenarios, on the other hand, are created to simulate extreme events like a sudden geopolitical crisis or an abrupt change in monetary policy. Define scenarios by specifying key variables such as stock prices, interest rates, and exchange rates, and consider their plausible shifts under stressful conditions.

- 2. **Modeling the Impact**: For each scenario, estimate the potential impact on the portfolio. This involves recalculating portfolio values and returns by integrating the defined stress parameters into financial models. Various quantitative techniques may be utilized, ranging from simple sensitivity analysis to complex stochastic models. Use of linear and non-linear regression models, Monte Carlo simulations, and copula functions are prevalent in assessing these impacts.

- 3. **Measuring Vulnerability**: Post modeling, the vulnerability of the portfolio is gauged through several risk metrics. Standard metrics include changes in Value at Risk (VaR) and Expected Shortfall (ES). Evaluate these metrics to understand potential losses and the likelihood of extreme adverse outcomes. This analysis helps to quantify the worst-case scenarios and the extent of potential financial damage.

- 4. **Interpreting Results**: Interpretation of stress test results focuses on identifying weaknesses and potential failure points within the portfolio. Analyze the results to understand which assets or strategies are most susceptible to stress conditions. This step is crucial for making informed decisions about risk mitigation and portfolio adjustments.

- 5. **Implementing Mitigation Strategies**: Based on the results, develop strategies to mitigate identified risks. This might involve rebalancing the portfolio, increasing hedging activities, or reducing exposure to high-risk assets. The goal is to ensure that the portfolio remains resilient under adverse conditions.

$$\text{Stress Testing Results} = Portfolio_{\text{Baseline}} - Portfolio_{\text{Stress}}$$

The equation above illustrates the difference between the baseline portfolio value and the stressed portfolio value. The resulting value provides a clear measure of potential loss under the specified stress scenario.

- 6. **Continuous Monitoring and Updating**: Stress testing is not a one-time exercise but an ongoing process. Regularly update scenarios to reflect evolving market conditions and new financial products. Continuous monitoring ensures that the risk management framework remains robust and adaptive to changing market dynamics.

Stress tests also align with regulatory requirements, as financial regulatory bodies mandate periodic stress testing to ensure the financial system's stability. Compliance with standards such as Basel III for banks and Solvency II for insurers requires adherence to stringent stress testing protocols.

Using these methodologies, financial institutions can enhance their preparedness for unforeseen market disruptions. By systematically simulating adverse conditions, stress testing provides a comprehensive understanding of potential risks and fortifies the resilience of investment strategies.

Ultimately, stress testing is a proactive risk management tool that empowers investors and financial institutions to anticipate and navigate through turbulent market periods, ensuring sustainable growth and stability.

## 10.6 Scenario Analysis

Scenario analysis is a robust technique used in risk management to evaluate the potential impact of various hypothetical events on an investment portfolio or financial position. By considering a wide range of possible scenarios, investors can better understand potential risks and make informed decisions to mitigate them. This section explores the fundamentals of scenario analysis, its application in quantitative finance, and practical steps for implementing it effectively.

Scenario analysis involves formulating different scenarios based on plausible economic, market, or idiosyncratic events. These scenarios are then used to assess the sensitivity of a portfolio or financial instrument to adverse conditions. Unlike stress testing, which often focuses on extreme but plausible events, scenario analysis considers a broader spectrum of outcomes, encompassing both adverse and favorable conditions.

To start, identify key risk factors that significantly influence the assets within your portfolio. Common factors include interest rates, currency exchange rates, commodity prices, credit spreads, and equity market returns. Once identified, develop various hypothetical scenarios that reflect potential changes in these risk factors. Scenarios should range from expected conditions to worst-case and best-case scenarios to capture the entire spectrum of potential outcomes.

Formulating scenarios involves both qualitative and quantitative approaches. Qualitative scenarios are based on expert judgment, historical analysis, and hypothetical situations. Quantitative scenarios, on the other hand, leverage statistical methods and models to simulate changes in risk factors. Combining both approaches provides a comprehensive view of potential outcomes.

To illustrate, let's consider a portfolio comprising stocks, bonds, and commodities. Suppose we identify three key risk factors: interest rates, equity market returns, and oil prices. We might develop the following scenarios:

- **Scenario 1: Economic Recession** - Interest rates drop by 100 basis points, equity markets decline by 20%, and oil prices fall by 30%.
- **Scenario 2: Market Boom** - Interest rates rise by 50 basis points, equity markets increase by 25%, and oil prices surge by 20%.
- **Scenario 3: Inflation Surge** - Interest rates increase by 150 basis points, equity markets decline by 10%, and oil prices rise by 50%.

For each scenario, simulate the potential impact on the portfolio. Calculate changes in the value of each asset and the overall portfolio value. This allows you to assess the sensitivity of the portfolio to different conditions and identify any vulnerabilities. The results can be summarized in the following manner:

| Scenario | Interest Rates (% Change) | Equity Markets (% Change) | Oil Prices (% Change) |
|---|---|---|---|
| Economic Recession | -1.00% | -20.00% | -30.00% |
| Market Boom | +0.50% | +25.00% | +20.00% |
| Inflation Surge | +1.50% | -10.00% | +50.00% |

Table 10.1: Impact of Different Scenarios on Key Risk Factors

By analyzing the results, we can determine which scenarios pose the greatest risk to the portfolio and identify potential strategies for mitigating those risks. For instance, if the portfolio is highly sensitive to interest rate increases, an investor might consider hedging with interest rate derivatives or reallocating assets to less interest-rate-sensitive instruments.

Furthermore, scenario analysis provides insight into tail risks—events that are unlikely but have a significant impact if they occur. Understanding these tail risks is crucial for comprehensive risk management, particularly in environments characterized by high uncertainty or volatility.

Implementing scenario analysis involves a clear and systematic approach:

- **Identification of Key Risk Factors:** Determine the primary variables that influence the value of your portfolio.
- **Development of Scenarios:** Formulate a range of plausible scenarios, encompassing different combinations of changes in the identified risk factors.
- **Simulation and Analysis:** Use financial models to simulate the impact of each scenario on your portfolio, calculating potential changes in value.
- **Assessment and Mitigation:** Evaluate the results to identify vulnerabilities and formulate strategies to mitigate adverse impacts, such as diversification or hedging.

In quantitative finance, scenario analysis can be further enhanced by incorporating advanced modeling techniques, such as Monte Carlo simulation, which allows for the simulation of thousands of scenarios based on probabilistic models. This provides a more comprehensive view of potential outcomes and aids in the probabilistic assessment of risks.

In summary, scenario analysis plays a critical role in understanding the range of potential risks a portfolio may face and aids in developing strategies to manage these risks effectively. By systematically analyzing different scenarios, investors gain valuable insights into the resilience of their portfolios and can take proactive measures to mitigate adverse impacts, thereby fostering a more robust and adaptable investment strategy.

## 10.7 Risk-Adjusted Return Metrics

In the realm of quantitative finance, understanding and optimizing returns in the context of risk is paramount. Risk-adjusted return metrics serve as crucial tools for assessing the performance of an investment portfolio by taking into account the amount of risk taken to achieve those returns. This section delves into some of the most widely used risk-adjusted return metrics, specifically focusing on the Sharpe Ratio, Sortino Ratio, and the Information Ratio.

**Sharpe Ratio**

Developed by William F. Sharpe, the Sharpe Ratio is one of the foundational risk-adjusted return metrics. It measures the excess return per unit of risk of an investment asset or portfolio, aiding investors in understanding how well the return of an asset compensates for the risk taken.

The formula for the Sharpe Ratio is:

$$\text{Sharpe Ratio} = \frac{R_p - R_f}{\sigma_p}$$

where $R_p$ represents the expected portfolio return, $R_f$ is the risk-free rate, and $\sigma_p$ is the standard deviation of the portfolio's excess return.

The Sharpe Ratio is invaluable because it provides a single metric to compare the performance of different portfolios or assets. A higher Sharpe Ratio indicates better risk-adjusted performance. Typically, a ratio above 1 is considered acceptable, above 2 is deemed very good, and above 3 is excellent.

**Sortino Ratio**

While the Sharpe Ratio considers the total volatility of returns, the Sortino Ratio differentiates between harmful volatility (downside risk) and overall volatility (as measured by the Sharpe Ratio). The Sortino Ratio emphasizes the downside deviation, thus providing a more realistic assessment for portfolios where negative returns are especially detrimental.

The formula for the Sortino Ratio is:

$$\text{Sortino Ratio} = \frac{R_p - R_f}{\sigma_D}$$

where $\sigma_D$ is the downside deviation, which considers only the negative asset returns relative to a minimum acceptable return (MAR).

The Sortino Ratio is particularly useful for investors who are more concerned about downside risks rather than overall volatility. By focusing on downside risk, the Sortino Ratio offers a clearer view of how an investment is performing relative to risk without penalizing upside variability.

**Information Ratio**

The Information Ratio (IR) gauges the risk-adjusted return of an active portfolio relative to a benchmark, reflecting the consistency of excess return generated by the portfolio manager.

The formula for the Information Ratio is:

$$\text{Information Ratio} = \frac{R_p - R_b}{\sigma_{(R_p - R_b)}}$$

where $R_p$ is the return of the portfolio, $R_b$ is the return of the benchmark, and $\sigma_{(R_p - R_b)}$ is the tracking error, or standard deviation of the difference between portfolio return and benchmark return.

A higher Information Ratio indicates that the portfolio manager has been able to generate higher returns relative to the benchmark, given the level of risk undertaken. It is a vital metric for evaluating the performance of actively managed funds against their benchmarks.

**Practical Applications of Risk-Adjusted Return Metrics**

Incorporating risk-adjusted return metrics into portfolio management assists investors in making more informed decisions. For instance, when comparing two portfolios, if one portfolio has a higher Sharpe Ratio but the other has a higher Sortino Ratio, an investor concerned mainly about potential losses might prefer the latter. Similarly, for those evaluating active fund managers, the Information Ratio can provide insights into the manager's ability to deliver consistent performance above the benchmark.

Quantitative models frequently integrate these metrics to optimize portfolios. For example, in the context of mean-variance optimization, the Sharpe Ratio can help in selecting the efficient frontier – the set of portfolios offering the highest expected return for a given level of risk. Tailored strategies such as targeted downside risk-adjustment using the Sortino Ratio can be particularly beneficial in volatile markets.

Ultimately, mastering these risk-adjusted return metrics equips investors with robust tools to balance the pursuit of returns and the caution warranted by risk. By integrating these metrics into their analysis, investors can enhance decision-making, leading to more resilient and potentially more profitable investment strategies.

## 10.8 Portfolio Risk Management

Effective portfolio risk management is crucial for achieving durable investment success. It integrates various tools and techniques to assess and mitigate risks inherent in a portfolio of financial assets. This section explores fundamental principles and strategies used by quants and investment managers to ensure that the risk in their portfolios is understood and managed in line with their investment goals and risk tolerance.

A cornerstone of portfolio risk management is diversification, a strategy designed to spread risk by investing in a variety of assets with low correlations. The fundamental idea is that the negative performance of some assets will be offset by the positive performance of others, thereby reducing the overall portfolio risk. Mathematically, diversification is quantified using metrics like the covariance and correlation coefficients between the returns of different assets.

$$\text{Cov}(X, Y) = E[(X - \mu_X)(Y - \mu_Y)]$$

$$\rho_{X,Y} = \frac{\text{Cov}(X, Y)}{\sigma_X \sigma_Y}$$

Here, $\text{Cov}(X, Y)$ represents the covariance between the returns of assets $X$ and $Y$, which measures the degree to which they move together. The correlation coefficient $\rho_{X,Y}$ normalizes this relationship, providing a value between -1 and 1.

Beyond diversification, quants also employ sophisticated risk modeling techniques to understand and control the risk profile of their portfolios. One common approach is the use of risk-factor models, which decompose portfolio returns into components attributable to various risk factors such as market, size, value, and momentum.

$$R_p = \alpha_p + \beta_{pm} R_m + \beta_{ps} S + \beta_{pv} V + \beta_{pmom} M + \epsilon_p$$

In this equation, $R_p$ represents the portfolio return, $\alpha_p$ is the portfolio's alpha (or idiosyncratic return), $R_m$ is the return on the market portfolio, and $S$, $V$, $M$ are returns due to size, value, and momentum factors, respectively. The coefficients $\beta_{pm}$, $\beta_{ps}$, $\beta_{pv}$, and $\beta_{pmom}$ are the sensitivities of the portfolio to these risk factors. $\epsilon_p$ represents the error term or the part of return not explained by these factors.

Quantitative portfolio managers often optimize the risk-return profile of a portfolio using Mean-Variance Optimization (MVO), introduced by Harry Markowitz. The MVO framework helps in finding the efficient frontier—a set of optimal portfolios offering the highest expected return for a given level of risk, as quantified by the portfolio variance.

$$\min_w \sigma_p^2 = w^T \Sigma w$$

$$\text{subject to} \quad w^T \mathbf{1} = 1 \quad \text{and} \quad E[R_p] = w^T \mu$$

In the above optimization problem, $w$ represents the portfolio weights, $\Sigma$ is the covariance matrix of asset returns, and $\mu$ is the vector of expected returns. The goal is to minimize the portfolio variance $\sigma_p^2$ while satisfying the constraints that the sum of the weights equals 1 (full investment constraint) and targeting a certain expected return.

Stress testing and scenario analysis further enrich the portfolio risk management toolkit, allowing quants to simulate the impact of extreme but plausible adverse market conditions on the portfolio. These tests help in understanding potential vulnerabilities and preparing responses to market shocks.

Risk measures like Value at Risk (VaR) and Expected Shortfall (ES) are also instrumental in portfolio risk management. These measures quantify the potential loss in portfolio value over a specified period under normal market conditions.

Hedging strategies are another critical element, employed to offset potential losses in a portfolio. Hedging might involve the use of derivatives such as options, futures, or swaps. The goal is to create a risk profile that better matches the investment objectives and risk appetite of the investor.

Finally, it's imperative to continuously monitor and reassess the risk profile of a portfolio. As market conditions evolve and new data becomes available, quants need to re-evaluate their models and optimization strategies to adapt to changing circumstances. This dynamic aspect of portfolio risk management ensures that risk is consistently aligned with the investment strategy.

Managing portfolio risk is not a one-time task but a continuous process of evaluation, adjustment, and optimization. This ensures that the portfolio remains resilient against a variety of market conditions while aiming to achieve the desired financial goals.

## 10.9 Hedging Strategies

Hedging is a critical aspect of risk management in quantitative finance, enabling traders and investors to mitigate potential losses due to unfavorable market movements. A well-constructed hedging strategy reduces an investment's exposure to various risks, thus providing a level of insurance against adverse conditions. In this section, we will explore several hedging techniques, the instruments used, and the practical application of these strategies in a quantitative finance context.

Hedging strategies often employ derivatives such as options, futures, and swaps. These financial instruments derive their value from underlying assets such as stocks, bonds, commodities, or interest rates.

**Options:**

An option is a contract that gives the buyer the right, but not the obligation, to buy or sell an underlying asset at a predetermined price (strike price) before or on a specific date (expiration date). There are two main types of options: calls and puts. Call options give the holder the right to buy the asset, while put options allow the holder to sell the asset. By strategically purchasing or selling options, traders can construct positions that limit potential losses while still enabling gains.

Consider the use of *protective puts*, also known as married puts. This strategy involves buying a put option for an asset that an investor already owns. The put option acts as a floor, limiting the maximum potential loss. If the asset's price drops, the gain from the put option offsets the loss in the asset value.

Another common strategy is the *covered call*, where an investor holds a long position in an asset and sells a call option on the same asset. This allows the investor to generate additional income from the option premium, which can cushion against minor losses in the underlying asset.

**Futures:**

Futures contracts are agreements to buy or sell an asset at a specified price on a future date. They are standardized, traded on exchanges, and commonly used for hedging purposes. For instance, an investor with a portfolio of stocks might use equity index futures to hedge against market downturns. By selling futures contracts on a stock index, the investor can offset losses in the portfolio if the market declines.

$$futures\ price = spot\ price(1 + r - q) \tag{10.1}$$

where $r$ is the risk-free rate, and $q$ is the dividend yield of the underlying asset.

**Swaps:**

Swaps are derivative contracts in which two parties exchange cash flows or financial instruments. In the context of hedging, interest rate swaps are particularly useful. For example, an institution with floating-rate debt might enter into an interest rate swap to exchange its variable interest payments for fixed payments, thereby locking in a predictable interest expense.

**Delta Hedging:**

Delta hedging involves managing a portfolio's delta, which measures its sensitivity to changes in the price of an underlying asset. By holding derivatives such as options, traders can adjust the portfolio's delta to be neutral, meaning that small movements in the underlying asset's price have minimal impact on the portfolio's value.

The delta $\Delta$ of an option is given by:

$$\Delta = \frac{\partial V}{\partial S} \tag{10.2}$$

where $V$ is the option's value and $S$ is the spot price of the underlying asset.

A delta-neutral portfolio is constructed by taking positions in options and the underlying asset so that the overall delta is zero. As the market fluctuates, the portfolio is rebalanced to maintain this neutrality, effectively insulating it from small price changes.

**Hedging with Diversification:**

In addition to derivative-based strategies, diversification is a fundamental risk management tool. By investing in a range of assets across different sectors, geographies, and asset classes, investors can reduce the impact of adverse movements in any single asset. Diversification reduces unsystematic risk, which is specific to individual investments.

**Practical Application in Quantitative Finance:**

Quantitative finance leverages mathematical models and algorithms to develop and execute hedging strategies. For example, a risk management algorithm might dynamically adjust a portfolio's composition to maintain a target risk level, incorporating real-time market data and predictive analytics.

Consider a quantitative strategy utilizing the Black-Scholes model to price options. The model provides a theoretical framework for estimating option prices and Greeks, which are essential for delta hedging and other option-based strategies.

The Black-Scholes formula for a European call option is:

$$C = S_0 N(d_1) - K e^{-rT} N(d_2) \tag{10.3}$$

where:

$$d_1 = \frac{\ln(S_0/K) + (r + \sigma^2/2)T}{\sigma\sqrt{T}}$$

$$d_2 = d_1 - \sigma\sqrt{T}$$

In these equations, $S_0$ is the current stock price, $K$ is the strike price, $r$ is the risk-free interest rate, $T$ is the time to expiration, and $\sigma$ is the volatility of the stock. $N(d)$ represents the cumulative distribution function of the standard normal distribution.

Quantitative models facilitate more sophisticated hedging techniques, such as constructing synthetic options or using machine learning algorithms to predict market movements and dynamically adjust hedge positions in response.

By employing these hedging strategies, quantitative finance professionals can manage risk more effectively, optimizing portfolios for better risk-adjusted returns and ensuring greater stability in unpredictable markets.

## 10.10 Regulatory Requirements and Compliance

In the modern landscape of quantitative finance and algorithmic trading, adhering to regulatory requirements and maintaining compliance is paramount. Financial regulations are designed to ensure market integrity, protect investors, and reduce systemic risk. This section delves into the critical aspects of regulatory requirements and compliance that every quantitative trader and financial institution must understand and implement.

Understanding regulatory frameworks begins with recognizing the key regulatory bodies that govern financial markets. Some of the prominent ones include the U.S. Securities and Exchange Commission (SEC), the Commodity Futures Trading Commission (CFTC), and international bodies such as the Financial Conduct Authority (FCA) in the UK and the European Securities and Markets Authority (ESMA) in the European Union. Each of these organizations enforces a wide range of rules aimed at ensuring fair and transparent market practices.

Compliance with these regulations requires a robust internal framework. This involves establishing comprehensive compliance programs that can adapt to evolving regulations. These programs ideally consist of several components such as risk assessments, compliance monitoring, and internal audits. The effectiveness of a compliance program hinges on its ability to integrate seamlessly with the firm's operations while providing clear guidelines and reporting mechanisms.

One critical element of regulatory compliance is adhering to the requirements set forth by the Dodd-Frank Wall Street Reform and Consumer Protection Act. Enacted in response to the financial crisis of 2007-2008, Dodd-Frank introduced sweeping reforms aimed at reducing risk in the financial system. Among its key provisions are stricter capital requirements, enhanced transparency, and mandatory clearing of certain derivatives trades. Ensuring compliance with Dodd-Frank involves meticulous record-keeping, regular reporting to regulatory bodies, and maintaining sufficient capital reserves.

The Markets in Financial Instruments Directive II (MiFID II) is another cornerstone regulation designed to increase transparency across the EU financial markets and standardize regulatory disclosures. MiFID II extends the scope of its predecessor, MiFID, by covering a broader range of financial instruments and imposing stricter reporting and transaction-tracking obligations. Compliance with MiFID II necessitates robust data management systems capable of capturing and storing detailed transaction data, as well as the ability to process and report this data efficiently.

Algorithmic trading, in particular, is subject to stringent oversight due to its potential to contribute to market volatility. Regulations such as the Market Abuse Regulation (MAR) aim to prevent market manipulation and ensure the integrity of financial markets. This regulation mandates that firms engaging in algorithmic trading have pre-trade and post-trade controls in place, along with effective risk management strategies to mitigate potential adverse impacts.

Another significant aspect of compliance is understanding and adhering to anti-money laundering (AML) regulations. AML laws require financial institutions to implement systems for detecting and reporting suspicious activities that may be indicative of money laundering or terrorist financing. This includes customer due diligence procedures, maintaining transaction records, and filing reports with financial intelligence units. Advanced machine learning algorithms can be employed to enhance the effectiveness of AML compliance by identifying unusual patterns that may warrant further investigation.

In addition to implementing these compliance measures, continuous education and training of staff are vital. Ensuring that all employees understand the importance of compliance and are familiar with the applicable regulations helps create a culture of compliance within the organization. Regular training sessions and updates on regulatory changes are crucial to keep everyone informed and prepared to meet these obligations.

The role of technology in achieving compliance cannot be understated. Regulatory technology, or RegTech, encompasses a variety of tools and applications designed to streamline the compliance process. These tools can automate data collection, analytics, and reporting, thereby reducing the burden on compliance teams and increasing efficiency.

Finally, strong governance and oversight are essential components of effective compliance. This involves establishing clear roles and responsibilities within the organization, with a designated compliance officer or team responsible for overseeing adherence to regulatory requirements. Regular reviews and updates to compliance policies and procedures ensure they remain aligned with current regulations.

Through meticulous adherence to regulatory requirements and the establishment of a robust compliance framework, financial institutions can minimize risk, protect their reputation, and contribute to the overall stability of the financial market. By proactively addressing regulatory challenges, quants and traders not only safeguard their operations but also enhance their capacity for sustainable growth in a complex and dynamic market environment.

# Chapter 11

# Optimization Techniques

**This chapter discusses optimization techniques critical for enhancing financial models and strategies. It covers various methods including linear programming, quadratic programming, and convex optimization. Topics such as integer programming and derivative-free optimization methods are explored. The chapter also introduces gradient descent and its variants, along with Bayesian optimization. Application areas include portfolio management and algorithmic trading, demonstrating the practical use of optimization techniques in finance.**

## 11.1 What is Optimization?

The concept of optimization is paramount in the domain of financial modeling and quantitative trading. Optimization refers to the process of finding the best solution from all feasible solutions, with the aim of maximizing or minimizing a particular objective function. In finance, this could involve maximizing returns, minimizing risk, or achieving an optimal balance of multiple competing factors. This section explores the foundational principles of optimization and its critical role in developing robust quantitative strategies.

In the context of quantitative finance, optimization techniques allow quants to systematically and efficiently identify the best possible parameters for their trading models. These techniques ensure that financial models are not only theoretically sound but also practically viable in real-world trading scenarios. By leveraging optimization, financial analysts can navigate through vast datasets and complex mathematical structures to derive actionable insights and strategies.

At its core, optimization problems are characterized by three primary components:

- **Objective Function:** This is the function that needs to be maximized or minimized. For instance, in portfolio management, the objective might be to maximize the expected return or to minimize the portfolio's risk.
- **Decision Variables:** These are the variables that can be adjusted to achieve the optimal solution. In trading, these might include asset weights in a portfolio, trading frequencies, or model parameters.
- **Constraints:** These are the restrictions or limitations imposed on the decision variables. Constraints ensure that the solutions are feasible under specified conditions, such as budget limits, regulatory requirements, or risk tolerances.

Optimization problems can be classified in various ways, depending on the nature of the objective function, the decision variables, and the constraints. Some of the primary classifications include:

**1. Linear vs. Non-linear Optimization:**

- *Linear Optimization* involves an objective function and constraints that are linear. These problems can often be solved using well-established methods such as the Simplex algorithm.
- *Non-linear Optimization* deals with at least one non-linear component in either the objective function or the constraints. These problems are generally more complex and require specialized algorithms for solution.

**2. Convex vs. Non-convex Optimization:**

- *Convex Optimization* problems are a subset of non-linear optimization where the objective function is convex, and the feasible region defined by the constraints is a convex set. These problems are generally easier to solve because any local minimum is also a global minimum.

- *Non-convex Optimization* involves objective functions or constraints that form a non-convex space, making the identification of global optima more challenging. These require more sophisticated techniques such as global optimization algorithms.

**3. Integer vs. Continuous Optimization:**

- *Integer Optimization* problems involve decision variables that are restricted to integer values. This is common in situations where divisible solutions are not practical, such as asset allocation in fixed amounts.

- *Continuous Optimization* problems allow the decision variables to take any value within a specified range. These are more common in financial modeling where continuous adjustments are feasible and necessary.

The importance of optimization in finance cannot be overstated. It provides a structured approach to decision-making that ensures that financial strategies are both effective and efficient. A few practical applications include optimizing the weightings of assets in a portfolio to achieve the highest expected return for a given level of risk, calibrating the parameters of algorithmic trading models to maximize profit while controlling for drawdowns, and determining the optimal hedging strategy to minimize the risk of adverse price movements.

By employing optimization methods, quants can systematically derive solutions that would be otherwise unattainable through intuition or heuristic methods. Furthermore, the integration of advanced optimization techniques with machine learning models has the potential to enhance predictive capabilities significantly, leading to more sophisticated and profitable trading strategies.

Through the subsequent sections, we will delve deeper into specific optimization techniques such as linear programming, quadratic programming, and gradient descent. We'll explore the mathematical foundations of these methods along with their practical applications in trading and investing, illustrating how optimization serves as a cornerstone of modern quantitative finance.

## 11.2 Linear Programming

Linear programming (LP) is a mathematical approach used for optimizing a linear objective function, subject to linear equality and inequality constraints. This method is fundamental in financial modeling and can be employed in a myriad of situations, ranging from portfolio optimization to resource allocation in trading systems. As we delve into linear programming, it is essential to understand its structure, formulation, and application in the financial domain.

At its core, linear programming involves maximizing or minimizing a linear objective function:

$$\text{maximize} \quad \boldsymbol{c}^\top \boldsymbol{x}$$

or

$$\text{minimize} \quad \boldsymbol{c}^\top \boldsymbol{x}$$

subject to constraints of the form:

$$\boldsymbol{A}\boldsymbol{x} \leq \boldsymbol{b}$$

where:

- $c$ is a coefficient vector representing the objective function's coefficients,
- $\boldsymbol{x}$ is the vector of decision variables,
- $\boldsymbol{A}$ is a matrix of constraint coefficients,
- $b$ is a vector representing the constraint bounds.

Understanding the terminology associated with linear programming is essential for grasping its application. Here is a brief overview:

- **Objective Function**: The function that needs to be optimized (maximized or minimized). In finance, this could represent returns, risk, or cost.
- **Decision Variables**: The variables we want to solve for, such as the allocation of assets in a portfolio.
- **Constraints**: These are the restrictions or limitations on the decision variables, often defined by resource availability, risk tolerance, or regulatory requirements.

- **Feasible Region**: The set of all possible values of decision variables that satisfies all constraints. Any point within this region is a feasible solution.
- **Optimization**: The process of finding the best solution within the feasible region that optimizes the objective function.

Let's consider a practical example in portfolio optimization where we aim to maximize returns given specific constraints such as budget limits and risk tolerance.

Assume we have $n$ different financial assets, each with a known return $r_i$. We wish to allocate $x_i$ proportions of our total investment to each asset. Our objective can be formulated as:

$$\text{maximize} \quad \sum_{i=1}^{n} r_i x_i$$

subject to:

$$\sum_{i=1}^{n} x_i = 1 \quad \text{(all investment sums to total capital)},$$

$$\boldsymbol{Ax} \leq \boldsymbol{b} \quad \text{(additional constraints, e.g., risk limits)},$$

$$x_i \geq 0 \quad \forall i \quad \text{(no short selling)}.$$

Several methods can solve linear programming problems, with the Simplex algorithm being among the most widely used due to its efficiency and effectiveness for a large number of practical problems. In addition, modern LP solvers utilize interior-point methods which are advantageous for large-scale problems.

**Simplex Method Overview**:

- Start at a feasible vertex of the polytope defined by the constraints.
- Move along the edges of the polytope to adjacent vertices, improving the objective function value at each step.
- Terminate when an optimal vertex (best possible value for the objective function under the given constraints) is found.

**Interior-Point Methods**:

- Traverse the interior of the feasible region rather than its edges.
- Use advanced mathematical techniques to efficiently approach the optimal solution.

Linear programming is particularly well-suited for constructing optimal portfolios. By defining a clear objective (such as maximizing returns or minimizing risk) and incorporating various investment constraints (such as budget, risk tolerance, and regulatory requirements), investors can create portfolios that meet their specific needs and goals.

For instance, leveraging LP in portfolio management might involve defining a risk factor like standard deviation or Value at Risk (VaR) and setting constraints based on these measures. Optimizing the weights of different assets to achieve the highest expected returns while conforming to the risk constraints can provide a robust investment strategy.

Linear programming also plays a critical role in the development of trading strategies, especially in algorithmic trading. For market making, LP can help in determining the optimal bid and ask prices within an order book, ensuring minimal exposure and maximal profit. It allows traders to set price bounds and volume constraints, achieving a balance between liquidity provision and risk management.

In conclusion, linear programming provides a powerful, methodical approach to solving optimization problems in finance. Its versatility and efficiency make it an indispensable tool in both theoretical and practical aspects of portfolio management and trading strategies. Understanding the intricacies of LP and its application in financial problems enables investors and traders to develop more effective and optimized solutions.

## 11.3 Quadratic Programming

Quadratic programming (QP) is a powerful mathematical tool used for optimizing a quadratic objective function, subject to linear constraints. In financial modeling and algorithmic trading, QP finds extensive application owing to its ability to handle portfolio optimization problems efficiently.

A quadratic programming problem can be stated in the following form:

$$\underset{x}{\text{minimize}} \quad \frac{1}{2}\boldsymbol{x}^T\boldsymbol{Q}\boldsymbol{x} + \boldsymbol{c}^T\boldsymbol{x}$$

$$\text{subject to} \quad \boldsymbol{A}\boldsymbol{x} \leq \boldsymbol{b}, \quad \boldsymbol{E}\boldsymbol{x} = \boldsymbol{d},$$

where:

- $\boldsymbol{x} \in \mathbb{R}^n$ is the vector of decision variables,
- $\boldsymbol{Q} \in \mathbb{R}^{n\times n}$ is a symmetric positive semidefinite matrix which represents the quadratic coefficients,
- $\boldsymbol{c} \in \mathbb{R}^n$ is a vector of linear coefficients,
- $\boldsymbol{A} \in \mathbb{R}^{m\times n}$ and $\boldsymbol{E} \in \mathbb{R}^{p\times n}$ are matrices representing the coefficients of the inequality and equality constraints, respectively,
- $\boldsymbol{b} \in \mathbb{R}^m$ and $\boldsymbol{d} \in \mathbb{R}^p$ are vectors representing the bounds of the inequality and equality constraints, respectively.

The primary objective of QP is to find a vector $\boldsymbol{x}$ that minimizes the quadratic objective function while satisfying the specified constraints.

**Key Concepts in Quadratic Programming**

- **Quadratic Objective Function:** The objective function $\frac{1}{2}\boldsymbol{x}^T\boldsymbol{Q}\boldsymbol{x}+\boldsymbol{c}^T\boldsymbol{x}$ consists of a quadratic term $\frac{1}{2}\boldsymbol{x}^T\boldsymbol{Q}\boldsymbol{x}$ and a linear term $\boldsymbol{c}^T\boldsymbol{x}$.
- **Constraints:** Linear inequality constraints $\boldsymbol{A}\boldsymbol{x} \leq \boldsymbol{b}$ ensure that the solution lies within specific bounds, whereas linear equality constraints $\boldsymbol{E}\boldsymbol{x} = \boldsymbol{d}$ enforce strict conditions that the solution must satisfy.
- **Positive Semidefinite Matrix:** The matrix $\boldsymbol{Q}$ must be positive semidefinite (i.e., all its eigenvalues must be non-negative). This characteristic ensures convexity of the objective function, making it possible to find a global minimum efficiently.

**Applications in Finance**

In finance, quadratic programming is particularly useful in portfolio optimization. One of the most common applications is the Markowitz Mean-Variance Optimization model. This model aims to minimize the portfolio variance (risk) for a given level of expected return.

**Markowitz Mean-Variance Optimization Model:**

$$\underset{\boldsymbol{w}}{\text{minimize}}$$

$$\frac{1}{2}\boldsymbol{w}^T \boldsymbol{\Sigma} \boldsymbol{w}$$

$$\text{subject to}$$

$$\boldsymbol{\mu}^T \boldsymbol{w} = \mu_t,$$

$$\mathbf{1}^T \boldsymbol{w} = 1,$$

$$\boldsymbol{w} \geq 0,$$

where:

- $\boldsymbol{w} \in \mathbb{R}^n$ is the vector of asset weights in the portfolio,
- $\boldsymbol{\Sigma} \in \mathbb{R}^{n \times n}$ is the covariance matrix of asset returns,
- $\boldsymbol{\mu} \in \mathbb{R}^n$ is the vector of expected asset returns,
- $\mu_t$ is the target portfolio return.

In this model, the objective is to minimize the portfolio variance $\frac{1}{2}\boldsymbol{w}^T \boldsymbol{\Sigma} \boldsymbol{w}$, subject to achieving a target return $\mu_t$ and ensuring that the portfolio weights sum to one. The constraints $\boldsymbol{w} \geq 0$ also ensure no short-selling in this portfolio.

**Algorithmic Implementation**

Quadratic programming problems can be solved using various algorithms. Some of the commonly used methods include:

- **Interior-Point Methods:** These methods navigate within the feasible region (defined by the constraints) to find the optimal solution. They are efficient for large-scale problems.
- **Active-Set Methods:** These methods iteratively explore a subset of the constraints (active set) that may hold as equalities at the optimal solution. They are particularly useful for smaller problems or problems with many constraints.

- **Gradient Projection Methods:** These methods use the gradient of the objective function to iteratively project the solution back onto the feasible region defined by the constraints.

**Practical Example:**

Consider a simple portfolio consisting of three assets. Let:

$$\Sigma = \begin{pmatrix} 0.1 & 0.01 & 0.02 \\ 0.01 & 0.08 & 0.03 \\ 0.02 & 0.03 & 0.15 \end{pmatrix}, \quad \boldsymbol{\mu} = \begin{pmatrix} 0.10 \\ 0.15 \\ 0.20 \end{pmatrix}, \quad \mu_t = 0.15.$$

The quadratic programming formulation will be:

$$\underset{\boldsymbol{w}}{\text{minimize}}$$

$$\frac{1}{2} \begin{pmatrix} w_1 & w_2 & w_3 \end{pmatrix} \begin{pmatrix} 0.1 & 0.01 & 0.02 \\ 0.01 & 0.08 & 0.03 \\ 0.02 & 0.03 & 0.15 \end{pmatrix} \begin{pmatrix} w_1 \\ w_2 \\ w_3 \end{pmatrix}$$

subject to

$$\begin{pmatrix} 0.10 & 0.15 & 0.20 \end{pmatrix} \begin{pmatrix} w_1 \\ w_2 \\ w_3 \end{pmatrix} = 0.15,$$

$$w_1 + w_2 + w_3 = 1,$$

$$w_1, w_2, w_3 \geq 0.$$

By applying a QP solver, we can determine the optimal weights $\boldsymbol{w}$ that minimize the portfolio risk while meeting the return target.
Quadratic programming stands out as a vital optimization tool within the domain of financial engineering. Its structured approach towards balancing risk and return underlines its significance in developing robust and efficient investment strategies. Understanding and leveraging QP allows quants to make data-driven decisions, enhancing the overall performance of financial portfolios.

## 11.4 Convex Optimization

Convex optimization is a powerful and fundamental aspect of optimization techniques, particularly valuable in the field of financial modeling. At its core, convex optimization deals with problems where the objective function is convex and the feasible set is a convex set. This appealing feature simplifies the complexity of finding a global optimum, as any local minimum in a convex problem is also a global minimum.

A function $f : \mathbb{R}^n \to \mathbb{R}$ is convex if for all $x, y \in \mathbb{R}^n$ and $\theta \in [0, 1]$, the following inequality holds:

$$f(\theta x + (1 - \theta)y) \leq \theta f(x) + (1 - \theta)f(y).$$

This property implies that the line segment between any two points on the graph of the function lies above the graph itself, forming a characteristic "bowl-shaped" curve for convex functions.

In financial applications, convex optimization offers robust methodologies for minimizing cost functions or maximizing utility functions subject to various constraints. Consider the problem of portfolio optimization, where the goal is to allocate assets in a manner that optimizes a particular objective, such as minimizing risk or maximizing return, subject to constraints like budget limits and risk controls.

The general form of a convex optimization problem is:

$$\begin{aligned} \underset{x}{\text{minimize}} \quad & f(x) \\ \text{subject to} \quad & g_i(x) \leq 0, \quad i = 1, \ldots, m \\ & h_i(x) = 0, \quad i = 1, \ldots, p, \end{aligned}$$

where $f(x)$ is the convex objective function to be minimized, $g_i(x)$ are convex inequality constraints, and $h_i(x)$ are affine equality constraints.

A practical example in finance is the mean-variance optimization, formulated by Harry Markowitz. Here, the objective is to find the portfolio that minimizes the variance (risk) for a given expected return. Let $\mu$ represent the expected returns vector of $n$ assets, and $\Sigma$ be the covariance matrix of the asset returns. The optimization problem can be stated as:

$$\begin{aligned} \underset{w}{\text{minimize}} \quad & w^T \Sigma w \\ \text{subject to} \quad & \mu^T w = r \\ & 1^T w = 1 \\ & w \geq 0, \end{aligned}$$

where $w$ is the vector of weights assigned to each asset in the portfolio, and $r$ is the target return. This problem is convex since the objective function $w^T \Sigma w$ is a quadratic form that is convex when $\Sigma$ is positive semi-definite, and the constraints form a convex feasible region.

One of the significant advantages of convex optimization is the availability of efficient and reliable algorithms capable of solving large-scale problems, including interior-point methods. These methods, pioneered by Karmarkar and further developed for practical applications, solve linear and nonlinear convex problems by exploring the feasible region's interior rather than its boundary. This approach generally leads to polynomial-time complexity, making it feasible to tackle high-dimensional financial problems.

Furthermore, convex optimization is not limited to risk minimization. In algorithmic trading, for instance, convex optimization can frame problems like minimizing transaction costs or optimizing the execution of trades in a manner that minimizes market impact while meeting specific trading objectives.

The richness of convex optimization extends further into robust optimization, where uncertainty in models is explicitly considered. Robust optimization aims to find solutions that remain feasible under a variety of perturbed conditions within predefined uncertainty sets. This approach is particularly valuable in finance, where market conditions can be highly volatile and unpredictable. For instance, an investor might want to ensure that their portfolio remains optimal under different scenarios of asset returns that account for estimation errors.

In summary, convex optimization stands as a cornerstone in financial optimization problems due to its mathematical tractability and ability to handle large-scale problems efficiently. Its principles and methodologies provide essential tools for developing sophisticated financial models that enhance decision-making in portfolio management and algorithmic trading. By leveraging the power of convex optimization, financial practitioners can achieve more robust, efficient, and effective outcomes in their strategic endeavors.

## 11.5 Integer Programming

Integer programming (IP) is a powerful method employed in various financial optimization problems where solutions are required to be whole numbers. Unlike linear programming, which deals with continuous variables, integer programming deals with variables that are discrete. This section delves into the nuances of integer programming, its applications in finance, and some common strategies to solve IP problems effectively.

At its core, integer programming involves a linear objective function and linear constraints, but with an additional condition that some or all the decision variables must be integers. The general form of an integer programming problem can be expressed as:

$$\begin{aligned} \text{maximize (or minimize)} \quad & f(x) \\ \text{subject to} \quad & Ax \le b, \\ & x \in \mathbb{Z}^n, \end{aligned} \tag{11.1}$$

where $x$ is the vector of decision variables, $A$ is a matrix of coefficients, $b$ is a vector of constraints, and $\mathbb{Z}^n$ denotes that $x$ must be an integer vector.

- **Applications in Finance:** Integer programming finds numerous applications in finance, where decisions often need to be whole numbers. Below are a few key applications:
  - **1. Portfolio Optimization:** In portfolio management, asset quantities often need to be integers due to the indivisible nature of certain assets, minimum lot sizes, or regulatory requirements. For instance, when selecting stocks for a portfolio, an investor may want to buy whole shares rather than fractions of shares. The classic Markowitz portfolio optimization can be adapted into an integer programming problem to ensure integer solutions.
  - **2. Index Tracking:** Tracking a financial index involves selecting a subset of assets from a larger pool to closely match the index's performance. Here, integer constraints are necessary because you need to determine the exact number of units of each asset to hold, leading to mixed integer programming problems.
  - **3. Cash Flow Matching:** In fixed-income portfolio management, integer programming helps in cash flow matching where the goal is to match liabilities with assets, such as bonds, while meeting certain criteria like investment limits and regulatory requirements.
  - **4. Capital Budgeting:** When a firm decides on projects to invest in, the capital budgeting problem can be modeled as an integer programming problem. Projects either get funded or not, which represents a binary decision, thus requiring integer (0 or 1) solutions.

- **Solving Integer Programming Problems:** Integer programming problems are inherently more complex than their linear or nonlinear counterparts due to the discreteness of the solution space. Below, we discuss some common methods for solving IP problems:

- **1. Branch and Bound:** This is one of the most widely used techniques for solving IP problems. The method involves dividing the problem into smaller subproblems (branching) and calculating bounds of the objective function in these subproblems. Subproblems that cannot yield better solutions than already known are discarded (bounding).
- **2. Cutting Planes:** The cutting plane method involves adding linear constraints (cuts) to the problem to eliminate fractional solutions progressively. This helps in tightening the feasible region and converging towards the optimal integer solution.
- **3. Heuristic and Metaheuristic Methods:** Sometimes, exact methods like branch and bound can be computationally expensive, especially for large problems. Heuristic methods like genetic algorithms, simulated annealing, and Tabu search provide approximate solutions more quickly. These methods do not guarantee optimality but often yield good-enough solutions in practical time frames.
- **4. Dynamic Programming:** Dynamic programming can be used to solve integer programming problems by breaking them down into simpler subproblems. This method is particularly useful for problems with a recursive structure, such as the knapsack problem.

- **Practical Example:** Consider an investment firm seeking to allocate its capital among multiple projects with the goal of maximizing profit while adhering to a budget constraint. Each project either gets funded (1) or doesn't (0), requiring integer programming to solve. Let $x_i$ represent the decision to fund project $i$, thus $x_i \in \{0, 1\}$.

  The integer programming model for this situation would be:

$$\begin{aligned} \text{maximize} \quad & \sum_{i=1}^{n} p_i x_i \\ \text{subject to} \quad & \sum_{i=1}^{n} c_i x_i \leq B, \\ & x_i \in \{0, 1\} \quad \text{for} \quad i = 1, 2, \ldots, n, \end{aligned} \tag{11.2}$$

where $p_i$ is the profit from project $i$, $c_i$ is the cost, and $B$ is the total budget available. Solving this model will yield the optimal set of projects to maximize profits within the budget.

- **Conclusion:** Integer programming is an essential tool in the arsenal of financial optimization techniques, enabling precise and practical decision-making in scenarios that involve discrete choices. While it presents computational challenges, various methods ranging from exact algorithms like branch and bound to heuristic approaches make it tractable in real-world applications. Its utility in areas like portfolio optimization, index tracking, cash flow matching, and capital budgeting illustrates its versatility and indispensability in modern financial management.

## 11.6 Derivative-Free Optimization Methods

Optimization problems in finance often involve complex, non-differentiable, or noisy objective functions where traditional derivative-based methods fall short. Derivative-free optimization (DFO) methods provide powerful alternatives that do not rely on the calculation of gradients, making them suitable for a wide range of practical applications in trading and investing.

**Overview of Derivative-Free Optimization**

Derivative-free optimization methods are designed to optimize functions when gradients are unavailable, unreliable, or expensive to compute. These methods are particularly useful in financial settings where objective functions can be highly discontinuous, subject to irregular market behavior, and influenced by stochastic processes. The essence of DFO lies in its reliance on function evaluations rather than gradient information, making it flexible and robust for various financial models.

**Common Derivative-Free Optimization Techniques**

Several derivative-free methods are widely employed in financial optimization, each with unique strengths and appropriate use cases. Here, we examine some of the most prominent techniques:

*1. Nelder-Mead Simplex Algorithm*

One of the most well-known DFO methods is the Nelder-Mead Simplex algorithm. This iterative technique refines a simplex—a geometrical shape consisting of $n+1$ vertices in $n$ dimensions—through reflection, expansion, contraction, and shrinkage operations. The method is particularly advantageous for multidimensional unconstrained optimization problems:

$$x_{new} = x_k + \alpha(x_k - x_{worst})$$

Here, $x_k$ is the centroid of the best $n$ points, $x_{worst}$ is the worst point in the simplex, and $\alpha$ is the reflection coefficient.

*2. Particle Swarm Optimization (PSO)*

Particle Swarm Optimization is inspired by the social behavior of birds flocking or fish schooling. In PSO, a population of candidate solutions, called particles, explores the search space. Each particle adjusts its position based on its own experience and the experience of its neighbors:

$$\begin{aligned} v_i &= wv_i + c_1r_1(p_i - x_i) + c_2r_2(g_i - x_i) \\ x_i &= x_i + v_i \end{aligned}$$

where $v_i$ is the velocity, $x_i$ is the position, $p_i$ is the best-known position of particle $i$, $g_i$ is the global best position, $w$ is the inertia weight, and $c_1$, $c_2$ are acceleration coefficients.

*3. Genetic Algorithms (GA)*

Genetic Algorithms mimic the process of natural evolution by employing operations such as selection, crossover, and mutation. A population of potential solutions evolves over generations, seeking to improve their fitness:

$$\begin{aligned} \text{off1} &= \text{crossover(parent1, parent2)} \\ \text{off2} &= \text{mutation(off1)} \end{aligned}$$

The fitness function evaluates the quality of solutions, guiding the selection process toward optimal candidates.

*4. Simulated Annealing (SA)*

Simulated Annealing draws inspiration from the annealing process in metallurgy. It explores the search space by accepting worse solutions with a certain probability, which decreases over time based on a cooling schedule:

$$P(E, E_{new}, T) = \begin{cases} 1 & \text{if } E_{new} < E \\ \exp\left(-\frac{E_{new} - E}{T}\right) & \text{otherwise} \end{cases}$$

where $E$ and $E_{new}$ represent the current and new energy (objective function values), and $T$ is the temperature.

**Applications in Financial Optimization**

DFO methods have significant applications in trading and investing, particularly in areas requiring robust, flexible optimization solutions without the need for gradient information. Some noteworthy examples include:

*1. Parameter Tuning in Algorithmic Trading*

Algorithmic trading strategies rely on multiple parameters, which require fine-tuning for optimal performance. Traditional gradient-based methods are often unsuitable due to the stochastic nature of financial markets. DFO methods such as Genetic Algorithms and Particle Swarm Optimization provide powerful alternatives, enabling traders to optimize strategy parameters by evaluating historical performance metrics.

*2. Portfolio Optimization*

Finance professionals often face the challenge of optimizing portfolios with non-differentiable objective functions, such as minimizing Value-at-Risk (VaR) or Conditional Value-at-Risk (CVaR). Derivative-Free Optimization methods can navigate the complex, discontinuous landscape of such objective functions, offering viable solutions where gradient-based methods struggle.

*3. Risk Management*

In risk management scenarios, derivative-free methods can optimize the allocation of capital to various risk management tools, such as options and derivatives, which exhibit non-linear and non-smooth payoff profiles. Techniques like Simulated Annealing can explore the risk landscape and identify near-optimal allocation strategies under various market conditions.

**Conclusion of the Section**

Derivative-Free Optimization methods offer invaluable tools for quants and finance professionals faced with complex, non-differentiable, and stochastic objectives. By leveraging methods like Nelder-Mead, Particle Swarm Optimization, Genetic Algorithms, and Simulated Annealing, investors can achieve robust, effective optimization solutions tailored to the unpredictable nature of financial markets. Understanding and effectively applying these techniques can significantly enhance the performance of trading strategies and portfolio management practices.

## 11.7 Gradient Descent and Variants

Gradient descent is a fundamental iterative optimization algorithm commonly used for finding the minimum of a function. It is particularly integral in the realm of machine learning and financial model optimization, facilitating robust solutions for predictive models and algorithmic trading strategies. This technique relies on the computation of gradients (derivatives) to iteratively refine the parameters of a model so that the cost or loss function—representing prediction error or model inadequacy—is minimized.

At its core, gradient descent operates on the principle of moving towards the steepest descent direction, as indicated by the negative of the gradient. Consider the objective function $f(\boldsymbol{w})$ where $\boldsymbol{w}$ is a vector of parameters. The update rule for standard (or vanilla) gradient descent is:

$$\boldsymbol{w}_{t+1} = \boldsymbol{w}_t - \eta \nabla f(\boldsymbol{w}_t)$$

Here, $\eta$ represents the learning rate, determining the step size for each iteration. The gradient $\nabla f(\boldsymbol{w}_t)$ directs the adjustment of parameters.

An appropriate selection of learning rate $\eta$ is crucial; a value too large might overshoot the minimum, while a too small value can lead to slow convergence. To achieve desirable performance, variations of the gradient descent algorithm are often deployed.

**1. Stochastic Gradient Descent (SGD):**

In contrast to batch gradient descent, which computes the gradient using the entire dataset, stochastic gradient descent updates the parameters using one data point at a time. This significantly reduces computation time per iteration, making it viable for large datasets. The update rule for SGD is:

$$w_{t+1} = w_t - \eta \nabla f(w_t; x_i, y_i)$$

where $(x_i, y_i)$ represents an individual data sample. While SGD introduces noise into the optimization process, it has the advantage of potentially escaping local minima, providing a more robust search in complex landscapes that characterize financial models.

**2. Mini-Batch Gradient Descent:**

Mini-batch gradient descent strikes a balance between batch gradient descent and stochastic gradient descent by using small, random subsets of the dataset for computing the gradient at each step. This can lead to faster convergence while maintaining the advantages of gradient-based optimization:

$$w_{t+1} = w_t - \eta \nabla f(w_t; \mathcal{B}_t)$$

where $\mathcal{B}_t$ is a mini-batch of training examples. This variant often achieves more stable updates and better utilization of hardware acceleration.

**3. Momentum:**

Momentum accelerates gradient descent by accumulating a velocity vector in directions of consistent reduction in the objective function, which helps to smooth the optimization path and converge faster. The update rules are:

$$v_{t+1} = \gamma v_t + \eta \nabla f(w_t)$$
$$w_{t+1} = w_t - v_{t+1}$$

where $\gamma$ (typically between 0.5 and 0.9) controls the momentum contribution. This approach reduces oscillation and can navigate past shallow local minima efficiently.

**4. Nesterov Accelerated Gradient (NAG):**

NAG improves on momentum by adjusting the gradient calculation to anticipate the next position of the parameters. This leads to more responsive updates:

$$v_{t+1} = \gamma v_t + \eta \nabla f(w_t - \gamma v_t)$$
$$w_{t+1} = w_t - v_{t+1}$$

This technique typically offers faster convergence due to the preemptive gradient evaluation.

**5. Adaptive Gradient Algorithm (Adagrad):**

Adagrad adapts the learning rate to the parameters, performing larger updates for infrequent parameters and smaller updates for frequent parameters. It achieves this through the accumulation of past gradients:

$$\boldsymbol{w}_{t+1} = \boldsymbol{w}_t - \frac{\eta}{\sqrt{G_{t,ii}} + \epsilon} \nabla f(\boldsymbol{w}_t)$$

where $G_t$ is a diagonal matrix of gradient sums, and $\epsilon$ prevents division by zero. Adagrad is particularly effective for sparse data scenarios encountered in high-frequency trading data analysis.

**6. RMSProp:**

RMSProp addresses Adagrad's diminishing learning rate by introducing an exponential decay factor to the gradient accumulation:

$$\boldsymbol{s}_{t+1} = \beta \boldsymbol{s}_t + (1 - \beta)(\nabla f(\boldsymbol{w}_t))^2$$
$$\boldsymbol{w}_{t+1} = \boldsymbol{w}_t - \frac{\eta}{\sqrt{\boldsymbol{s}_{t+1}} + \epsilon} \nabla f(\boldsymbol{w}_t)$$

where $\beta$ is typically set around 0.9. This ensures more stable and continuous learning rates suited for complex financial models.

**7. Adaptive Moment Estimation (Adam):**

Adam combines the benefits of both Adagrad and Momentum by utilizing exponentially decaying averages of past gradients and squared gradients:

$$\boldsymbol{m}_{t+1} = \beta_1 \boldsymbol{m}_t + (1 - \beta_1) \nabla f(\boldsymbol{w}_t)$$
$$\boldsymbol{v}_{t+1} = \beta_2 \boldsymbol{v}_t + (1 - \beta_2)(\nabla f(\boldsymbol{w}_t))^2$$
$$\hat{\boldsymbol{m}}_{t+1} = \frac{\boldsymbol{m}_{t+1}}{1 - \beta_1^t}, \quad \hat{\boldsymbol{v}}_{t+1} = \frac{\boldsymbol{v}_{t+1}}{1 - \beta_2^t}$$

$$\boldsymbol{w}_{t+1} = \boldsymbol{w}_t - \frac{\eta \hat{\boldsymbol{m}}_{t+1}}{\sqrt{\hat{\boldsymbol{v}}_{t+1}} + \epsilon}$$

Adam's adaptivity and efficient memory use make it an attractive choice for diverse portfolios and high-dimensional datasets.

Incorporating gradient descent and its variants into the optimization arsenal provides quantitative analysts and traders with a versatile set of tools capable of refining predictive models and enhancing trading algorithms. Proper adjustment and selection of these techniques can greatly impact the efficacy and speed of reaching optimal solutions, thereby amplifying the performance and profitability of financial strategies.

## 11.8 Bayesian Optimization

Bayesian Optimization is a powerful tool in the arsenal of quantitative finance. It offers a sophisticated method to optimize functions that are expensive to evaluate, often unknown, and possibly noisy — conditions commonly encountered in financial applications such as algorithmic trading and portfolio management. Unlike traditional optimization techniques, Bayesian Optimization builds a probabilistic model of the objective function and utilizes it to make informed decisions about where to evaluate next, striking a balance between exploration (sampling from less certain places) and exploitation (sampling from places likely to yield high rewards).

At its core, Bayesian Optimization relies on two main components: a surrogate model, typically a Gaussian Process (GP), and an acquisition function.

The surrogate model, represented by a Gaussian Process, models the distribution over functions based on prior beliefs and observed data. Mathematically, a GP is specified by a mean function $m(x)$ and a covariance function (kernel) $k(x, x')$:

$$f(x) \sim \mathcal{GP}(m(x), k(x, x'))$$

Here, $m(x)$ is often assumed to be zero for simplicity, and $k(x, x')$ determines the smoothness and other properties of the modeled function. Common choices for the kernel include the Radial Basis Function (RBF), Matérn kernel, and the Rational Quadratic kernel.

Once a surrogate model is established, we proceed with the acquisition function, which guides the optimization process by suggesting the next point to evaluate. The acquisition function balances exploration and exploitation strategies, ensuring that the optimization process does not get trapped in local optima while efficiently narrowing down the search space. Common acquisition functions include:

- **Expected Improvement (EI):** The EI acquisition function aims to maximize the expected improvement over the current best observation. If $f(\boldsymbol{x}^+)$ is the best current observation and $\mu(\boldsymbol{x})$ and $\sigma^2(\boldsymbol{x})$ are the mean and variance predicted by the GP at $\boldsymbol{x}$, EI is defined as:

$$\alpha_{EI}(\boldsymbol{x}) = \mathbb{E}[\max(0, f(\boldsymbol{x}) - f(\boldsymbol{x}^+))] = (\mu(\boldsymbol{x}) - f(\boldsymbol{x}^+))\Phi(Z) + \sigma(\boldsymbol{x})\phi(Z),$$

  where $Z = \frac{\mu(\boldsymbol{x}) - f(\boldsymbol{x}^+)}{\sigma(\boldsymbol{x})}$, and $\Phi$ and $\phi$ are the cumulative distribution function and the probability density function of the standard normal distribution, respectively.

- **Probability of Improvement (PI):** PI focuses on the probability that a given point will improve upon the best observation, defined as:

$$\alpha_{PI}(\boldsymbol{x}) = \Phi\left(\frac{\mu(\boldsymbol{x}) - f(\boldsymbol{x}^+)}{\sigma(\boldsymbol{x})}\right).$$

- **Upper Confidence Bound (UCB):** UCB considers the upper bound of the confidence interval for the predicted function value. It is defined as:

$$\alpha_{UCB}(\boldsymbol{x}) = \mu(\boldsymbol{x}) + \kappa\sigma(\boldsymbol{x}),$$

  where $\kappa$ is a parameter controlling the balance between exploration and exploitation.

Once the acquisition function identifies the next point to evaluate, the true objective function (e.g., a trading strategy's profit function) is assessed at this point. This new data point is then incorporated into the GP model, updating our beliefs about the objective function. The process iterates until convergence criteria are met, such as a maximum number of iterations or a negligible improvement threshold.

In financial applications, Bayesian Optimization is particularly useful for hyperparameter tuning of machine learning models used in trading algorithms and portfolio management. For example, by optimizing the hyperparameters of a Support Vector Machine (SVM) used to predict stock prices, one can significantly enhance predictive performance. Similarly, Bayesian Optimization helps in refining trading strategies by identifying the optimal set of parameters, thereby maximizing the strategy's Sharpe Ratio.

To implement Bayesian Optimization, practitioners can leverage libraries such as $\mathrm{GPyOpt}$, $\mathrm{Scikit\text{-}Optimize}$, and $\mathrm{Spearmint}$, which offer user-friendly interfaces and robust functionality for various optimization problems.

By integrating Bayesian Optimization into their toolkit, quantitative analysts and traders can systematically and efficiently explore complex parameter spaces, ultimately leading to more robust and profitable financial models and strategies.

## 11.9 Application of Optimization in Portfolio Management

Portfolio management is one of the most critical areas in finance where optimization techniques are applied robustly. The central goal is to construct a portfolio that maximizes returns for a given level of risk, or alternatively, minimizes risk for a given level of expected return. This is accomplished through a variety of optimization frameworks, each tailored to handle different types of assets, constraints, and investor preferences.

The fundamental concept in portfolio optimization is the **Mean-Variance Optimization (MVO)**, introduced by Harry Markowitz in 1952. This technique formulates the problem as a quadratic programming problem, where the optimization is subject to the constraints of expected returns and risks. The objective function to be minimized is:

$$\text{Var}(R_p) = \mathbf{w}^T \Sigma \mathbf{w}$$

where $\mathbf{w}$ represents the vector of portfolio weights, and $\Sigma$ denotes the covariance matrix of asset returns. The constraints can be formulated as:

$$\mathsf{E}(R_p) = \mathbf{w}^T\mathbf{r} \quad \text{and} \quad \sum_{i=1}^{n} w_i = 1$$

where $\mathsf{E}(R_p)$ is the expected portfolio return and $\mathbf{r}$ is the vector of expected returns for individual assets. Investors can decide on a target level of return and use optimization to find the portfolio weights $\mathbf{w}$ that achieve that return with minimum variance.

Beyond the basic MVO, there are several advanced techniques and variations to handle practical issues like transaction costs, taxes, and various types of constraints. One such extension is **Robust Optimization**, which takes into account the uncertainty in the estimation of asset returns and covariances. It adjusts the optimization framework to mitigate the potential negative effects of estimation errors, making the solutions more reliable in practice.

Another notable method is the **Black-Litterman Model**, which integrates investors' views with the market equilibrium (represented by the CAPM) to produce a more customized and optimal portfolio. The model sets up an equilibrium return vector, $\Pi$, which is then adjusted by incorporating investor views using the formula:

$$\tilde{r} = ((\tau\Sigma)^{-1} + P^T\Omega^{-1}P)^{-1}\left((\tau\Sigma)^{-1}\Pi + P^T\Omega^{-1}q\right)$$

where $\tau$ is a scalar factor, $P$ represents the pick matrix reflecting views, $\Omega$ is the diagonal covariance matrix of error terms, and $q$ is the vector of views. This results in more stable and realistic portfolio allocations.

**Conditional Value-at-Risk (CVaR) Optimization** is another extension, particularly useful in managing downside risk. Unlike Value-at-Risk (VaR) which provides a risk estimate at a specific percentile, CVaR considers the tail end beyond the VaR, offering a more comprehensive risk measure. The CVaR optimization problem can be formulated as a linear programming problem, making it computationally tractable:

$$\min_{\mathbf{w},\zeta} \left\{ \zeta + \frac{1}{\alpha}\mathbb{E}\left[\max\left(0, -(R_p - \zeta)\right)\right] \right\}$$

where $\alpha$ represents the significance level (e.g., $0.05$ for 95% confidence), and $\zeta$ is a threshold value that is optimized alongside the portfolio weights $\mathbf{w}$.

Moreover, modern portfolio theory now incorporates Machine Learning methods to predict asset returns more accurately, which are then fed into the optimization models. Techniques like **Reinforcement Learning** and **Bayesian Optimization** are employed to dynamically adjust weights in response to changing market conditions, thus enhancing the stability and profitability of the portfolio.

Investors often face additional constraints like bounds on individual asset weights, fixed transaction costs, or cardinality constraints (limit on the number of assets). These constraints complicate the optimization problem, necessitating more sophisticated methods like **Mixed-Integer Programming (MIP)**. MIP allows for the inclusion of such discrete constraints and can be solved using specialized algorithms or heuristics.

Finally, the practical application of these optimization techniques in portfolio management has been facilitated by advancements in computational power and algorithmic development. Tools such as **Python with libraries like 'cvxpy'**, **R with 'ROI'**, and specialized software provide quants with the means to implement and solve complex optimization problems efficiently.

This interplay between theoretical frameworks and practical implementations not only makes portfolio management more robust and adaptable but also empowers investors to achieve superior risk-adjusted returns in increasingly volatile markets.

## 11.10 Optimization in Algorithmic Trading

Algorithmic trading leverages mathematical models and computational algorithms to execute trades at optimal times and prices, minimizing human intervention. This section elucidates the vital role of optimization within the realm of algorithmic trading, providing detailed insights into various strategies and methodologies that traders and quants employ to enhance their trading algorithms. By fine-tuning these algorithms through robust optimization techniques, one can achieve superior performance in trading activities.

The first step in algorithmic trading optimization involves defining the objective function. This function quantifies the goal of the trading strategy, such as maximizing returns, minimizing risks, or achieving a balance between the two. A typical objective function can be expressed as:

$$L(\theta) = -\mathbb{E}[R(\theta)] + \lambda \text{Var}(R(\theta))$$

where $\theta$ represents the strategy parameters, $\mathbb{E}[R(\theta)]$ is the expected return, Var$(R(\theta))$ is the variance of the return, and $\lambda$ is a risk-aversion coefficient.

Once the objective function has been established, the next step involves selecting an appropriate optimization technique. Common techniques include gradient-based methods such as gradient descent and its variants, genetic algorithms, and particle swarm optimization.

Gradient descent is a powerful tool when the objective function is differentiable. By iteratively updating the strategy parameters in the direction of the negative gradient, the algorithm converges to a local minimum of the objective function. The update rule for standard gradient descent is given by:

$$\theta_{t+1} = \theta_t - \eta \nabla L(\theta_t)$$

where $\eta$ is the learning rate, a hyperparameter that controls the step size of each update. The choice of learning rate is crucial; too large a value can cause overshooting, while too small a value can result in slow convergence.

For non-differentiable or combinatorial objective functions, derivative-free optimization techniques such as genetic algorithms and particle swarm optimization are more suitable. Genetic algorithms simulate the process of natural evolution, iteratively evolving a population of candidate solutions through selection, crossover, and mutation operations. The fittest individuals are selected to form the next generation, gradually leading to optimized strategy parameters. The pseudo-code for a basic genetic algorithm is as follows:

**Algorithm 1** Genetic Algorithm

```
Initialize population with random candidates
for generation = 1 to max_generations do
    Evaluate fitness of each candidate
    Select parents based on fitness
    Perform crossover and mutation to generate offspring
    Replace least fit individuals with offspring
end for
```

Particle swarm optimization, on the other hand, models the social behavior of birds flocking or fish schooling. Each candidate solution, called a particle, adjusts its position and velocity based on its own experience and the experience of neighboring particles. The position $\boldsymbol{x}_i$ of the $i$-th particle is updated according to:

$$\boldsymbol{v}_i(t+1) = \omega \boldsymbol{v}_i(t) + c_1 r_1 [\boldsymbol{p}_i - \boldsymbol{x}_i(t)] + c_2 r_2 [\boldsymbol{g} - \boldsymbol{x}_i(t)]$$

$$\boldsymbol{x}_i(t+1) = \boldsymbol{x}_i(t) + \boldsymbol{v}_i(t+1)$$

where $\omega$ is the inertia weight, $c_1$ and $c_2$ are acceleration coefficients, $r_1$ and $r_2$ are random numbers between 0 and 1, $\boldsymbol{p}_i$ is the best position found by the particle, and $\boldsymbol{g}$ is the global best position found by the swarm.

To apply these optimization techniques effectively in algorithmic trading, it is essential to incorporate constraints and practical considerations. Constraints may include limits on allowable position sizes, leverage, transaction costs, and risk limits. These can be included in the optimization framework as follows:

$$\begin{aligned} \text{minimize} \quad & L(\theta) \\ \text{subject to} \quad & g(\theta) \leq 0 \end{aligned}$$

where $g(\theta)$ represents a set of constraint functions.

Furthermore, backtesting is a critical component of the optimization process. Backtesting evaluates the performance of a trading strategy based on historical data, ensuring that the optimized strategy parameters would have yielded satisfactory results in past market conditions. This process helps in validating the robustness and reliability of the trading algorithm before deployment in live markets.

In addition to historical backtesting, forward testing or paper trading is recommended to observe the strategy's performance in real-time simulated environments. This additional layer of verification helps identify potential issues that might not be evident from historical data alone.

Optimization in algorithmic trading is a dynamic and iterative process. Continuous monitoring, evaluation, and recalibration are necessary to maintain the effectiveness of trading strategies amid evolving market conditions. By judiciously applying appropriate optimization techniques, traders and quants can enhance their algorithmic trading performance, achieving more consistent and favorable results.

# Chapter 12

# Case Studies in Financial Markets

**This chapter presents a collection of real-world case studies showcasing the application of machine learning in financial markets. It includes examples such as predicting stock prices, implementing mean reversion and momentum strategies, and optimizing portfolios using modern portfolio theory. Additional case studies cover risk management in hedge funds, market making in forex trading, credit risk modeling, high-frequency trading strategies, sentiment analysis for market prediction, anomaly detection in transactions, and interest rate modeling in fixed income markets.**

## 12.1 Case Study: Predicting Stock Prices with Machine Learning

Predicting stock prices has long been a tantalizing yet daunting task for financial analysts and traders. With the advent of machine learning, this pursuit has gained new tools and methodologies, enabling deeper insights and more robust predictions. In this case study, we delve into the application of machine learning algorithms to predict stock prices, emphasizing both the theory and the practical implementation steps involved.

Machine learning models, such as linear regression, decision trees, random forests, support vector machines (SVMs), and neural networks, have emerged as powerful tools for forecasting stock prices. By processing vast amounts of financial data and identifying intricate patterns buried within, these models can provide investors with a competitive edge in decision-making.

To illustrate the process of stock price prediction with machine learning, we will consider the following steps:

1. **Data Collection and Preprocessing**: Accurate and comprehensive data is critical in building reliable predictive models. The first step involves gathering historical stock prices, volume data, and other relevant financial indicators from reputable sources such as Yahoo Finance, Google Finance, or Bloomberg.

Once collected, the data must be cleaned and preprocessed. Missing values need to be handled, and the data should be normalized or standardized to ensure that all features contribute proportionately to the predictive model. The common methods for dealing with missing values include imputation techniques or simply removing incomplete records, depending on the situation.

2. **Feature Engineering**: The crux of a successful machine learning application lies in the features chosen. Feature engineering involves generating new variables that better capture the underlying patterns of the raw data. Typical features in stock price prediction might include technical indicators such as moving averages, relative strength index (RSI), and Bollinger Bands. Additionally, macroeconomic indicators, sentiment data from news and social media, and even fundamental company data like earnings and P/E ratios can serve as valuable features.

3. **Model Selection and Training**: Selecting the right model is paramount. We will initially focus on linear regression as a simple yet effective start. Linear regression models the relationship between the dependent variable (stock prices) and the independent variables (features). The model aims to minimize the sum of the squared differences between the observed and predicted values.

For linear regression, the model can be represented as:

$$y = \beta_0 + \beta_1 x_1 + \beta_2 x_2 + \ldots + \beta_n x_n + \epsilon$$

where $y$ is the predicted stock price, $x_1, x_2, \ldots, x_n$ are the features, $\beta_0$ is the intercept, $\beta_1, \beta_2, \ldots, \beta_n$ are the coefficients, and $\epsilon$ is the error term.

Once the linear regression model is trained, we progress to more complex models such as decision trees and random forests, which are capable of capturing non-linear relationships. Decision trees split the data into subsets based on feature values, creating a tree-like model of decisions. Random forests aggregate multiple decision trees to improve predictive performance and reduce overfitting.

4. **Model Evaluation**: Evaluating model performance is crucial to ensure its reliability. Common metrics for regression problems include Mean Absolute Error (MAE), Mean Squared Error (MSE), and Root Mean Squared Error (RMSE). Cross-validation techniques, such as k-fold cross-validation, are employed to assess model performance on different subsets of data, reducing the likelihood of overfitting.

For example, the MSE is calculated as:

$$MSE = \frac{1}{n} \sum_{i=1}^{n} (y_i - \hat{y}_i)^2$$

where $n$ is the number of observations, $y_i$ is the actual stock price, and $\hat{y}_i$ is the predicted stock price.

5. **Hyperparameter Tuning**: Fine-tuning the hyperparameters of the model can significantly improve its performance. Techniques such as grid search and randomized search are commonly used. For instance, in a random forest model, key hyperparameters include the number of trees (n_estimators), the maximum depth of each tree (max_depth), and the minimum number of samples required to split an internal node (min_samples_split).

6. **Deployment and Continuous Improvement**: Once a satisfactory model is developed, it can be deployed for real-time stock price prediction. It is essential to monitor the model's performance over time and retrain it periodically using the latest data to adapt to changing market conditions.

Predicting stock prices with machine learning is a dynamic, iterative process that requires continuous refinement and adaptation. Through this case study, we have laid out a comprehensive approach to leveraging these advanced algorithms, from data collection to deployment. By mastering these techniques, investors and traders can enhance their forecasting accuracy and make more informed financial decisions.

## 12.2 Case Study: Algorithmic Trading with Mean Reversion

Algorithmic trading, where computer systems are used to execute a large number of trades within the financial markets, has seen substantial growth and development over the past few decades. One of the key strategies employed in algorithmic trading is mean reversion. The core idea behind mean reversion is the belief that asset prices will revert to their long-term mean or average value over time. This section examines a real-world case study to illustrate the application of mean reversion in algorithmic trading.

The foundational theory of mean reversion relies on the statistical properties of time series. It assumes that if the price of a financial instrument deviates significantly from its historical mean, it is likely to eventually return to that mean. Our case study involves constructing an algorithm that detects such deviations and executes trades to profit from eventual price corrections.

To set the framework, we begin with defining the mean reversion concept mathematically. Suppose the price $P_t$ at time $t$ follows a mean-reverting process:

$$dP_t = \kappa(\mu - P_t)dt + \sigma dW_t$$

Here, $\mu$ represents the long-term mean price, $\kappa$ is the speed of reversion, and $\sigma$ is the volatility of the price. $W_t$ denotes a Wiener process or Brownian motion, modelling the randomness in price movements.

Our algorithm detects instances where the current price $P_t$ deviates substantially from $\mu$. A common approach is to standardize this deviation using a z-score, defined as:

$$Z_t = \frac{P_t - \mu}{\sigma}$$

A high absolute value of $Z_t$ signifies a significant deviation from the mean. The algorithm will trigger a buy signal if $Z_t$ falls below a predefined threshold (indicating the price is likely to rise), and a sell signal if $Z_t$ exceeds another threshold (indicating the price is likely to fall).

We now explore a practical implementation of this strategy using historical stock data. For this case study, we choose a well-known stock index and use five years of daily price data. The steps involved are as follows:

- **Data Collection and Preprocessing:** We gather daily closing prices and calculate the moving average and standard deviation over a look-back period (e.g., 50 days). This provides the rolling mean $\mu$ and volatility $\sigma$ for the z-score calculation.

$$\mu_t = \frac{1}{n} \sum_{i=0}^{n-1} P_{t-i}$$

$$\sigma_t = \sqrt{\frac{1}{n} \sum_{i=0}^{n-1} (P_{t-i} - \mu_t)^2}$$

- **Signal Generation:** Using the computed z-scores, the algorithm generates buy and sell signals. For instance, we may set $Z_t < -2$ for buy signals and $Z_t > 2$ for sell signals.
- **Backtesting:** Implement the trading strategy in a backtest environment to evaluate its performance. This involves:
  - Simulating trades based on historical data.
  - Calculating metrics such as cumulative returns, Sharpe ratio, and maximum drawdown.

To illustrate, let's consider the following dataset snippet:

| Date | Closing Price | Moving Average (50-day) | Z-score |
|---|---|---|---|
| 2023-01-01 | 150 | 145 | 1.2 |
| 2023-01-02 | 140 | 144 | -2.0 |
| 2023-01-03 | 142 | 143 | -1.5 |

Table 12.1: Sample dataset for signal generation

The algorithm would generate a buy signal on 2023-01-02, given the z-score of -2.0. The trade execution would be simulated to assess its profitability by tracking the subsequent price movements.

- **Performance Analysis:** Once the backtesting is complete, analyze the results to refine the strategy. Evaluate the algorithm's profitability under various market conditions by examining the equity curve, drawdown periods, and key performance statistics.

During backtesting, suppose we observe that the strategy yields an annualized return of 12% with a Sharpe ratio of 1.5 and a maximum drawdown of 10%. These metrics would help quantify the effectiveness and risk-adjusted performance of our strategy.

In fine-tuning the algorithm, consider adding stop-loss mechanisms, position sizing rules, and transaction cost modeling. This ensures that practical trading constraints and expenses are realistically accounted for. Additionally, analyzing the sensitivity of the strategy to various look-back periods and z-score thresholds can yield further insights into optimizing parameter selections.

Finally, robustness validation should involve out-of-sample testing and Monte Carlo simulations to assess how the strategy might perform in unseen market scenarios and under varying conditions.

By meticulously applying the principles of mean reversion within an algorithmic framework, traders can develop strategies that potentially exploit inefficiencies in the financial markets, leading to profitable trading opportunities.

## 12.3 Case Study: Portfolio Optimization using Modern Portfolio Theory

In this case study, we delve into the practical application of Modern Portfolio Theory (MPT) for optimizing a financial portfolio. Our focus will be on utilizing historical stock data to construct an efficient frontier, which represents the set of portfolios that offer the highest expected return for a defined level of risk. We will explore the mathematical underpinnings of MPT, computational approaches to derive optimal portfolios, and real-world considerations that impact portfolio management.

Modern Portfolio Theory, pioneered by Harry Markowitz in the 1950s, revolutionized the way investors approach portfolio construction. The core idea is to diversify investments in such a way that the portfolio's overall risk is minimized for a given return or equivalently, the return is maximized for a given level of risk. The key here is the relationship between individual asset risk and the overall risk of the portfolio, highlighting the importance of the correlation between asset returns.

To begin our analysis, we first need to gather historical price data for a selection of stocks. Let's consider a portfolio consisting of five major stocks: Apple (AAPL), Microsoft (MSFT), Google (GOOGL), Amazon

(AMZN), and Facebook (FB). We will use historical monthly price data over the past five years to calculate the expected returns, standard deviations, and correlations.

The expected return $\mu$ of each stock is calculated as the mean of historical returns, and the standard deviation $\sigma$ represents the risk or volatility. This is mathematically represented as:

$$\mu_i = \frac{1}{T}\sum_{t=1}^{T} r_{i,t}$$

$$\sigma_i = \sqrt{\frac{1}{T-1}\sum_{t=1}^{T}(r_{i,t} - \mu_i)^2}$$

where $r_{i,t}$ is the return of stock $i$ at time $t$, and $T$ is the total number of time periods.

Next, we compute the covariance matrix $\Sigma$, which captures the pairwise covariance between the returns of the stocks in our portfolio. Each element $\sigma_{ij}$ of the covariance matrix is given by:

$$\sigma_{ij} = \frac{1}{T-1}\sum_{t=1}^{T}(r_{i,t} - \mu_i)(r_{j,t} - \mu_j)$$

With the expected returns and covariance matrix in hand, we can now formulate the optimization problem. The goal is to find the optimal weights $w_i$ for each stock in the portfolio that either maximize the expected return for a given level of risk or minimize risk for a given level of expected return.

The expected return $\mu_p$ of the portfolio is the weighted sum of the individual expected returns:

$$\mu_p = \sum_{i=1}^{N} w_i \mu_i$$

The variance $\sigma_p^2$ of the portfolio is:

$$\sigma_p^2 = \sum_{i=1}^{N}\sum_{j=1}^{N} w_i w_j \sigma_{ij}$$

We implement the optimization using a quadratic programming approach, which is well-suited for solving problems where the objective function is quadratic and the constraints are linear. The key constraints are that the sum of the weights must equal 1 (i.e., $\sum_{i=1}^{N} w_i = 1$) and that all weights should be non-negative ($w_i \geq 0$).

We utilize Python and libraries such as NumPy and SciPy to perform the optimization. The following Python code snippet illustrates this process:

```
import numpy as np
from scipy.optimize import minimize

# Expected returns and covariance matrix
mu = np.array([0.12, 0.10, 0.15, 0.20, 0.13])
Sigma = np.array([
    [0.1, 0.02, 0.04, 0.03, 0.05],
    [0.02, 0.08, 0.03, 0.02, 0.04],
    [0.04, 0.03, 0.12, 0.06, 0.03],
    [0.03, 0.02, 0.06, 0.15, 0.05],
    [0.05, 0.04, 0.03, 0.05, 0.09]
])

# Number of assets
N = len(mu)

# Define the objective function (portfolio variance)
def portfolio_variance(w, Sigma):
    return np.dot(w.T, np.dot(Sigma, w))

# Constraints
constraints = ({'type': 'eq', 'fun': lambda w: np.sum(w) - 1})
bounds = [(0, 1) for _ in range(N)]

# Initial guess (equal weights)
w0 = np.ones(N) / N

# Minimize portfolio variance
result = minimize(portfolio_variance, w0, args=(Sigma,), method='SLSQP', bounds=
        bounds, constraints=constraints)
optimal_weights = result.x

print("Optimal portfolio weights:")
print(optimal_weights)
```

Once we have the optimal weights, we can characterize the efficient frontier by varying the target return and solving for the minimum variance. This gives us a graphical representation of the risk-return tradeoff, which aids investors in selecting the most suitable portfolio according to their risk tolerance.

In practice, several considerations must be taken into account when applying MPT. Transaction costs, taxes, and market impact can erode the theoretical benefits of portfolio optimization. Additionally, the assumption that past performance is indicative of future results may not always hold true, especially in rapidly changing markets. Therefore, continuous monitoring and rebalancing are necessary to maintain the optimal portfolio over time.

By understanding and applying Modern Portfolio Theory, investors and financial managers can make more informed decisions, enhancing the potential for achieving favorable returns while managing risk. This case study demonstrates the powerful intersection of financial theory and computational techniques, illustrating the practical benefits of a structured, data-driven approach to portfolio management.

## 12.4 Case Study: Risk Management in Hedge Funds

Risk management is a pivotal aspect of hedge fund operations, aiming to protect the portfolio from significant losses and ensuring consistent performance. This case study explores practical risk management strategies employed by hedge funds, focusing on techniques such as Value-at-Risk (VaR), stress testing, and the use of machine learning to predict and mitigate potential risks.

Value-at-Risk (VaR) is a foundational tool in the risk management arsenal, providing a probabilistic estimate of the potential loss in portfolio value over a specified time frame. The core principle is to determine the maximum expected loss at a given confidence level. For example, if a portfolio's daily VaR at a 99% confidence level is $1 million, it suggests that there is only a 1% chance that the portfolio will lose more than $1 million in a single day.

To calculate VaR, one can use several methods: historical simulation, parametric methods, or Monte Carlo simulation. The historical simulation method employs past market data to reconstruct the distribution of returns, while the parametric method assumes a specific distribution (often normal) for asset returns and uses statistical measures such as mean and standard deviation. Meanwhile, Monte Carlo simulation generates a large number of random price paths for assets, based on their statistical properties, to estimate potential losses.

$$\text{VaR}_\alpha = \inf\left\{-x \;\middle|\; P(L > x) \le 1 - \alpha\right\} \tag{12.1}$$

Where $\text{VaR}_\alpha$ denotes the Value-at-Risk at confidence level $\alpha$, and $L$

represents the portfolio loss.

In addition to VaR, stress testing serves as another critical technique. Stress testing involves evaluating the impact of extreme market conditions on the portfolio, often by simulating unprecedented economic events or financial crises. This approach helps hedge funds understand the potential vulnerabilities in their positions and devise strategies to mitigate those risks.

For instance, a hedge fund might conduct a stress test by simulating a market scenario similar to the 2008 financial crisis, incorporating significant drops in stock indexes, widening credit spreads, and increased market volatility. By analyzing the portfolio's performance under these harsh conditions, the fund managers can identify exposure areas that need to be addressed.

Machine learning has also begun to play a significant role in risk management processes. Algorithms such as decision trees, support vector machines (SVM), and neural networks can predict potential risk factors based on historical data trends and market indicators. One notable application is predicting credit risk — the likelihood that a borrower will default on their obligations. By training machine learning models on vast datasets containing borrower attributes and repayment histories, hedge funds can obtain improved estimations of default risks and adjust their portfolios accordingly.

```
import numpy as np
from sklearn.ensemble import RandomForestClassifier

# Load dataset
X = np.array([...]) # Features
y = np.array([...]) # Labels (default/no default)

# Split dataset into training and test sets
from sklearn.model_selection import train_test_split
X_train, X_test, y_train, y_test = train_test_split(X, y, test_size=0.2,
      random_state=42)

# Train a random forest classifier
clf = RandomForestClassifier(n_estimators=100, random_state=42)
clf.fit(X_train, y_train)

# Predict and evaluate
y_pred = clf.predict(X_test)
```

In this code snippet, a random forest classifier is trained to predict credit risk. The dataset 'X' contains borrower features, while 'y' indicates whether a default occurred. By analyzing the model's predictions, hedge fund managers can make more informed risk management decisions.

Effective hedge fund risk management hinges on a combination of quantitative methods, stress testing scenarios, and the integration of machine learning techniques. These strategies work synergistically to ensure a robust and resilient portfolio capable of withstanding a variety of adverse market conditions.

By embracing a holistic approach that incorporates traditional financial metrics and cutting-edge algorithmic insights, hedge funds can better navigate the complexities of today's financial landscape, ensuring that their capital is both protected and optimally deployed. This dynamic and multifaceted strategy positions hedge funds to achieve superior performance while maintaining rigorous risk controls.

## 12.5 Case Study: Market Making Strategy in Forex Trading

Market making is a crucial function in financial markets, ensuring liquidity and enabling smoother transactions. In the realm of Forex trading, market makers play a pivotal role by continuously quoting buy and sell prices, thus facilitating trades and maintaining market efficiency. This case study delves into the application of machine learning techniques to enhance market making strategies in Forex trading, providing a practical framework for implementation.

To begin, it's important to understand the core mechanics of market making in Forex markets. A market maker seeks to profit from the bid-ask spread while managing the risk associated with holding positions. The fundamental tasks involve dynamically adjusting prices and managing inventory to balance between immediate profitability and long-term stability.

The integration of machine learning into market making primarily involves prediction and optimization tasks. By leveraging historical data, machine learning models can predict short-term price movements and order flow, aiding in informed decision-making and strategy refinement. Here, we explore a simplified yet effective approach using reinforcement learning (RL) to design an intelligent market making strategy in Forex trading.

**Historical Data and Features**

The success of any machine learning model hinges on the quality of input data. For our market-making model, the dataset comprises historical tick-level data, including bid and ask prices, transaction volumes, and timestamps. Additionally, derived features such as volatility measures, order book depth, and trading imbalances are incorporated to enrich the information available to the model.

### Reinforcement Learning Framework

Reinforcement learning, a subset of machine learning, is well-suited for market-making as it involves sequential decision-making under uncertainty. The RL framework consists of an agent (the market maker) interacting with an environment (the Forex market), with the objective of maximizing cumulative rewards over time.

- **States and Actions:**
    - *States* are representations of the market's current condition, encapsulating features like current bid-ask spread, order flow, and inventory levels.
    - *Actions* include adjusting the bid or ask prices, accepting or rejecting trades, and managing inventory.
- **Reward Function:** Designing an appropriate reward function is crucial. It should account for:
    - *Profitability*: The immediate profit from the bid-ask spread.
    - *Inventory Holding Costs*: Penalties for holding large or risky positions.
    - *Liquidity Provision*: Rewards for actions that contribute to market liquidity and stability.
- **Training the Agent:** The RL agent is trained using historical data through a process known as simulation-based learning. The training involves simulating numerous trading sessions where the agent iteratively improves its strategy based on the rewards received.

### Model Evaluation and Backtesting

Evaluating the performance of the RL-based market making strategy is carried out through backtesting. Backtesting involves simulating the strategy on historical data to assess its profitability and robustness. Key metrics to evaluate include:

- *Profit and Loss (P&L)*: The net earnings over the testing period.

- *Sharpe Ratio*: A measure of risk-adjusted returns.

- *Inventory Turnover*: Frequency of inventory turnover, indicating the strategy's liquidity.

Through backtesting, it was observed that the RL-based market making strategy effectively manages inventory, stabilizes bid-ask spreads, and enhances profitability compared to baseline static strategies. Additionally, the adaptive nature of the RL model allows it to respond to varying market conditions, demonstrating resilience and adaptability.

**Implementation Considerations**

Implementing an RL-based market making strategy in a live trading environment presents several challenges:

- *Execution Latency*: Ensuring low-latency execution to capitalize on the bid-ask spread effectively.

- *Regulatory Compliance*: Adhering to regulatory standards and maintaining transparency in operations.

- *Risk Management*: Employing robust risk management protocols to mitigate market exposure and operational risks.

### Conclusion

The incorporation of machine learning, particularly reinforcement learning, into market making strategies offers significant enhancements in decision-making and efficiency. By leveraging historical data and predictive models, market makers can achieve better management of inventory and bid-ask spreads, ultimately contributing to more liquid and stable Forex markets. As technology advances, the continuous refinement of these models will further elevate the capabilities and competitiveness of market makers in the dynamic landscape of Forex trading.

## 12.6 Case Study: Predictive Modeling for Credit Risk

Assessing credit risk accurately is paramount in the financial industry. Credit risk refers to the possibility of a loss resulting from a borrower's failure to repay a loan or meet contractual obligations. Financial institutions use predictive modeling to evaluate the likelihood of default, thus enabling better decision-making when it comes to lending and risk management.

In this case study, we explore the process of developing and validating a predictive model for credit risk using machine learning techniques. We will cover data preprocessing, feature selection, model training, validation, and interpretation, providing practical insights and strategies that readers can apply to their own projects.

To illustrate these concepts, we will work with a dataset of loan application records. Each record contains various features such as loan amount, interest rate, borrower's credit history, employment status, and income level, among others.

### Data Preprocessing and Feature Engineering

The first step in developing a credit risk model involves preparing the dataset for analysis. This includes handling missing values, encoding categorical variables, and normalizing numerical features.

% Code Snippet for Data Preprocessing

```
import pandas as pd
from sklearn.preprocessing import MinMaxScaler, LabelEncoder

# Load dataset
```

```
data = pd.read_csv('loan_data.csv')

# Handle missing values
data.fillna(data.median(), inplace=True)

# Encode categorical variables
label_encoders = {}
for column in ['employment_status', 'credit_history']:
    label_encoders[column] = LabelEncoder()
    data[column] = label_encoders[column].fit_transform(data[column])

# Normalize numerical features
scaler = MinMaxScaler()
numerical_features = ['loan_amount', 'interest_rate', 'income']
data[numerical_features] = scaler.fit_transform(data[numerical_features])
```

Feature engineering is crucial as it can significantly impact the model's performance. We can create new features based on domain knowledge. For example, the ratio of loan amount to income can be an informative feature, indicating the borrower's debt burden relative to their earnings.

$$\text{loan\_to\_income\_ratio} = \frac{\text{loan\_amount}}{\text{income}}$$

**Model Selection and Training**

Once preprocessing is complete, the next step is to build the predictive model. For credit risk prediction, logistic regression is often a great starting point due to its interpretability and efficiency. However, more sophisticated models like decision trees, random forests, and gradient boosting machines (GBMs) can also be employed to capture non-linear relationships.

% Code Snippet for Model Training

```
from sklearn.model_selection import train_test_split
from sklearn.ensemble import RandomForestClassifier
from sklearn.metrics import roc_auc_score

# Prepare features and target
X = data.drop('default', axis=1)
y = data['default']

# Split data into training and test sets
X_train, X_test, y_train, y_test = train_test_split(X, y, test_size=0.3,
     random_state=42)

# Train RandomForest model
model = RandomForestClassifier(n_estimators=100, random_state=42)
model.fit(X_train, y_train)

# Evaluate model performance
```

```
y_pred_proba = model.predict_proba(X_test)[:, 1]
auc_score = roc_auc_score(y_test, y_pred_proba)
print("AUC Score: ", auc_score)
```

The Area Under the Receiver Operating Characteristic Curve (AUC-ROC) is a common evaluation metric for binary classification models. It measures the model's ability to distinguish between classes, with values closer to 1 indicating better performance.

**Model Validation and Interpretation**

Validation is an essential part of the model development process, as it ensures the model's generalizability to unseen data. We use techniques like cross-validation to assess model robustness.

For interpretability, especially in regulated industries like finance, understanding how different features impact the prediction is vital. Tools like SHAP (Shapley Additive ExPlanations) values provide an interpretable and consistent way to explain model predictions.

% Code Snippet for Model Interpretation

```
import shap

# Explain model predictions using SHAP values
explainer = shap.TreeExplainer(model)
shap_values = explainer.shap_values(X_test)

# Plot summary of SHAP values
shap.summary_plot(shap_values, X_test)
```

SHAP values help identify which features are driving the model predictions. For instance, a high loan-to-income ratio might significantly increase the probability of default, highlighting the critical role of this feature in the model's decision-making process.

Predictive modeling for credit risk is a multifaceted task that requires careful consideration of data quality, feature engineering, model selection, and validation. By leveraging machine learning techniques, financial institutions can more accurately assess credit risk, thereby making more informed lending decisions and maintaining financial stability.

## 12.7 Case Study: High Frequency Trading Strategy

High Frequency Trading (HFT) represents the pinnacle of modern financial technology, utilizing powerful algorithms to execute trades at extremely high speeds and frequencies. The goal here is to capitalize on small price discrepancies that may exist for very short durations. This case study explores the design, implementation, and performance of a high frequency trading strategy in equity markets, emphasizing key components such as data acquisition, trade execution, risk management, and backtesting.

The first step in developing an HFT strategy involves the acquisition of high-quality, low-latency data. The data used must be tick-level, capturing every market event including trades and quotes. This granularity is necessary to detect the fleeting opportunities HFT algorithms exploit. The data is often sourced directly from exchanges or through specialized data providers with connectivity solutions that meet the stringent requirements for timeliness and accuracy.

Once the data is in place, the next step is to develop the trading algorithm. A common strategy in high frequency trading is statistical arbitrage, where the algorithm identifies price inefficiencies between correlated securities and executes trades to profit from their convergence. Here, we implement a basic pairs trading strategy, which involves monitoring the price spread between two historically correlated stocks.

We start by defining our model:

$$\text{Spread}_t = P_{A,t} - \beta P_{B,t}$$

where $P_{A,t}$ and $P_{B,t}$ are the prices of stocks $A$ and $B$ at time $t$, and $\beta$ is a coefficient derived from historical data, typically using an Ordinary Least Squares (OLS) regression.

The algorithm continuously monitors the spread and triggers trades when the spread deviates significantly from its historical mean, indicating a temporary market inefficiency. Specifically, the trading rules are:

- **Entry Signal:** Enter a long position on stock A and a short position on stock B if the spread is greater than a threshold $\mu + k\sigma$, where $\mu$ is the mean spread and $\sigma$ is the standard deviation. Conversely, enter a short position on stock A and a long position on stock B if the spread is less than $\mu - k\sigma$.

- **Exit Signal:** Close the position when the spread reverts to the mean.

Executing these trades efficiently requires robust infrastructure. Low-latency execution is critical, necessitating colocated servers in close proximity to exchange matching engines to minimize delays. The system architecture typically includes a direct market access (DMA) layer for rapid order routing, and an order management system (OMS) to handle order lifecycle and status.

Risk management in HFT is automated and real-time. Position limits, stop-loss levels, and exposure constraints are predefined and enforced by the trading system. Ensuring compliance with regulatory requirements, such as pre-trade risk checks, is also integral to the setup.

The final step is backtesting the strategy against historical data to evaluate its performance. This involves simulating the algorithm's trades and assessing metrics such as profitability, Sharpe ratio, maximum drawdown, and win/loss ratio. Suppose our backtest shows:

| Metric | Value |
|---|---|
| Annualized Return | 18% |
| Sharpe Ratio | 2.5 |
| Maximum Drawdown | 3% |
| Win/Loss Ratio | 1.2 |

These results suggest a robust strategy with a high reward-to-risk ratio. It is crucial to conduct rigorous stress testing to model potential market scenarios and ensure the algorithm's robustness to different market conditions.

In developing a high frequency trading strategy, a confluence of algorithmic prowess, technological infrastructure, and rigorous risk management is paramount. While the potential for high returns is significant, so too are the operational complexities and risks. This case study underscores the necessity for meticulous planning, continuous monitoring, and adaptive strategies to exploit fleeting market inefficiencies profitably.

## 12.8 Case Study: Sentiment Analysis for Stock Market Prediction

The financial world is increasingly recognizing the power of sentiment analysis, especially with the proliferation of social media and online news sources that provide real-time information about market sentiment. This section delves into a comprehensive case study that demonstrates the application of sentiment analysis for predicting stock market movements. Our focus will be on the practical integration of natural language processing (NLP) techniques with machine learning models to extract valuable insights and make informed trading decisions.

Sentiment analysis involves computationally identifying and categorizing opinions expressed in a piece of text, especially to determine whether the writer's attitude towards a particular topic is positive, negative, or neutral. In the context of stock markets, the sentiment expressed in news articles, social media posts, analyst reports, and other text sources can have a profound impact on stock prices.

Imagine you're tasked with predicting the price movements of a specific stock using sentiment analysis. First, you need to gather a comprehensive dataset consisting of both stock prices and corresponding sentiment data. For this case study, consider using a combination of historical stock price data for a particular company and textual data sourced from financial news websites and social media platforms such as Twitter.

The first step is to preprocess the textual data. Preprocessing involves cleaning the text by removing stop words, punctuation, and other nonessential elements. Tokenization is then performed to break down the text into individual words or tokens. Next, these tokens can be converted into numerical representations using techniques like term frequency-inverse document frequency (TF-IDF) or word embeddings such as Word2Vec or GloVe.

Once the data is prepared, a sentiment analysis model needs to be trained. For this case study, a supervised learning approach can be employed using a labeled dataset containing texts and their corresponding sentiment scores. A common technique is to use a classification algorithm such as logistic regression, support vector machines (SVM), or more advanced methods like deep learning models (e.g., recurrent neural networks or transformer-based models).

Assuming we use a logistic regression model, the sentiment classification model is trained on the labeled dataset to predict whether a given piece of text is positive, negative, or neutral regarding the stock's future performance. The performance of the sentiment classification model can be evaluated using metrics like accuracy, precision, recall, and the F1-score.

After training the sentiment analysis model, the next step is integrating the sentiment scores with stock price data. Each piece of textual information is analyzed using the sentiment model to obtain a sentiment score. These scores can then be aggregated over specific time windows (e.g., daily, weekly) to create sentiment features that reflect the overall market sentiment towards the stock over those periods.

The resulting dataset, combining historical stock prices and sentiment features, can be used to train a predictive model for stock price movements. Machine learning algorithms such as random forests, gradient boosting machines, or neural networks can be employed for this task. The model learns the relationship between sentiment features and stock price changes, enabling it to predict future price movements based on new sentiment data.

Consider the following example in which historical stock prices and aggregated daily sentiment scores are used to train a predictive model. We denote the stock price at time $t$ as $P_t$, and the aggregated sentiment score for the same period as $S_t$. The predictive model can be represented as follows:

$$P_{t+1} = f(P_t, S_t) + \epsilon_t$$

where $f$ is the predictive function learned by the model and $\epsilon_t$ is the error term.

To evaluate the model, divide the data into training and testing sets. The model is trained on the training set, and its performance is measured on the testing set using metrics such as mean absolute error (MAE) or root mean squared error (RMSE). It's crucial to ensure the model generalizes well to unseen data to make reliable predictions in real-world scenarios.

Finally, let's discuss deploying the sentiment-based predictive model in a practical trading strategy. For instance, you can use the model's predictions to inform buy or sell decisions. If the predicted price is significantly higher than the current price, it might signal a buying opportunity. Conversely, if the predicted price is significantly lower, it could indicate a good time to sell.

To further illustrate, consider a trading strategy where you buy the stock when the sentiment score exceeds a certain threshold and sell when it falls below another threshold. Backtesting this strategy on historical data helps analyze its profitability and risk. It's important to account for transaction costs, slippage, and other real-world trading factors to ensure the strategy is viable.

Through this case study, we have covered the entire workflow of applying sentiment analysis for stock market prediction—from data collection and preprocessing to model training and deployment in a trading strategy. This practical example highlights the powerful synergy between natural language processing and machine learning, offering valuable insights that can significantly enhance trading and investment decisions.

## 12.9 Case Study: Anomaly Detection in Financial Transactions

In the increasingly complex landscape of financial markets, the ability to detect anomalies in transactions is vital for mitigating risk and ensuring the integrity of financial systems. Anomaly detection involves identifying transactions that deviate significantly from normal behavior, which could indicate fraud, market manipulation, or operational errors. This case study demonstrates the application of machine learning algorithms to detect anomalies in financial transactions with a focus on practical implementation and real-world results.

Understanding the types of anomalies is crucial. In finance, anomalies often manifest as sudden spikes in transaction volume, unusual trading patterns, or deviations from expected financial metrics. Detecting these anomalies in real-time can help organizations respond swiftly to potential threats.

To illustrate the machine learning approach to anomaly detection, we begin with a dataset of financial transactions, which includes attributes such as transaction time, amount, sender, recipient, and transaction type. The goal is to develop a model that can automatically flag potentially fraudulent transactions.

Machine learning algorithms, particularly unsupervised learning methods, are well-suited for this task because they do not require labeled anomaly data, which can be scarce. Commonly used algorithms include Principal Component Analysis (PCA), k-means clustering, and

Autoencoders. For this case study, we will focus on using an Autoencoder neural network due to its effectiveness in capturing complex patterns within high-dimensional data.

An Autoencoder consists of two main parts: the encoder, which compresses the input data into a lower-dimensional representation, and the decoder, which reconstructs the original data from this representation. Training the model involves minimizing the difference between the input and the reconstructed output, measured by the reconstruction error. Transactions with high reconstruction error are considered anomalous.

Here is how the Autoencoder model is constructed and trained in a financial anomaly detection scenario:

Autoencoder for Anomaly Detection in Financial Transactions

```
import numpy as np
import pandas as pd
from sklearn.preprocessing import StandardScaler
from tensorflow.keras.models import Model
from tensorflow.keras.layers import Input, Dense

# Load and preprocess the dataset
data = pd.read_csv('financial_transactions.csv')
scaler = StandardScaler()
data_scaled = scaler.fit_transform(data)

# Split data into training and test sets
train_data = data_scaled[:int(0.8*len(data))]
test_data = data_scaled[int(0.8*len(data)):]

# Build the Autoencoder model
input_dim = train_data.shape[1]
input_layer = Input(shape=(input_dim,))
encoded = Dense(14, activation='relu')(input_layer)
encoded = Dense(7, activation='relu')(encoded)
decoded = Dense(14, activation='relu')(encoded)
decoded = Dense(input_dim, activation='sigmoid')(decoded)

autoencoder = Model(input_layer, decoded)
autoencoder.compile(optimizer='adam', loss='mean_squared_error')

# Train the Autoencoder
autoencoder.fit(train_data, train_data,
                epochs=50,
                batch_size=256,
                shuffle=True,
                validation_data=(test_data, test_data))

# Compute reconstruction error on the test set
reconstructions = autoencoder.predict(test_data)
reconstruction_error = np.mean((test_data - reconstructions) ** 2, axis=1)
```

After training the Autoencoder, the next step involves defining a threshold for the reconstruction error to classify an anomaly. This threshold can be set based on the error distribution observed in the training data, often using methods such as the 95th percentile or by visual inspection.

$$\text{Threshold} = \text{percentile\_score}(\text{reconstruction\_error}, 95)$$

Transactions with a reconstruction error above this threshold are flagged as anomalies. This method allows us to identify suspicious transactions that require further investigation.

Detecting Anomalies

```
# Set the anomaly detection threshold
threshold = np.percentile(reconstruction_error, 95)

# Identify anomalies
anomalies = test_data[reconstruction_error > threshold]
print(f"Number of anomalies detected: {len(anomalies)}")
```

Ultimately, the success of an anomaly detection system hinges on its accuracy and usability. Regular evaluation and tuning of the model, considering new data and emerging patterns, are critical. In practical scenarios, integrating this model into a real-time monitoring system could involve using stream processing frameworks like Apache Kafka or Apache Flink to manage and analyze transaction flows continuously.

This case study exemplifies the power of machine learning in maintaining financial security. By deploying sophisticated models, financial institutions can proactively detect and respond to potential threats, thereby safeguarding their operations and maintaining trust with their stakeholders. The methodologies covered here not only serve to elucidate practical machine learning applications but also empower practitioners to innovate and adapt these techniques to their specific needs in the ever-evolving financial landscape.

## 12.10 Case Study: Interest Rate Modeling in Fixed Income Markets

Interest rate modeling is an essential aspect of fixed income markets, crucial for pricing, risk management, and strategic decision-making in financial institutions. This case study delves into how machine learning techniques can be effectively employed to model interest rates, and by extension, enhance the performance of fixed income portfolios.

Fixed income securities, such as bonds, derive their value from the underlying interest rates, which often exhibit complex, non-linear dynamics. Traditional models, like the Vasicek or Cox-Ingersoll-Ross (CIR) models, have been fundamental in understanding these movements. However, the advent of machine learning provides a more flexible and precise toolset for capturing the intricate patterns present in the data.

The first step in interest rate modeling involves understanding the term structure of interest rates, which represents the relationship between bond yields and their maturities. The term structure is paramount as it drives the pricing of bonds and derivative instruments. Here, we begin our exploration by focusing on the yield curve, a graphical representation of this relationship.

### Yield Curve Construction and Preliminary Analysis

The yield curve typically takes three shapes: upward sloping, downward sloping, and flat. An upward sloping curve indicates growing confidence in the economy, while a downward sloping curve, often seen as an indicator of an impending recession, suggests the opposite. A flat yield curve happens when short-term interest rates are very close to long-term rates and generally indicates uncertainty in economic conditions.

We start by collecting historical yield curve data for a diverse set of maturities, from short-term Treasury bills to long-term Treasury bonds. Assume our dataset comprises the daily interest rates for maturities of 3 months, 6 months, 1 year, 2 years, 5 years, 10 years, and 30 years over a period of multiple decades.

Conducting an exploratory data analysis (EDA) on this dataset allows us to visualize the data patterns, recognize missing values, and understand the overall distribution.

```
# Python code snippet for EDA
import pandas as pd
import matplotlib.pyplot as plt

# Load the dataset
data = pd.read_csv('historical_yield_curve.csv')
# Display the first few rows
print(data.head())

# Plot yield curves for different dates
dates = ['2000-01-01', '2010-01-01', '2020-01-01']
for date in dates:
    plt.plot(data['Maturity'], data[date], label=date)

plt.xlabel('Maturity (Years)')
plt.ylabel('Yield (%)')
plt.title('Yield Curve Over Different Dates')
```

```
plt.legend()
plt.show()
```

This preliminary analysis helps identify significant shifts and trends in the yield curve over time, providing insights into the economic conditions and the evolving behavior of interest rates.

### Machine Learning Model Selection and Training

To model the term structure of interest rates, various machine learning algorithms can be employed, such as regression trees, support vector machines, and more recently, deep learning techniques. In this case study, we opt for a Long Short-Term Memory (LSTM) network, a type of recurrent neural network well-suited for time series data due to its ability to learn long-term dependencies.

The dataset is divided into training, validation, and test sets. The LSTM model is trained to predict yields based on historical data, including the yields of various maturities and relevant macroeconomic indicators such as GDP growth rates, inflation, and unemployment rates.

Here is an outline of the LSTM model implementation:

```
# Python code snippet for LSTM model implementation
import numpy as np
from keras.models import Sequential
from keras.layers import LSTM, Dense, Dropout

# Prepare data for LSTM
def prepare_data(data, n_steps):
    X, y = list(), list()
    for i in range(len(data)):
        end_ix = i + n_steps
        if end_ix > len(data) - 1:
            break
        seq_x, seq_y = data[i:end_ix], data[end_ix]
        X.append(seq_x)
        y.append(seq_y)
    return np.array(X), np.array(y)

n_steps = 10
X, y = prepare_data(yields, n_steps)

# Define the LSTM model
model = Sequential()
model.add(LSTM(50, activation='relu', input_shape=(n_steps, 1)))
model.add(Dropout(0.2))
model.add(Dense(1))
model.compile(optimizer='adam', loss='mse')

# Fit the model
model.fit(X, y, epochs=300, verbose=1)
```

The performance of the model is evaluated using metrics such as Mean Absolute Error (MAE) and Root Mean Squared Error (RMSE), providing a quantitative measure of the prediction accuracy.

### Use Case: Pricing and Hedging Strategies

Accurately modeled interest rates form the cornerstone of various financial strategies. One of the primary applications is in the pricing of interest rate derivatives such as swaps, options, and futures. Moreover, these models assist in the construction of hedging strategies to mitigate interest rate risk.

An organization can leverage the predictions from the LSTM model to determine the appropriate yields for new bond issuances, optimize its fixed income portfolio allocations, and generate hedging positions to minimize exposure to adverse interest rate movements.

Consider a portfolio manager tasked with building a fixed income portfolio that balances yield generation with risk management. Using the predicted yield curves, the manager can simulate different market scenarios and devise strategies that ensure favorable outcomes even under fluctuating interest rates.

### Conclusion

This case study highlights the transformative potential of machine learning in modeling the complex dynamics of interest rates in the fixed income market. By employing advanced techniques like LSTM, we can achieve more precise and insightful predictions, ultimately driving better-informed financial decisions. Such models not only enhance the pricing and risk management of fixed income securities but also provide a robust framework for developing resilient financial strategies in an ever-evolving market landscape.

Made in the USA
Monee, IL
05 November 2026

67911527R00174